INSURRECTION

INSURRECTION

Rebellion, Civil Rights, and the
Paradoxical State of Black Citizenship

Hawa Allan

W. W. NORTON & COMPANY
Independent Publishers Since 1923

For information about permission to reproduce selections from this book, write to Permissions, W. W. Norton & Company, Inc., 500 Fifth Avenue, New York, NY 10110

For information about special discounts for bulk purchases, please contact W. W. Norton Special Sales at specialsales@wwnorton.com or 800-233-4830

Manufacturing by Lakeside Book Company
Book design by Daniel Lagin
Production manager: Lauren Abbate

ISBN 978-1-324-00303-8

W. W. Norton & Company, Inc.
500 Fifth Avenue, New York, N.Y. 10110
www.wwnorton.com

W. W. Norton & Company Ltd.
15 Carlisle Street, London W1D 3BS

1 2 3 4 5 6 7 8 9 0

CONTENTS

INSURRECTION

In the Beginning Was the Word

On Monday, June 1, 2020, in front of the historic St. John's Episcopal Church in Washington, D.C., then-president Donald Trump held up a bible, seemingly upside down, in his right hand and posed rigidly before a barrage of camera flashes. Then, ensconced by Secret Service agents, Trump walked away from the church and back through the adjacent Lafayette Park, where he was flanked by a line of riot police standing at attention behind clear shields. Not long beforehand, some of these very same riot police had likely participated in clearing the park of peaceful protesters with rubber bullets, flash grenades, and tear gas. All of this was occurring in the midst of global protests sparked in response to Derek Chauvin's brutal killing of George Floyd in Minneapolis, with massive demonstrations against police brutality coinciding with vandalism, looting, and arson—in other words, with "riots."

The weekend immediately prior to the bizarre photo op, a part of St. John's Episcopal Church itself—known as "the church of the presidents"—had been briefly set afire during protests in D.C., prompting Trump's press secretary to select it as a site for the media spectacle. When later questioned about the staged photo, Trump responded that it "was very symbolic" but never elaborated on what, exactly, this imagery represented. The cryptic symbolism, however, followed a press conference in which Trump—referring to himself as the "president of law and order"—threatened to invoke a "beautiful law" to restore "order" to states where governors were unable or unwilling to do so: the Insurrection Act of 1807. The Act allows the president to domestically deploy federal troops and deputize the state National Guard to suppress any "insurrection, domestic violence, unlawful combination, or conspiracy."

Trump's threatened invocation of the Insurrection Act during the George Floyd protests incited an uproar among numerous commentators who decried the federal government's use of military power against its "own people." The use of federal troops as a civilian police force, according to many commentators at the time, is an unwarranted trespass on the rights and freedoms of American citizens and contravenes the values upon which the United States was founded.

It is true that the military power set forth in the Insurrection Act is an extraordinary exception from the normal state of federal affairs. The power, among other things, upends the conventions of federalism, in line with which domestic deployments of the "militia"—or the modern-day National Guard—are authorized by the state governor. This power also represents a significant departure from the constitutional aversion to standing armies, which some framers feared would result in the arbitrary use of force against civilians and thereby re-create the same sort of authoritarian menace, in the form of the British Army, that American revolutionaries had just sought to free themselves from. The Insurrection Act, then, is both an exception and a rule—it represents a radical deviation from the principles of federalism and aversion to using military forces to police civilians, while authorizing a purportedly necessary use of federal military power to restore "law and order" amid a domestic crisis.

Unlike contemporary legislation, the 1807 law is fairly spare and markedly devoid of the definitions, articulated exceptions, and other technicalities that characterize more recent statutes. So, an "insurrection" (or "domestic violence" or an "unlawful combination," etc.) is effectively undefined, left to be envisioned in the eye of the beholder—whether that of the state governor who might request that the president dispatch federal troops pursuant to the Act, or of the president who can unilaterally deploy such troops under this authority. This exceptional power is not without its limitations, because any such insurrection or other civil disturbance, if suppressed unilaterally by the president, must technically either deprive citizens of constitutional rights (which a given state has failed or refused to protect), or violate federal law. Nonetheless—and especially in the midst of some emergency or other domestic upheaval—an "insurrection" is, effectively, what the executive says it is.

An insurrection, under the Act, is a definitional vacuum waiting to be filled by the executive. The incidents taken to warrant domestic federal military intervention betray just as much, if not more, about the predilections of those wielding power as they do about the threatening nature of such events. From Nat Turner's rebellion to violent clashes over slavery in "Bleeding Kansas" to white paramilitary resistance during Radical Reconstruction to the desegregation of public schools in Alabama, Arkansas, and Mississippi to the Los Angeles "riots" in 1992, the events across history that have been interpreted to warrant the domestic deployment of federal troops under the Insurrection Act reveal a pattern: the prevailing invocation of the Act, on the one hand, to suppress revolts against the slave system and so-called race riots, and, on the other, to enforce the civil rights of African Americans. So, although what constitutes an insurrection is technically undefined in the text of the Act itself, the term has been defined in practice through its historical application. What has been interpreted to constitute an insurrection is a mirror reflecting the ongoing and often bloody battle to fully incorporate black Americans into the citizenry of the United States—a struggle that, in this light, appears more like an open-ended civil war than a history of "progress."

An "insurrection," however, is also defined by omission. Where the Trump administration, for example, threatened to invoke the Act in response to nationwide demonstrations against police brutality, the same inclination was nonexistent in response to, say, deadly protests in Charlottesville, North Carolina, by white nationalists, or to the storming of the Michigan state capitol by armed mostly white men protesting ongoing COVID-19 pandemic lockdowns. Although the Insurrection Act does not need to be invoked for the president to deploy the D.C. National Guard or federal troops within the District of Columbia, the absence of any military presence during the riots—or, as commentators called it, the "insurrection"—at the Capitol on January 6, 2021, was certainly glaring. As commander in chief of the D.C. National Guard, it is clear that Trump and his administration could have authorized its deployment—that is, if they actually intepreted the riot to be a threat to law and order.

Given this context, an "insurrection," under the Act, means more than its textbook definition—that being "a violent uprising against an authority or government." Legal pronouncements of "insurrection" are not merely descriptive. They have material consequences in the physical world—as they warrant the use of violence to enforce a normative state of affairs. To proclaim an "insurrection," to borrow from renowned legal scholar Robert Cover, is to deploy the power to create and destroy worlds through the use of force. "Legal interpretive acts," writes Cover in his seminal essay "Violence and the Word," "signal and occasion the imposition of violence upon others." When government officials articulate their understanding of the law, they establish or reestablish the world in which we already live, or, at times, newly construct the world in which we ought to live. Inversely, however, such legal pronouncements also threaten to destroy worlds that deviate from prescribed norms, upholding law and order by subjecting actual and would-be defectors to violence or its threat.

Along these lines, a proclamation of "insurrection," historically,

helped to destroy the worlds of staunch segregationists for whom
the mere presence of Negro students in schools represented a death
blow to their "way of life," and, for the students themselves, such a
proclamation worked to create at least a semblance of equal opportunity. A proclamation of "insurrection" also threatened to destroy
the worlds of protesters assembling to decry George Floyd's killing
and police brutality, and promised to reify the world of officials
and observers more concerned about the sanctity of property than
black lives.

—————

THE WORD OF LAW, HOWEVER, DOES NOT ALONE CREATE WORLDS. "NO SET
of legal institutions or prescriptions exists apart from the narratives
that locate it and give it meaning," writes Cover, again, this time in
another seminal essay called "Nomos and Narrative." "Every [legal]
prescription is insistent in its demand to be located in discourse—to
be supplied with history and destiny, beginning and end, explanation
and purpose." Many "worlds" and the meanings made within them
preexisted the legal construct, which, pervasive as it has become, still
does not fully occupy the field of meaning and narrative possibility
once it has been initiated. Whenever a legal construct is first established (such as that which governed human bondage), rabble-rousers
and rebels may rally against it, appealing to some higher authority or
natural law that transcends the earthly one mandated by violence and
its threat. And when an established legal construct is modified (such
as when slavery was abolished), new rabble-rousers and rebels then
arise, demanding a return to the prior rule and regulations that had
governed their preferred way of life. In other words, a given world
purportedly destroyed by the legal construct is never truly eliminated
but nonetheless persists, coexisting in parallel with the newly created
one. And, like an erratic and menacing poltergeist, the world that the
legal construct was supposed to have destroyed continues to make

itself known, persists as a ghostly reassertion into the new legally ordained world.

The many "insurrections" that mark the ongoing battle to incorporate black Americans as full citizens of the United States are, in themselves, ghostly reassertions—whether as resurgent demands for the respect of black humanity, which always seem to beckon to a higher authority and divine right that precedes and eclipses the formal rights of citizenship, or violent irruptions of white supremacy.

———

THOUGH I AM A LAWYER BY TRAINING, THE WORLD I LIVE IN HAS ALWAYS seemed to clash with the one prescribed by the legal construct. I once verbally sparred with a fellow law clerk, with whom I was hired to serve a federal judge, over the concept of "guilt"—not that sensation of remorse that arises from within, but the external pronouncement, the firm declaration made alongside the pounding of the gavel that redefines a presumptively innocent defendant as a convict. While he insisted that a judicial finding of guilt amounted to actual guilt, I contended that being "found guilty" meant just that—a finding of guilt that is distinguishable from *actual* guilt, which may be ultimately unknowable by any judge or jury or spectator observing a trial from the courtroom pews. After we each made the same points, going back and forth, finally he asked me how I expected there to be any sense of finality, from the perspective of the legal system, if I did not accept its verdicts.

At this juncture, I remained silent—not because I didn't have a response, but because the law clerk finally said something I agreed with. This conversation represented my existential antagonism with The Law. Legal interpretations are bolstered by the assumptions of certainty, reliability, and, above all, legitimacy, arrived at by jurists after they have sifted through an otherwise disorganized medley of facts. Once isolated, certain relevant facts are placed into a box that is then closed and labeled "truth"—as if they were the conclusive pronouncements of an Old Testament God.

Meanwhile, the orientation of my mind has always been to uncover and open closed systems, and to continue to pry ajar and scrutinize what I find inside, which, like an endless succession of Russian dolls, are yet more shut boxes waiting to be explored. In this way, the closest thing to truth that I have ever been able to divine is what I have observed from patterns, and how they repeat.

Considering both history and my own story through the theme of "insurrection," I have continued to recognize patterns. And within them, those well-known events that are supposed to constitute the "progress" made to invest black Americans with the entitlements of full citizenship, and a glint of the American Dream, start to appear as a kind of recurring nightmare.

Part I

"PROGRESS"

CHAPTER 1

Be Not Afraid or Dismayed

When I was a little girl, a recurring theme in my dreams was running away from some would-be captor and straight into my inevitable demise by way of falling off of a tall building. The dream itself wasn't recurring, because the scenery would change. Different pursuers, different backdrops, different buildings—but the running and falling remained unchanged. And even as I would be fully absorbed within the dream, afraid of being caught, and absconding to higher ground, I would at some point become of two minds. Still running, sporadically turning my head to gauge the distance between me and whoever was chasing, I would suddenly become aware of both the fact that I was dreaming and what would be the dream's well-worn ending. "Oh," I would think, "I know how *this* is going to end." Soon enough, flailing mid-plummet, I would startle awake in my bed.

I no longer have this particular kind of nightmare. I do, however, still suffer from a fear of heights. When on skyrise observation decks or roads that skirt steep cliffs, a static-like tingling swarms up my legs and attempts to steal my balance. I have learned this fear of heights is a "natural environment" phobia, which can also refer to a fear of thunder, lightning, water, or the dark. It is also a "simple" phobia, which typically arises from an encounter with a specific object and, therefore, is reducible to a single, identifiable trigger—one always knows *what* exactly is scary, if not exactly why. The association between such a fear and its object is presumed to be self-evident, devoid of mystery, tautological: spiders, for example, are scary because they are spiders.

———

AT A PANEL DISCUSSION I ATTENDED ON THE TOPIC OF ANTISLAVERY POLItics in the decades leading up to the Civil War, one of the two panelists cited heightened panic among white society of the time about the potential for mass slave insurrections. This panelist, an up-and-coming historian of the period, highlighted this fear as one of the factors that contributed to a more fervent push by abolitionists for emancipation on the eve of the war. The other panelist, a more senior and prominent historian of the era, responded that fear was a psychological inference, not a historical fact—and therefore an insubstantial basis on which to formulate a hypothesis about why past events unfolded the way they did.

This statement gave me pause. What would be the motivation behind restricting the movement and congregation of the enslaved, preventing them from bearing arms, and, of course, sanctioning their "correction" to the point of dismemberment and death, if not some underlying fear? Historical discourse, as with many other academic disciplines, has tended to erect impassable barriers between "fact" and "emotion," denying the plausible association between the two in order to avoid recklessly concluding what might lurk in the heart or mind of any given person, much less an entire society. If fear could not be seen or touched, this discourse seems to be asking, albeit subtextually, was it ever really there?

———

OTHER FEARS HAVE OTHER NAMES. SOCIAL PHOBIAS, FOR EXAMPLE, ARE deemed "complex" insofar as they tend to be more disabling than their simple counterparts, and they are more likely to concern a fear of situations—fears of being scrutinized, rejected, or embarrassed. Someone suffering from a complex phobia usually can't pinpoint what is scary about a given set of circumstances, like speaking in public, meeting new people, or even eating in front of others. The fear, here, is not of the other people in and of themselves but, rather, of their judgment. Judgment, like a spider, is a "thing"; but unlike a spider, judgment is not physical, or concrete. Judgment is abstract and lacks any physical reality, even notwithstanding the concrete existence of the person from whom one fears such judgment will exude.

Therein lies the question: if judgment can't be seen or touched, then is it really there? Absent convenient scapegoats like spiders or thunderclaps, sufferers of complex social phobias are more likely to be tasked with turning within to determine the cause of their fear—and to have a hard time locating it.

When fear goes unnamed and, by association, denied, fear becomes an antonym to fact. Yet that amorphous sense of dread—denied to exist but nonetheless existing—goes in search of an object to which to fasten, from which to become indistinguishable, and with which to become synonymous. The finger is pointed away from the self and at the external enemy. Toward something that has already been named.

———

"FOR A LONG TIME IN COLONIAL AMERICA," LERONE BENNETT JR. WRITES in *Before the Mayflower: A History of Black America*, "there was no legal name to focus white anxiety." The first Africans on colonial American soil—around twenty or so people who landed in the first permanent English settlement in the Americas, Jamestown, Virginia, in August 1619—were not yet consistently "Negro." "Blackamoors" or "Moors," at times, or perhaps "Negers" or "Negars." These first Africans were also not yet "slaves." The first Africans to set foot in the British portion of what was not yet the United States were, instead, indentured servants—who, like the poor whites with whom they worked side by side, traded their labor for a fixed number of years, not their very lives until death. Also, white people were not yet universally "white" but, say, "Englishmen" or "Christians." They were men and women who had nationalities and religions, but not yet races. Not yet.

"Slave insurrection," also, was not yet a trigger of collective fear in the new colony. There would first have to be "slaves" and "slavery"— and, even before that, the "Negro," who, easily distinguishable and unprotected, made the most able candidate for the unfree labor that would establish the economic foundation of that particular tract of the so-called New World. And defining the "Negro" as "brutish," "bestial," "heathen," and "savage" helped forestall a guilty conscience among those who were, by definition, becoming "white" and, by association, relatively "free."

There were, however, "insurrections," and the fear of them was not yet predominantly affixed to the enslaved. The first recorded "slave" revolt, which occurred in 1633, was actually a joint conspiracy among enslaved Negroes and white indentured servants in Gloucester County, Virginia. However, as Winthrop D. Jordan recounts in *White Over Black: American Attitudes toward the Negro 1550–1812*, after the 1660s and 1670s any particular fear of enslaved Negroes and white servants joining forces in rebellion had abated, at least for the time being. By that point, the "Negro" had been not only legally defined as "slave," but the architecture of law enforcement to ensure the fulfillment of this designation had been already erected and fortified.

During this same period, laws were first passed in colonial Jamestown to codify the enslavement of Africans. Among such laws, passed in 1669 was "[a]n act about the casuall killing of slaves," which held that enslavers who killed persons they had enslaved could not be found guilty of any crime. This was among the first, and certainly far from the last, of the slave codes in the United States—which regulated the movement of the enslaved and, in many cases, the extent of brutality that white men could exact upon them. As the 1669 law stated, the laws in force governing the punishment of white servants by their masters were insufficient to discipline Negroes, given the "obstinacy of many of them," who could not "by other then [sic] violent meanes [be] supprest." The reasoning set forth in the law was that malice could not be presumed of an enslaver who managed to kill his "slave" when "correcting him," because it was illogical for anyone with malicious intent to "destroy his owne estate."

Of course, writes Edmund S. Morgan in *American Slavery, American Freedom*, an enslaver would have found it necessary to beat, maim, and even kill "in order to get work out of men and women who had nothing to gain but the absence of pain." White servants were by no means treated with kid gloves—they were also subjected to violence in order to compel them to work. White servants in colonial Virginia also could be sold without their consent, be subject to physical abuse; they were, as Morgan writes, "a machine for making tobacco for somebody else," subject to "a system of labor that treated people like things." However, despite having been committed to long terms of servitude, such servants could still anticipate freedom on the horizon. This also explains why the laws governing white servants were deemed inadequate to the task of punishing Negroes. As Morgan notes, unlike white servants, the enslaved had "absolutely no incentive to work."

White servants, by contrast, still had the chimerical antecedent of what we now call the American Dream to entice them to persevere under grueling conditions, to trade immediate dignity for the future promise, however distant and faint, of one's very own plot of land, of one's very own servants and, perhaps, even of one's very own slaves. By contrast, there was no carrot to dangle before the Negro slave, only the stick.

THE ENSLAVED HAD DUAL NATURES. THEY WERE, AT THE SAME TIME, BOTH property and persons. As property, the enslaved were jealously protected. As persons, the enslaved were brutally violated. As property, the enslaved increased in value when multiplied. As persons, the enslaved became more of a potential liability the more populous they became. As property, the enslaved were deemed as docile as cattle. As persons, the enslaved were potential rebels to be feared. And this duality, what James Madison called "the mixt character of persons and of property," wrought a system of governance with an internally contradictory mission: protect the property by suppressing the human.

This mission was as dubious in theory as it evidently was in practice. For a seminal source, what better text to consider than that of seventeenth-century English philosopher John Locke—the conceptual forefather of the Declaration of Independence and the theoretical purveyor of private property. In his *Two Treatises of Government,* Locke stated that all persons had an inalienable property interest in themselves, to which no other person had any right. Any freedoms one forfeited, according to Locke, could only be legitimately relinquished subject to one's consent—and even then, said Locke, the "freedom from absolute, arbitrary power" was inviolable and therefore could never be surrendered, willingly or otherwise.

For Locke, slavery was both unjust and intolerable, warranting someone threatened with enslavement to "destroy" his would-be enslaver. Even considering a scenario where someone who had committed a grievous act was by punishment consigned by some overlord to slavery, Locke maintained that this unfortunate person still had the freedom to kill himself rather than suffer indefinite bondage—to exercise his liberty to end his own life. And so this tenuous liaison between freedom and death is what Locke stated was the consummate state of slavery: a "state of war" between conqueror and captive.

Locke's theoretical aversion notwithstanding, his theory of private property happens to outline a moral justification of the slave system. The uncultivated commons, existing in the state of nature, said Locke, belonged to all mankind. Having coronated man in general as the divine beneficiary of the untilled earth, he went on to state that what made any particular man the proprietor of any particular piece of land, or anything at all, was that person's labor. According to Locke, one's labor—the work of one's hands—transformed, as if by magic, some portion of the public common into a private good. This theory, of course, has served as justification for white settlers' continual appropriation of land that had been the dominion of indigenous peoples—or, as Locke put it, of "the wild Indian, who knows no enclosure [. . .]."

Similarly branded as savage, what was an enslaved person but someone who had been removed from "the state of nature"—whether the physical geography of Africa or the carnal state of barbarism—and who had been made useful by his captors via compulsory labor? For Locke, the labor of beasts of burden and servants was considered an extension of the labor of their "masters," so that "the grass my horse has bit" or "the turfs my servant has cut" then becomes the property of said enslaver. Similarly, so was the enslaved's labor the enslaver's labor, and the fruit of enslaved labor the enslaver's fruit.

There is, however, one leap of logic, or perhaps of faith, that must be taken to arrive at this conclusion—and that would be, again, over the personhood of the one targeted for conversion into property. To be traded, sold, bought, and bred, consigned to a plantation backdrop as if a mule or a willow tree, is to be not fully human, certainly not in the Lockean sense. (In theory, that is. In practice, Locke had investments in the Royal African Company, the mercantile enterprise almost wholly devoted to the transatlantic slave trade.) There were myriad efforts to bypass this inconvenient tenet, all of which involved concocting some rationale to deny the enslaved's humanity.

The enslaved, again, was savage and uncivilized, was heathen and not saved, was a biological and intellectual inferior to white men and thus unsuited for full membership in society. However, these were all ex post facto justifications, evidence concocted to reinforce a system that already had been forged by one originary force. What is the labor that the enslaver "hath mixed" with the enslaved? What was this something of his own that the enslaver had "joined to" the enslaved? What preliminary "work" did the enslaver do in order to convert both the enslaved and the yield of the enslaved's toil into his property? There is one answer: violence.

Humanity is not stripped like a loose cape. Nor is humanity merely denied and ignored into inexistence. Humanity, rather, first succumbs to the force of a bludgeon. Violence—and, thereafter, its threat—was the enslaver's initial bit of labor that transformed the enslaved into his possession, which seized the enslaved's labor as his own. Violence was the absolute and arbitrary force that both waged war on the humanity of the enslaved—and, once put down, violence was continuously employed and threatened to keep this humanity suppressed.

———

I CAN'T BLAME THE RENOWNED HISTORY SCHOLAR FOR HIS BLINDNESS TO fear. It's hard to decipher the cause of something when you're steeped in its effect. As for my own fear—even if originally arising from traumatic experiences or conditioned reactions—my direct experience of it has always been as something inextricable from my body, innate to my very being. I have never known any space between my fear and me. If my fear had been, at one point, separate and unattached from my person, then I don't recall. When I look through a thick glass pane at slow, rolling multicolored dots of traffic hundreds of feet below, the swimming in my limbs is immediate. There is no delay between my bird's-eye perception and the sensation of doom.

Yet I must admit that my fear of heights is much more complex and not that simple at all. Rather than a simple fear of some tall perch, I'm really more afraid of my relationship to this set of circumstances. Some say that a fear of heights is closely related to a fear of falling and its disastrous consequences. But in attempting to index this fear, I can say that while I am afraid of plunging to my death, it's not necessarily due to fear of slipping or accidentally tumbling off a ledge. Instead, what I sense when nerves fire up my lower limbs is an urge to dispense with all the drama and suspense misfiring in my veins, and just jump.

BLACK OVER WHITE

I was a summer associate at a New York law firm that had been bombarding its wide-eyed recruits with a sufficient variety of amusements to distract us from how dull the work was. I had danced around purchased tables at exclusive clubs with champagne flutes in my hand. I had been waited on by waiters who waltzed in synchronized movements around our dining table. I had watched *Avenue Q*.

One afternoon, I was invited via group email to the top floor of the building to hear from a candidate for Senate. A partner had been supporting the Senate hopeful's campaign and was helping him raise funds. So, I took a break from researching a very dry memorandum and shot up in the elevator to go check it out. After a brief introduction and tepid applause from the gathered audience, the candidate stepped to the front of the conference room. I remember listening to standard fare for a political address as the speaker promised what he would do if elected, his words weaving some nearby future that all of us, in that very room, could help bring into existence with our combined civic and financial efforts. What stands out most in my memory, however, is his emphasis on his heritage, which became a refrain of his speech. "My mother is from Kansas," he kept saying, "and my father is from Kenya."

The candidate was eventually interrupted by the partner who had invited him to speak. New York law firms all had personalities, I had been told. This one, though relatively prestigious, was known to be a bit "rough and tumble," or, plainly, full of jocks. Accordingly, this man who had been made partner found it fitting to inform the audience, head shaking and hands waving in the air, as if preventing a bar brawl, that *this man right here* was the only candidate who could bring together the voters of Illinois behind a progressive platform. This partner should know; after all, he was from there, and, as he knew, it was rare for the voters he was familiar with to rally behind a progressive, much less "a Black."

"A Black??" I remember asking angrily, rhetorically. "A Black what? A black shoe? A black dog?" This is what I asked later that afternoon at another one of our scheduled amusements, holding hostage the sympathetic ear of a fellow summer associate. He listened intently, but appeared circumspect about carrying on the conversation. I couldn't blame him. Whenever I gathered with one or more other black summer associates to chitchat in the hallway, I would periodically crane my neck to check for any disapproving onlookers and was always poised to disperse.

In any case, right then, in the conference room, I remained silent along with everyone else, and simply scanned the other attendees to see if anyone was visibly offended. The candidate was as poker-faced as the rest of us; after all, he was there to raise funds and the rest of us were getting paid actual corporate salaries. He did, however, invite all of us to his fundraiser later that night.

———

PRELIMINARY LEGAL DISTINCTIONS BETWEEN "NEGRO" AND "WHITE" NOT-withstanding, one major uprising in 1676 proved that the interests of white servants and African slaves had not yet been entirely divided. An upstart named Nathaniel Bacon sought to exploit the political quandary of then–Virginia governor William Berkeley. Local indigenous tribes, including the Doeg peoples, had been waging intermittent raids on frontier settlements in order to defend against the westward encroachment of white settlers, and Berkeley declined to launch armed campaigns against them despite the urging of his constituents. While it's unclear whether Berkeley was content to keep recently freed white servants who were scrambling for land on the frontier as a human buffer against such tribes, or hesitant to organize and arm such restless, poorer whites to defend "their" territory, it's clear that Berkeley ignored the white settlers' requests for intervention.

Ambitious and resentful, Bacon disliked Berkeley for thwarting his political aspirations as well as his economic mobility—Berkeley had excluded him from beaver trading with indigenous locals, which Bacon alleged was due to the governor's attempt at maintaining a monopoly on the trade. Meanwhile, white servants at the conclusion of their indentures were also ambitious and resentful, having found scant land available once they were "free"; many saw Berkeley's reluctance to battle on the frontier as an obstacle to their becoming landed men.

Seizing upon such discontent, Bacon marshaled support from a growing number of former white servants, and by 1677, he had assembled a militia of white men and enslaved Africans he led into the frontier, indiscriminately killing indigenous men, women, and children. The bloody crusade not only turned its sights westward but also inward toward the colony's capital, Jamestown, which this rag-tag militia—after chasing Berkeley out of town—looted and burned to the ground. The rebels were eventually repressed by soldiers dispatched from England. As Morgan chronicled in *American Slavery, American Freedom*, "[o]ne of the last groups to surrender was a band of eighty negroes and twenty English servants."

Bacon's Rebellion was, in effect, a battle in a larger class war, for which indigenous peoples and the land they fought to preserve were a mere territorial backdrop. Yet, as some scholars have argued, indigenous peoples would not be the sole scapegoats of this battle, as the mere fact of white men and African slaves uniting in battle provoked further legal delineations between the two groups.

By 1680, for instance,"[a]n act for preventing Negroes Insurrections" was passed in Virginia in an attempt to restrict the congregation of slaves, given that "the frequent meeting of considerable numbers of negroe slaves under pretence of feasts and burialls [was] judged of dangerous consequence." The Act went on to prohibit any enslaved persons from bearing arms or leaving his or her master's grounds without a certificate, and further stated that any enslaved person who resisted apprehension after being found "lurking in obscure places" could be lawfully killed. To be clear, the "dangerous consequence" was an uprising against, and potential disruption of, the then-recently codified institution of slavery.

———

LATER THAT WORKDAY EVENING, I ENTERED A LARGE EVENT SPACE WHERE Barack Obama's fundraiser was being held. The event was sponsored by an African American lawyers' association, one of many such identity groups convened to professionally encourage black lawyers, who at the time comprised a single-digit percentage of all lawyers in the United States. We still do, only an estimated 5 percent. Black women make up only 2 percent of the profession. Though absurdly low, these statistics don't mean anything to me. If "equality" and "diversity" are truly noble goals, then they will never amount to any particular number. Having spent a lifetime accustomed to being the only or, at most, one of a few black people in any given room full of white people, I never believed that having more of "us" there would do anything other than cause alarm for everyone else. Given the widespread presumption in the United States of a white majority, there is an implicit threshold tolerance for diversity. Up to said threshold, my majoritarian hosts might view my statistical presence as an extension of benevolence, a reflection of their tolerance and good nature. And after this tipping point, my presence would be a threat.

I attended the fundraiser by myself, drawn by promised networking and the guest of honor. There were hors d'oeuvres, drinking, and sporadic dancing before an MC ascended to a spotlighted stage and hushed the crowd. When Obama finally came to the microphone, I didn't necessarily expect innovation. I didn't really have expectations at all, having just heard him speak that afternoon. But I ended up being very surprised. I stood there and listened to him give the same exact speech that he had given earlier that day, with one exception. And that was inflection: "My mama's from Kansas, and my daddy's from Kenya . . ."

He said everything I had heard before, but in African American vernacular English. He code-switched.

AS MENTIONED EARLIER, THE FIRST RECORDED SLAVE REBELLION TOOK place in 1633 in Virginia. However, white fear of slave insurrection is often said to have another origin story, and its Adam was named Gabriel, who became known for leading the first major slave revolt in the newly "free" America. Born the same year as the United States, in 1776, Gabriel lived on a tobacco plantation in Henrico County, just outside of Richmond, Virginia. Having been taught to read and write, Gabriel was also a trained blacksmith. His trade brought him in close contact with white artisans and Negro freedmen of similar skill in Richmond—a city he often traveled to when his "master," Thomas Henry Prosser, loaned out his labor for a fee.

The practice was called "self-hiring" because, although the enslaved's labor was being rented by his master, the enslaved were often at liberty to choose their part-time enslaver, whether by comparing their offered wages or their reputations for cruelty. Also, Gabriel was able to keep a portion of his self-hire fee, which might have elevated his own perception of his status into the twilight zone between enslaved and free wage laborer. So, both enslaved and literate, born on the plantation but no longer fully of the plantation, Gabriel had tasted the forbidden fruit of knowledge and relative freedom, or, as Douglas Egerton calls it in *Gabriel's Rebellion,* "a crude quasi freedom."

Many historians have presumed that Gabriel's glimpse of, in particular, the lives of free Negro laborers—many of whom were surely aware of the slave rebellion in Saint-Domingue, not to mention the very revolution in America, which birthed a free white nation that codified his enslavement—inspired him to hatch a plan to overthrow his own captors. Over the course of several months in 1800, at twenty-four years of age, Gabriel recruited coconspirators of primarily skilled Negro artisans and together they devised a plot: surround the city of Richmond, seize its arsenal, and kidnap governor James Monroe, killing anyone who dared obstruct them along the way.

Historical accounts differ as to how indiscriminate such killing would be, with some noting that Gabriel intended to spare Quakers, Methodists, and Frenchmen—groups that were expressly abolitionist, or, in the case of French "Jacobins," implicitly perceived to be so—as well as poor white women who were not enslavers. Some records indicate that Gabriel, upon trapping Governor Monroe, intended to persuade the former American revolutionary to emancipate the enslaved, whereafter, as Egerton writes, Gabriel and his makeshift troops would "hoist a white flag [. . .] and dine and drink with the merchants of the city."

What is more certain, however, is that the insurrection was to begin on the night of August 30, 1800. Gabriel and his top men had recruited rebels from Henrico and Richmond, as well as nearby counties including Hanover, Caroline, Norfolk, and Petersburg. Some of his coconspirators, including his brother Solomon, put their trades to use by smithing swords out of scythes, typically used by field hands to cut wheat. On the appointed date, which was a Saturday—commonly a half day of work for the enslaved—Gabriel's recruits were to assemble at the Brook Bridge, a popular meeting place for Negro Henrico residents, who would hold picnics, religious services, and other festivities or venture into the city of Richmond for the weekend. Marching together with his band of righteous soldiers, Gabriel was to hoist a silk flag that read "Death or Liberty."

Gabriel's plan, however, was foiled by two enslaved men who informed their enslavers of the plotted revolt, as well as by torrential rainfall that gave Virginia officials sufficient time to mobilize militia in and around Richmond. The insurrection was quickly suppressed, resulting in plotters dispersing upon getting word of slave patrols and militia that had been called forth to stop them. Around thirty alleged conspirators were ultimately arrested after patrols and militia engaged in what one enslaved person characterized as an indiscriminate manhunt: "[A] man can't but go out of his house now but he is taken up to be hanged."

In the end, twenty-seven enslaved Negroes were executed, including Gabriel himself, who from the time of his apprehension to the date of his hanging hardly divulged any details about his plans for revolt. Much of the evidence Virginia officials relied upon in trying and executing alleged coconspirators, according to Lacy K. Ford in *Deliver Us From Evil: The Slavery Question in the Old South*, "came from either black testimony given under duress or from preconceived white notions about how and why such plots developed." Ford also relays the conclusion of John Randolph of Roanoke on Gabriel's insurrection, which, he quipped, "had been quieted without any bloodshed, but that which has streamed from the scaffold."

Again, Gabriel was not the first enslaved person to rebel, and he certainly would not be the last. But the context of the conspiracy— which involved the rising population of Negroes in proportion to whites in the southern states, as well as the ongoing slave rebellion in Saint-Domingue—worked to exaggerate already-present fears among white citizens.

THERE ARE MOMENTS IN LIFE THAT ARE ANTICIPATED WHILE WHOLLY
unexpected, and which, while intelligible in the abstract, are unintelligible in so-called reality. One such date was November 4, 2008. I
was sitting on the floor of an acquaintance's apartment awaiting the
results of the presidential election. It would become a historic day,
but I was nonplussed. Having lived through George W. Bush's first
presidential contest—with the ensuing days of uncertainty, hanging
chads, and eventual binding decision of the Supreme Court—I had
been primed to expect a long night, if not week or month, ahead. Even
as the numbers continued to be tallied, tipping the weighted scale of
electoral votes in the Illinois senator's direction, the logical outcome
was still denied by my emotional truth.

And then it happened. Without much bureaucratic fanfare,
Barack Hussein Obama was proclaimed the forty-fourth president of
the United States. The results were definitive and uncontested.

What we call history are moments that are accumulated in hindsight, rearranged to betray some narrative coherence and, perhaps,
affective resonance. But that night, after the election was called, I felt
history as it was happening. That said, I'm not a sentimental person.
In fact, I still have a sullen, sarcastic, fourteen-year-old version of
myself defending my underlying sensitivity against any mainstream
incitement of "hope." And yet, that evening, I cried. Barack, Michelle,
Malia, and Sasha walking out onto a large stage in varying shades of
black and red, before a cheering crowd of supporters, bypassed my
cynicism, for the time being.

My myriad critiques of the eventual Obama administration aside,
I can't deny the power of its symbolism. Or at least I can't deny how its
symbolism apparently affected me in those early days. I cried when the
election results were confirmed; I cried when the Obamas stepped out
before similarly sobbing yet elated crowds; I cried when he stepped out

from the armored vehicle that was ferrying him along in a motorcade on inauguration day and he waved at the crowd.

———

SLAVE CODES WERE ABUNDANT IN NUMBER BUT REPETITIVE IN SUBSTANCE. The specific language and qualifications varied from state to state, but their content was ever similar. The enslaved could not move about without some kind of pass or "certificate" authorizing their passage. The enslaved were prohibited from assembling in large numbers, unless, perhaps, a white person was in attendance. The enslaved were subject to curfews, limiting their movement to specified times of day. The enslaved were often barred from reading or writing. The enslaved could not testify against a white person. The enslaved, since they were property, could not own property themselves. The enslaved could not own weapons. And, of course, the enslaved could not raise their hand to strike a white person.

In the aftermath of Gabriel's plot, slave codes in southern states were tightened even further. Such tightening involved not only additional legislation across the South, but also more stringent application of laws that had been long enacted. Of course, laws restricting and policing the movements and activities of the enslaved would have been dead letters without a machinery of enforcement to give them viability; and enforcement waxed and waned with the social, economic, and political weather. Gabriel himself rose up at a time when, according to Egerton, "[s]lave controls were in a state of collapse in Virginia at large," due in part, perhaps, to a postrevolutionary wave of antislavery and humanitarian sentiment, growing discourse about "gradual" emancipation, a flurry of private manumissions, and/or challenges to the institution from an evangelical movement known as the Great Awakening. Whatever the cause, such controls in Virginia were in a waning season, which abruptly shifted after Gabriel's conspiracy was foiled.

After Gabriel's plot, restrictions were not only tightened with respect to the enslaved, but also especially for free Negroes, who in their very person were a dangerous symbol of relative freedom that stoked existing discontent. Free Negroes—who might have been granted freedom through private manumission, or were born free of parents who had been themselves manumitted—were also restricted in their movements, activities, and, dare one say, rights. Though not enslaved, free Negroes generally were not exactly citizens, and were banned from voting and interracial marriage. Free Negroes also were required to carry some pass or certificate validating their freedom. Free Negroes were subject to segregation in housing and public places. Free Negroes were restricted in pursuing certain trades and educational opportunities. And, of course, free Negroes could not enlist in any militia. The tightening of slave codes after Gabriel involved restrictions on private manumissions to stem the further occurrence of such dangerous symbols, as well as, in some states, limitations on the practice of "self-hire," which represented a "crude quasi freedom" that was similarly ominous.

Four operatives facilitated the enforcement of slave codes: state-funded militia; patrols of white men (not all necessarily enlisted in the military) who policed Negroes; and the enslavers and overseers themselves, aided by the complicity of the larger white society. Though Negroes were the "objects" the codes sought to repress, white citizens were the subjects tasked with enforcing them. "[T]he law told the white man, not the Negro, what he must do," writes Jordan in *White Over Black*. "It was the white man who was *required* to punish his runaways, prevent assemblages of slaves, enforce the curfews, sit on the special courts, and ride the patrols." Indeed, it was illegal for the enslaved to become literate—to learn to read and write words—making it doubly clear to whom the written word of the law was ultimately addressed. White citizens must have been aware that the ultimate intent of the slave codes was to prevent a slave insurrection.

The state militias in the South, which were more organized than their counterparts in the North, were emblematic of a southern society that was militaristic in character. "The fact is, they are all soldiers," British scientist Francis Baily wrote of the white men during his tour of the South in 1796–1797. Of his journey through the American South from 1852 to 1857, journalist and social critic Frederick Law Olmsted observed this about the city of Charleston, South Carolina: "There is [. . .] nearly everywhere [in the South], always prepared to act, if not always in service, an armed force with a military organization, which is invested with more arbitrary and cruel power than any police in Europe." (Olmsted added: "Yet the security of the whites is in a much less degree contingent on the action of the patrols than upon the constant, habitual, and instinctive surveillance and authority of all white people over black.") The militaristic trait, again, was often associated with the slave system that it was time and again called upon to uphold. "[N]ominally created to defend the state in a national emergency," Egerton said of state militia in his account of Gabriel's rebellion, "the Virginia militia, like that of all southern states, in reality existed to prevent slave insurrections."

———

VOTING EARLIER THAT DAY—THE DAY OBAMA WAS ELECTED—HAD BEEN rather uneventful. The organized confusion of checking in by last name, long slow lines, the recording and casting one's vote within cubicle-like slots. But that election day featured one peculiar element. It had taken me some time to register; there were repeated incidents on my way to the subway, on the subway, walking down the sidewalk to work, and so on: white people kept smiling at me. Once I'd started to notice, my last-minute blank-faced recognition was replaced with a civil stretch of my lips and, after some time, with the willful yet casual avoidance of a B-list celebrity. The supposedly secret ballot notwithstanding, it was clear who had voted for whom.

IF ENSLAVEMENT IS A DECLARATION OF WAR, THEN G. W. F. HEGEL'S master-slave dialectic offers a more nuanced philosophical depiction of the protagonists in this epic battle—one elegantly described by David Brion Davis in his epilogue to *The Problem of Slavery in the Age of Revolution 1770–1823*. Before the declaration of war, before the "master" bludgeoned man into property, there was, initially, an encounter. A time before one was "master" and the other "slave." There have been numerous theoretical reenactments of this encounter, attempts to reimagine and deduce what particular set of circumstances, both internal and external, combined to transform the Englishman into "master" and the Blackamoor into "slave." As for the external conditions, slavery, of course, was an expedient—and "free"—means of exploiting land and reaping profit from the export of its fruit. That Negroes were later all marked as "slaves" was a mere convenience, an easy demarcation that both defined a permanent productive underclass and created an artificial division between Negroes and poor whites, both of whose interests were more aligned than their new legal designations implied. Whatever the seeming external justifications, certain internal conditions—inner landscapes and psychological frontiers—helped reinforce and perpetuate the slave system once established.

For Hegel, when one consciousness initially encounters another, it first views this other person as "an undifferentiated extension of himself," perhaps, as Davis interpreted, in the way that babies initially view their parents, or, as Locke might have understood, as "men" view the natural world. "[T]hey are for one another," said Hegel, "like ordinary objects, independent shapes [. . .]." Yet once it becomes apparent that the other is not some inert object among others in the background scenery, that one is not readily manipulable to meet such person's desire, then there are two possible outcomes. The ideal outcome, according to Hegel, would be that a person encountering the "other" would, somehow, see himself in this other being—and by recognizing the "other" as himself, become aware of a deeper sense of his own self, and attain a transcendent notion of his own very being.

The other possible outcome, however, is what Hegel called a life-and-death struggle, where instead of a person merely recognizing himself in the other, he engages in a battle to impose his solipsistic certainty of himself onto the other, to compel this other person to submit to his own visions and desires. The victor of this battle, Hegel calls the "lord," and the defeated one the "bondsman." For the enslaved Negro, defeat did not necessarily result in a physical death, but rather a social one—the death of his humanity within a living body, which had become property, a mere extension of the lord.

So, Hegel's theory goes, the consciousness of the victorious lord is one that exists *for itself*, while, for the lord, the bondsman has been restored to his rightful place—as an object consigned to a plantation backdrop, like a mule or a willow tree—so that the lord once again reigns over all of nature, uncontested. However, the bondsman—forced into a state of subservience and fear—must adopt the consciousness of the lord. The bondsman is "infected by the lord's consciousness through and through." The bondsman, then, adopts the lord's vision of truth to ensure his own survival.

There is, yes, recognition, but it is largely one-sided—from the bondsman only, and not, of course, from the lord. It is, for the most part, the enslaved one who learns how to code-switch.

———

THERE IS A REASON WHY I FOUND MYSELF CRYING ON INAUGURATION DAY, when the Obamas stepped out of their car, which had emerged from a line of sturdy black cars lined up in the slow-moving presidential motorcade. I was afraid for his life. Obama, beaming and waving at the crowd as he walked, carefree, with panache, had me choked in tears, as I imagined him being centered within some sniper's crosshairs, the target of some hidden assassin.

Does this sound dramatic? I don't care, because it's true.

―――――

THOUGH THE LORD APPEARS, TO HIMSELF, TO BE SOVEREIGN, TO BE INDE-pendent insofar as he has become the "master" of the bondsman, the lord is, in fact, dependent upon the bondsman, whose slave consciousness enables the lord's sense of power and freedom—the paradoxical unfree freedom wrought by the legacy of slavery in the United States. Though not entirely consumed with fear, the lord has only experienced a "lesser dread," perhaps a simple phobia triggered by the bondman's mere existence, which is in itself a constant reminder of the threat of revolt. So, it follows that the lord's consciousness "is only an empty self-centered attitude" that never discovers its essential being, and therefore remains dependent. This kind of consciousness does not bring about transformative fear, only a lesser kind that looks outward and seeks to control and eliminate any perceived external threats.

Meanwhile, the bondsman has been "seized with dread," has "trembled in every fibre of its being," having had "everything solid and stable [. . .] shaken to its foundations." Perhaps this fear is the complex kind, as the bondsman has been forced into a situation where his subjection to pain and death has been left to the judgment of the lord. To address this fear would not be akin to turning on the light when one is afraid of the dark, but to turning within in order to overcome it.

Consumed with fear and compelled to labor by violence and its threat, the bondsman becomes absorbed with his labor. Through "discipline of service and obedience," the bondsman becomes aware of his transformative power. His labor has a tangible effect on the natural world; he begins to remember himself as distinct and apart from that world, not as an object, but as an agent. Through this acknowledgment, according to Hegel, the bondsman begins to engage in the process of transmuting his "absolute fear" into personal power. The bondsman's discovery of his essential being, meanwhile, eventually spurs him to fight for independence, for insurrection.

———

AFTER THE ELECTION, I WAS HANGING OUT WITH MY WHITE BOYFRIEND AT the time, browsing online and scanning various news coverage and images of all the carnivalesque street celebrations we'd managed to miss. I joked that all the white people were going to be afraid now that a black person was in charge. There was silence as I browsed and clicked some more, having already forgotten what I'd said. I soon snatched my fingers out of harm's way as he slammed closed the top cover of my laptop. I looked at him, bemused; he was seething with anger.

I had, he said, ruined what was up to that point a very beautiful moment, and what I had said, he said, was totally unacceptable. Or something along those lines. I stared at him, quiet but inwardly laughing. It's not like I was being abused or anything. In fact, it was the first time I had ever seen him that angry. Irritated, perhaps, maybe frustrated, but never angry to the point of shaking. He, in fact, usually seemed to have the perpetual disposition of all the people who had been smiling at me all day.

I eventually laughed outwardly, asked him if he was scared.

———

SO, THE BONDSMAN'S FULL ASSERTION OF HIS HUMANITY BECOMES SYNON- ymous with revolt, and the ascending sense of his own humanity comes to correlate with the lord's mounting fear of loss. Freedom or death is not only a zero-sum game for the bondsman. The lord cannot conceive of the bondsman's freedom without fearing a kind of death— whether the physical kind brought about by violent retribution or the existential kind caused by a loss of identity. The bondsman's freedom, then, is synonymous with the lord's death.

———

AS IT TURNED OUT, MY EARLY FEARS FOR OBAMA'S LIFE WERE NOT unfounded. News outlets eventually reported that Obama was experiencing a sharp uptick in death threats—up to four times more than George W. Bush, according to one account. In fact, Obama's election coincided with the formation of a new, far-right extremist group called the Oath Keepers, which, according to the hate-group monitor Southern Poverty Law Center, was founded in 2009 by a Yale Law School graduate named Stewart Rhodes. Self-described on its website as a "non-partisan association of current and formerly serving military, police, and first responders," the Oath Keepers are committed to fulfilling vows taken to "defend the Constitution of the United States against all enemies, foreign and domestic." The group's express enemies are the federal government and the threat of its overreaching powers, which they state include martial law.

My fear for his life, however, was apparently intertwined with the spectacle of his inauguration, because I eventually forgot about it completely as I started to scrutinize the policies of his administration. As far as I was concerned, no amount of charm and intelligence could eclipse the fact that the president of the United States was, in all cases, a figurehead for a gargantuan bureaucratic apparatus that translates corporate priorities into policy and wages foreign wars for profit. It was, in hindsight, a startling shift: from a former version of myself doing voter registration drives in some of the poorest, and mostly black, neighborhoods in Philadelphia, purchasing seven different newspapers after Obama won, then buying and framing a screenprinted image of his face above a caption reading "We Made History," to a later incarnation who would feel a numb jadedness spread through her body while reading that this same man was helming an administration that deported more persons than any prior one.

———

"THE SPECTRE OF NEGRO REBELLION PRESENTED AN APPALLING WORLD turned upside down," writes Jordan in *White Over Black*, "a crazy nonsense world of black over white, an anti-community, which was the direct negation of the community as white men knew it." In other words, it threatened a world where the concrete reality of white power and black insubordinacy would flip. Where the world would be one of "black over white."

Gabriel, though, did not seek to become the master of his enslavers; his ambitions were rather unambitious in that regard. Gabriel only sought to have the same rights and relative freedoms as his fellow white artisans—in other words, the right to be a free wage laborer, to autonomously sell his labor on equal terms. He did not seek dominance, only a semblance of equality—albeit by any means necessary.

Perhaps, in having seen or recognized the enslavers as he saw or recognized himself, Gabriel did not seek to obliterate them. That journey within, for the bondsman, does not always result in one's fear turning into projection, or turning a complex phobia into a simple one. Yet the "master," never having beheld the "slave" as anything other than an object, was not forced to contend with the slave's worldview, much less empathize with him.

Perhaps this is why the enslaver could not imagine any other motive of the rebellious enslaved than revenge.

———

I KNEW, OF COURSE, THAT ONE MAN COULD NOT BEAR THE FULL WEIGHT OF representing my aspirations or be the sole cause of my disappointments. This is likely why my sudden and unanticipated excitement about Obama's election quickly evaporated. Perhaps it's the same anticlimax that comes from applying for a job where your interviewer assures you that your role will be highly valued and your coworkers like "family," only for the friendly façade to give way almost immediately to the daily grind of mundanity and office rivalries.

All that said, I wondered about the mindset of someone who would actually want to kill the president. I didn't know the details of the threats, which were not disseminated at the time, but I assumed they came from white nationalists of some kind. That in and of itself should be an answer: they were white racists wanting to harm the first black president.

Yet the question still lingered unanswered. The intransigence of congressional leaders notwithstanding, I didn't see how Obama's presidency was a significant departure from prior ones. What, exactly, did these people think he was going to do? What were they so afraid of?

———

WHY ALL THIS FEAR OF A SLAVE INSURRECTION, WHAT WITH THE SANCtion and armed backing of the state? With a legal apparatus built to restrict the assembly, movement, and education of Negroes? With so many enslaved persons intimidated by the threat of harsh and indiscriminate retribution always ready to blow the whistle on planned revolts? With legions of armed civilians often required by law to patrol upon a whisper of revolt? With squadrons of state militiamen who could be swiftly called forth to put down any insurrections that actually occurred? Why?

The annals of history can be scoured for names, dates, locales, and events, but they often provide scant corroboration for why anything happened. This is particularly true when seeking rationales for fear, an emotion that often runs deep below the consciousness of whomever it grips. The "what" of fear—along with all of history's "whens," "wheres," and "whos"—is among a constellation of dots awaiting a narrative through line to draw an intelligible portrait of the past, and hopefully reveal an archetype of our contemporary moment.

———

THE ENSLAVER, IN ESSENCE, IS TRULY ENSLAVED. MEANWHILE, THE enslaved is put into the complex position of transforming all-consuming fear into courage. Even so, the enslaved's subsequent fight for outward independence was then, and sometimes feels even now, like a suicide mission—or, perhaps, a sign of supernatural faith. Akin to leaping off the top of a building with the intention to fly.

CHAPTER 2

So That Every Mouth
May Be Silenced

Silence is defined as the complete absence of sound. Yet unless one is diving in some deep-sea cavern or locked in an anechoic chamber, what is often registered as silence is in fact pervaded by noise. The chirping of birds and crickets; the low drone of a plane or refrigerator; here and there a distant blare of a car horn. Silence is rarely the complete absence of sound. Silence, rather, is the absence of the sound to which one is attuned to listen.

Put another way, silence is the sound of what has not been foregrounded. Silence is the sound of what has been relegated to the backdrop. And, of course, whether a sound's volume is internally raised or muted depends on who is doing the listening. In that light, it makes sense that one meaning of the word "observe" is to notice or perceive something *and* register it as being significant. In this sense, a thing is not observed merely by being in the field of one's perception, but also by having been deemed worth observing in the first place.

Neurologists have a term for this kind of hearing, which they call selective auditory attention. Because the brain would be overwhelmed by sensory omniscience, it acknowledges certain sounds and ignores others—a function that is crucial for human beings to make sense of the world. Perhaps this capacity stems from an early human need to differentiate the rustle of dead leaves in subtle wind from their crunch underfoot by an approaching predator. Selective listening, perhaps, is a matter of survival.

———

NEITHER THE WORD "SLAVERY" NOR "SLAVE" IS USED IN THE DECLARATION of Independence, that foundational pronouncement which, with mere words, birthed a nation separate from British rule. This is a rational omission. The primary tenet of the instrument—the avowal, borrowed from John Locke's *Two Treatises of Government*, that "all men are created equal"—is, of course, inimical to both the peculiar institution and to those who were forcibly subjected to it. Thomas Jefferson himself, the Declaration's author, enslaved more than one hundred people. In drafting the "truths" the Declaration holds to be self-evident, Jefferson replaced Locke's assertion that governments should be instituted to secure "life, liberty, and property" with "Life, Liberty and the pursuit of Happiness," arguably to further elide the glaring contradiction between these pronouncements and present practices. Slavery, then, was silenced in order to amplify self-evident "truths."

What a rhetorical sleight of hand—as something "self-evident" is, by definition, so obvious that it does not require any explanation. What is self-evident, for the most part, may be seen or touched, or is otherwise indisputable as to its existence. What is self-evident does not require declaration; it is simply acknowledged, usually in silence.

So, it is slavery, and not the equality of "men," that was, by definition, self-evident—and, thereby, consistent with the document's silence on the infernal institution. Slavery obviously was not absent as a historical fact, but it was present as an inconvenient truth.

———

AS THE CONTEXT FOR HUMAN SURVIVAL HAS SHIFTED WITH THE IMPOSItion of history, so this ability—that is, selective auditory attention—

must have continued to evolve. We assume that what is heard and not heard in the name of survival continues, over time, to correspond to the actual threat connected to a given sound. Yet, moving out of natural environments and into legally constructed ones—out of the "state of nature" and into systems of governance and control—what is not heard is not necessarily silent because it is inherently nonthreatening and can therefore be ignored. Rather, what is silent is often not heard because it has been silenced.

The word "silence," of course, is not only a noun. It is also a verb. Just as "slaves" were not a priori "slaves," but rather enslaved, "silence" does not necessarily exist in and of itself. Silence can be imposed by force—by violence or its threat. A subversive sound, if made, may be swiftly punished. Certain words are not spoken for fear of wrath. Similar to a brain striving to make meaning, silence imposed selectively by force creates the illusion of a lack of sound. Silence, then, is also a construct.

———

"SLAVERY," IN THE END, WAS EDITED OUT OF THE DECLARATION OF INDE-pendence. Jefferson initially had proposed including an indictment of the institution in the text. His censure of slavery, though, was truly a disavowal of British rule, damning the crown for having "waged cruel war against human nature itself, violating its most sacred rights of life and liberty in the persons of a distant people who never offended him, captivating & carrying them into slavery in another hemisphere, or to incur miserable death in their transportation thither. . . ." The Continental Congress chose to omit this passage, thereby, as described by Don Fehrenbacher and Ward McAfee in *The Slaveholding Republic*, "leaving a document that exalted liberty and equality but said nothing about the presence of slavery in the new nation." Representatives of South Carolina and Georgia, according to Jefferson, had insisted that this language be struck. Why jeopardize an actual institution for the sake of a rhetorical point?

The year was 1776. Historians have identified the decade or so leading up to that pivotal year as characterized by heightened slave "resistance," with increasing reports, for example, of fugitivity and unrest among the enslaved. The scare quotes around "resistance" are intentional. For one, the reality and rumor of plotted slave revolts often blurred, leaving the two indistinguishable among fearful white residents and their political representatives. Also, the spectrum between "resistance" and "insurrection" was wide—encompassing, as Herbert Aptheker notes in *American Negro Slave Revolts*, anything from individual acts of sabotage, stealing, suicide, and strikes to grand conspiracies reportedly agreed upon by larger collectives.

It is true that, by definition, the term "resistance" implies a much smaller scale of revolt than "insurrection." (Aptheker, for the sake of clarity, established a threshold in his foundational text on American slave revolts, a numerical tipping point at which "resistance" became "insurrection"—in his words, a minimum of ten slaves conspiring with "freedom" as their apparent aim.) Yet, in practice, one person's "resistance" is another's "insurrection." And when the terms are applied by historians, not only does the presence of one or the other label minimize or magnify a given event, the absence of either can eliminate it from the perceptual continuum altogether.

Take the American Revolutionary War, which spanned from 1775 to 1783. "As the British military occupied coastal cities in the South during the Revolutionary War," writes Michael Klarman in *The Framers' Coup*, "many thousands of slaves seized the opportunity to flee their masters in what one historian has called 'the greatest slave insurgency in North American history.'" This statement refers to the trend of British governors and generals issuing proclamations to liberate slaves who fought on the royal side of the war against American "rebels." Indeed, the year prior to the Declaration's drafting, in November

1775, royal governor of Virginia Lord Dunmore famously issued one such proclamation, which is considered to be the first large-scale offer of slave emancipation in the British colonies. Yet while the historical record is clear that large numbers of the enslaved did actually escape from and fight against their enslavers on the word of such British promises, this mass defection has rarely been deemed sufficient by historians for the label "insurrection."

The British arming of slaves in the Revolutionary War did not escape the attention of the Continental Congress, however. As Donald Waldstreicher noted in *Slavery's Constitution: From Revolution to Ratification*, Benjamin Franklin, who served on the drafting committee, suggested the insertion of "[He has] excited domestic insurrections among us" into the list of grievances against the king. With this small revision, and the omission of Jefferson's indictment, the Declaration of Independence—still formally silent on "slaves" and "slavery"—transitioned from scolding British rule for the peculiar institution to blaming British rule for instigating slave uprisings.

———

SILENCE UNDER THE LAW MAY BE CONSIDERED AN AFFIRMATIVE RIGHT—for instance, the right to remain silent in the face of criminal allegations. Also, in the context of legal interpretation, silence may be considered the absence of contemplation, as when the text of case law or a written agreement is "silent" on one matter or another. However, silence is not just a right prescribed by law or indicative of some absence of deliberation. Silence is fundamental to upholding the very construct of legal rule.

Look no further than the ultimate contract, the so-called social contract—the theoretical pact between peoples and the systems that govern them, which establishes the concept of law in the first place. Under the law, or, rather, "within" the legal construct, silence generally is not construed to indicate acceptance of a contract. If an offer is made, its acceptance must be expressly granted in order for the contract to be enforceable. There is a principle of free will that is said to underlie such everyday agreements, which are supposed to be mutual and voluntary.

Yet the opposite is true with respect to the social contract. The social contract does not require the express acceptance of all the peoples to whom it applies. It is—after its initial inception—unilateral, not mutual. It is imposed upon the peoples it subsequently governs involuntarily: if not necessarily against their will, then without their consent.

The social contract also relies on the peoples' silence. Silent acceptance helps constitute the social contract, and, thereafter, silent acceptance is the norm that fortifies the social contract's continuing legitimacy. An offer is made, laws are established, and every mouth thereupon is silenced.

THE CONSTITUTION ALSO DOES NOT MENTION THE WORD "SLAVERY" OR "slave." James Madison, one of the chief drafters, later explained this conspicuous absence, stating that some of the delegates "had scruples against admitting the term 'slaves' into the instrument." While the words themselves are absent, the deed is nonetheless addressed throughout the document. Euphemism was deployed.

Where Article 1, Section 2, ties apportionment of members of the House of Representatives to the population of the several states, the infamous three-fifths clause allowed each state to include in its headcount not only "citizens," who were typically defined under state law as white landed men, but also three-fifths of "all other persons." (Counting each slave as three-fifths of a person also implicated Article 1, Section 9, which apportions direct taxes Congress may levy according to state population.) The clause in Article 1, Section 9, preventing Congress from prohibiting the foreign slave trade until 1808, refers to such trade as the "migration or importation of such persons as any of the states now existing shall think proper to admit." Article 4, Section 2, requires each state to return any "person held to service or labour" back to the state from which he or she fled, hence its reference as the Fugitive Slave Clause.

The omission of the words "slavery" and "slave" at the time was not unremarkable. It was an absence, for example, that Delaware delegate John Dickinson stated would "be regarded as an endeavor to conceal a principle of which we are ashamed." Yet slavery was not initially on the agenda of those attending the Constitutional Convention of 1787. Delegates at this Philadelphia gathering were present to establish another form of governance, not to debate the propriety of the peculiar institution—a topic that would have surely derailed the aim of uniting northern and southern states under a newfound federalist government. As Waldstreicher writes: "Silence about slavery would emphasize what the Americans had in common, such as a desire for equitable taxation grounded in the consent of the people."

And the "people" and "citizens" referenced in the Constitution were, at the time, understood to be white, although the word "white" does not appear in the document, or in the Declaration for that matter. The Tenth Amendment—which reserves all powers not expressly delegated to the federal government to the states—allowed the framers to conveniently bypass the issue of who, under the founding documents, could and could not be considered a "citizen."

———

LAWS THEMSELVES ARE SILENT. YES, THEY ARE WRITTEN, EVIDENCED IN words, but our experience of them generally has no sound. Our compliance with, and acceptance of, the law is silent. What is perceptible, rather, is the violence exacted when the law is broken. Laws are only as apparent as the punishment of those who violate them, and perhaps as the ongoing policing of all others who silently observe them.

Retributive justice is the hand over the speaking mouth. Surveillance is the beat cop who strolls by and, with his presence, compels one to swallow the word before it can be spoken. The law is silent. The law silences. And the law is legitimized in silence.

Together with violence, silence is foundational to the law's very existence. It makes sense, then, that another definition of the word "observe" is to maintain silence in compliance with a rule or custom. As when a temple or church is hushed as solemn parishioners kneel and pray, so do laypersons fulfill or comply with the law in silence. The silent observer makes slow, deliberate movements, stifles routine urges, and seems to apologize for her very existence. The silent observer watches herself, yes, but also watches others to verify that she is not the only one adhering to the ritual of compliance. Whether such silence is reverent or resentful, however, it is nonetheless the sound made by those who obey.

———

IN LATE 1786, TAX COLLECTORS DOING THEIR ROUNDS IN CENTRAL MASSA-chusetts were faced down by bands of armed "debtors" and "taxpayers" (i.e., white "citizens"). It was a culmination of escalating events that arose from a combination of the state's imposition of heavy taxes to service its debt, a rigorous and unforgiving tax enforcement, and a state administration overrepresented by mercantilists who were impervious to the pleas for relief from debt-strapped farmers. Several thousand rebels—many of whom were veterans of the Revolutionary War—stormed courthouses from August 1786 to February 1787, interrupting proceedings related to tax and debt collection. In response, the governor of Massachusetts enacted the Riot Act, which, among other things, suspended the writ of habeas corpus to allow for warrantless arrests of rebels, who could also face indefinite detention without a hearing.

Enter Daniel Shays, himself a Revolutionary War veteran, who in January 1787 attempted to take over a federal arsenal of weapons and ammunition with a group of protesters. When civilians refused to respond to the Massachusetts governor's call to bear arms against Shays and his followers, a private militia was assembled, financed by many of those prominent members of Massachusetts society who owned state bonds and had the most to gain from all levied taxes being collected. The privately financed army dispersed Shays and his fellow rebels in February of that year.

In the aftermath of this uprising, attendees of the Constitutional Convention—including Madison, George Washington, and John Jay—were documented as having expressed grave concerns about the extent of Shays' Rebellion, how it exposed the weakness of state governments to suppress domestic uprisings, and, finally, how it evidenced the critical need for a strong national government.

———

LAW INDUCES SILENCE, AND LAW AMPLIFIES SOUND. OUTSIDE THE LEGAL construct, the click of a lighter inside a restaurant would be imperceptible in the background chatter; within the construct the very same sound pricks the nearby ears of those wary of smoking bans. Yet to survive within the construct is not simply a matter of foregrounding what is illicit and relegating what is licit to the backdrop. It is not just a matter of highlighting the abnormal and muting the norm— itself a facet of internal and external policing. Survival under law also involves a silencing of one's conscience—that is, to the extent that it runs counter to that which has been designated as lawful.

———

OTHER THAN THE CONSTITUTION'S FOREIGN-SLAVE-TRADE CLAUSE (WHICH prevented Congress from prohibiting the foreign slave trade until 1808), the regulation of slavery itself was relegated to the states, a convenient way to sidestep any prolonged federal debate over the legitimacy of the institution itself. From the perspective of federal governance, the question of whether slavery should continue could be skirted or, at least with respect to foreign slave trade, delayed. The fact that slavery actually existed, however, could not be avoided insofar as the institution inevitably touched on those central issues of representation, taxation, and the overall balance of power in Congress. Apportionment of state representatives to the House chiefly amounted to whether any one or more regional interests would be advanced or undermined. As to the southern interest in slavery, while Congress was not empowered to directly regulate the institution, it could indirectly frustrate its viability—for example, by increased taxes on southern exports, the fruits of enslaved labor.

The three-fifths clause, in particular, was cause for much debate between northern and southern delegates—and not necessarily because any were expressly opposed to the concept of counting a "person" as a fraction of a human. That was a side issue. The main point of contention between the regional factions was their relative political power, and whether agrarian or increasingly industrial economic interests would gain representative favor in Congress. The quandary of the slave's dual nature as both property and person was largely discussed in relation to this power struggle.

"Are they [slaves] men?" In *The Framers' Coup*, Klarman quotes the rhetorical interrogation of delegate Gouverneur Morris of Pennsylvania, who questioned the three-fifths clause. "Then make them citizens and let them vote. Are they property? Why then is no other property included?" Further, delegate Elbridge Gerry of Massachusetts argued that if the enslaved counted toward the apportionment of representatives to the House, then so should "the cattle and horses of the North." Whether highlighting their character as property or as people, the enslaved, to the delegates, were always pawns. At the Convention and beyond, the peculiar and dual character of the enslaved was not a moral quandary, but a power play.

There are other clauses of the Constitution that are interpreted to regulate slavery. The three-fifths, slave trade, and fugitive slave clauses are the most recited ones, with express signifiers of "slavery" and "slaves" clearly replaced with more euphemism. And yet there are also the clauses regarding "domestic violence" and "insurrection." While Article 1, Section 8, of the Constitution allows Congress to "provide for calling forth the militia to execute the laws of the union, suppress insurrections and repel invasions," Article 4, Section 4, obligates the federal government to protect each of the states "against domestic violence." Shays' Rebellion is often cited as the source for such language, since it occurred shortly before the Convention took place. A Virginia delegate, for example, emphasized the need for a strong government to suppress such uprisings. However, the debate over these clauses during the constitutional ratification process tells a different story—they were primarily discussed in terms of their application to slave revolts.

Gouverneur Morris, among other northern delegates, objected to their having to "march their militia for the defense of southern states" in the event of a slave insurrection. With some exceptions—including the conscientious Quakers and abolitionists largely vocal in the Northeast—the concerns of Morris and others about such clauses were framed in terms of cost burden. Why should nonslave states have to contribute to the collective defense against slave insurrections? This criticism was ultimately overruled, and the "insurrection" and "domestic violence" clauses became among those praised by southern representatives for protecting their slaveholding interests.

The state militias were not the only military forces intended to suppress insurrections. As elaborated in *The Federalist Papers*, Alexander Hamilton advocated for "a force constituted differently from the militia to preserve the peace of the community and to maintain the just authority of the laws against those violent invasions of them which amount to insurrections and rebellions." In other words, framers advocated for the establishment of a federal military force, which was eventually enumerated in Article 1, referring to the power of Congress to "raise and support Armies" and "provide and maintain a Navy." The concerns raised at the time about establishing federal military forces—the modern-day equivalent to the federal military corps that includes the Army, Navy, and Coast Guard—had less to do with the enslaved and seemed to generally arise from the threat that such an armed body could pose to white citizens themselves.

To dispel concerns about any abuse of federal military power, James Madison surmised in *The Federalist Papers* that the state militia together with armed civilians would be sufficiently numerous to repel a federal army. In other words, federal military forces could be easily repelled by the "people." Hamilton, however, also sought to quell fears about the federal military by assuring doubters that the federal military would, in fact, be constituted by the "people." "Where in the name of common sense are our fears to end if we may not trust our sons, our brothers, our neighbors, our fellow-citizens?" Hamilton rhetorically asked in *The Federalist Papers*. "What shadow of danger can there be from men who are daily mingling with the rest of their countrymen and who participate with them in the same feelings, sentiments, habits and interests?"

The silence at the end of that question surely has a sound.

BIRTH OF AN ACT

The Insurrection Act of 1807 was enacted in silence. It has no legislative history—that is, there is no record of any congressional debate on Congress's intent in introducing and passing the law. Under the Act, the president can federalize the militia (now the National Guard) and deploy federal troops to suppress an insurrection or other "unlawful combinations" upon the request of the state governor, or unilaterally if such incidents are either causing the deprivation of constitutional rights that a state is either unwilling or unable to protect, or are obstructing the enforcement of federal law. In all cases, the president must first make a proclamation under the Act, ordering insurgents to "disperse and retire peaceably to their abodes," and only after this official utterance may the president follow up with an executive order authorizing the domestic deployment of federal troops.

Though lacking legislative history, the Insurrection Act does have antecedents—the Militia Acts of 1792. Under the First Militia Act of 1792, Congress delegated its constitutional authority under the "insurrections" and "domestic violence" clauses to the president, who was thereby authorized to call forth the militia of the states in order to suppress insurrections, as well as to repress "invasion from any foreign nation or Indian tribe." The Second Militia Act of 1792 later required "each and every free able-bodied white male citizen" of the several states between the ages of eighteen and forty-five to enroll in the militia and procure the prescribed arms, including "a good musket or firelock, a sufficient bayonet and belt, two spare flints, and a knapsack, a pouch with a box therein to contain not less than twenty-four cartridges." There is scant record of debate about some of the language of these initial Militia Acts; the record does not reveal the underlying motivation for their enactment.

That said, the Haitian Revolution had begun one year before, in 1791. In that year, writes Gerald Horne in *Confronting the Black Jacobins: The U.S., the Haitian Revolution, and the Origins of the Dominican Republic*, South Carolina governor Charles Pinckney warned then-president George Washington about how similar Hispaniola was to South Carolina in terms of demographics, insofar as Negroes outnumbered whites. He warned that "a day may arrive when mainlanders too would be exposed to the same insurrections as the 'flame' of sedition spread northward."

Legal scholars, for the most part, reference Shays' Rebellion as a likely trigger for the Militia Acts and the subsequent Insurrection Act.

THE SELECTIVE ATTENTION THAT CONSTRUCTS SILENCE IS ALSO A CONDI-
tion precedent for denial. With troubling emotions kept at bay,
the person in denial does not even have to suffer from cognitive
dissonance—that liminal experience of holding two contradictory
beliefs at the same time. Someone can refuse to acknowledge that
which would trigger fear or guilt or shame or, perhaps, even an inkling
of courage. Denial is a defense mechanism that protects one's physical self or sense of self against any other "realities" that threaten to
violate either of them.

Denying the existence of something, and thereby silencing it in
the mind, does not resolve the contradiction. Whether it manages
to infiltrate consciousness or is forever exiled to the dimension of
an ignored reality, the contradiction persists and recurs, resulting in
repeating patterns in the lives of those suffering from denial—or even
from cognitive dissonance, denial's close sibling. It's a recurring nightmare, where similar themes arise and taunt the dreamer to address
and perhaps resolve her discordance once and for all.

So it is the perfect trifecta. The ability of the brain to render
something "silent." The confluence of law and violence to "silence."
And the human ability to block or silence certain thoughts and events
from conscious awareness in order to avoid uncomfortable emotions.

SHAYS' REBELLION, AS WIDELY DOCUMENTED, DEEPLY TROUBLED THE
founders. It was an uprising that reverberated through the Constitutional Convention, bolstering federalist arguments for a national
government. It was by definition an "insurrection," a violent uprising
against domestic authority.

Yet in the intermittent silence—the absolute silence that birthed

the Insurrection Act and the relative silence from whence its antecedents emerged—over a period of time that spanned about fifteen years
from 1792 to 1807, could there not have been any other motivations?
It's true that George Washington invoked the first Militia Act in order
to suppress the Whiskey Rebellion—an uprising of about five hundred
armed "taxpayers" resisting a tax on whiskey consumption and distri-
bution, which is also often cited in tandem with the Shays uprising to
affirm the executive power to suppress insurrections. Yet, in consistently amplifying the influence of Shays' Rebellion on the "insurrections" and "domestic violence" clauses, could legal scholars be muting
other factors?

The silence at the end of that question surely has a sound.

———

LIBERTÉ! ÉGALITÉ! FRATERNITÉ! THIS BATTLE CRY OF THE FRENCH REVO-
lution, the collapse of the Declaration of the Rights of Man into
a tripartite principle, was also the rebel yell of the revolution in
Saint-Domingue. "When drawing up the constitution of the French
people," said deputy of the National Convention René Levasseur to
members of France's early government, "we paid no attention to the
unhappy Negroes."

French revolutionaries may not have been paying attention to "the
unhappy Negroes" of colonial Saint-Domingue, but the "unhappy
Negroes" were paying attention to the revolutionary fervor of the
French masses. Indeed, the internal fire that overthrew feudalism and
monarchal rule in France was also sparked among the enslaved in
Saint-Domingue, who wrested liberty from their own infernal enslavers in an uprising that is said to have begun in August 1791. "[T]he
liberty and equality which these blacks acclaimed as they went into
battle," writes C. L. R. James in *The Black Jacobins*, "meant more to
them than the same words in the mouths of the French."

The Saint-Domingue revolution had its own founding father— the much loved, very mysterious, and seemingly ubiquitous Toussaint L'Ouverture. However, Jacques Dessalines would become the first leader of the independent country reborn as Haiti, which became independent on New Year's Day 1804. "It was therefore an important result of the reverberating disaster of St. Domingo," writes Jordan in *White Over Black*, "that many Americans came increasingly to feel that slavery was a closed subject, entirely unsuitable for frank discussion." Jordan details the mounting fear among white citizens in America as the revolution in Hispaniola raged and was eventually won. Starting in 1793, he lists one after another southern state that had taken legal moves to restrict or outright ban the entry of Negroes from the West Indies, with some residents of Wilmington, North Carolina, petitioning the House of Representatives in 1803 to prevent the arrival of Negroes from the then-revolting French Guadeloupe. To make it easier to identify any potential firebrands visiting from the insurrectionary islands, the House soon introduced a bill barring "any negro, mulatto, or other person of color" from the ports of the United States, which was later modified to apply only to Negroes who were nonnative. That version of the bill passed the Senate.

In short, in the 1790s into the early 1800s there is some historical record of white citizens and representatives showing concern about international Negro revolts. Jordan quotes Thomas Jefferson himself, who, in response to Congress passing a bill opening trade with L'Ouverture in 1799, told Madison "[w]e may expect therefore black crews, and supercargoes and missionaries thence into the southern states. . . . If this combustion can be introduced among us under any veil whatever, we have to fear it."

One reaction to this fear, as Jordan describes, is denial; a Richmond newspaper accused American editors of fomenting unrest among Virginia slaves by printing the Saint-Domingue constitution.

"[B]eyond a reasoned fear of domestic insurrection seems to have been a desire to banish the reality of St. Domingo."

CONSPIRACY OF SILENCE

I have an ear for what is not said. For what is couched, qualified, skirted, deflected. I even know what silence sounds like. The pauses, the hesitations, the stalling intakes of breath all bear their own messages that often belie the spoken word. I can even read what has not been written. What is between the lines, as they say, is often more important than what is being communicated in them. The proverbial elephant in the room. I vividly remember stumbling upon one such silence while attending a semester-long class on property in law school. Slavery was not mentioned once.

—————

ONE SUNDAY EVENING IN CHARLESTON, SOUTH CAROLINA, WRITES LACY K. Ford in *Deliver Us from Evil*, was "marked by rumors of danger and the 'passing of patrols on the street' throughout the night, rendering 'every slight noise' a matter of so much concern that 'no one, not even the children, ventured to retire' that evening." The foregoing describes panic incited by rumors of insurrection on the night of June 16, 1822, when Denmark Vesey was supposed to have led an insurrection in the port city. Born into slavery in St. Thomas, Vesey was sold to work in Bermuda, then Saint-Domingue, then back to Bermuda before accompanying his master to Charleston, where he bought, if not his freedom, at least the absence of slavery. Like Gabriel Prosser, Vesey was literate and had a trade; after using six hundred dollars in lottery winnings to purchase himself out of slavery, he worked as an independent carpenter. Vesey's wife and subsequent children, however, remained slaves when their "master" refused to allow Vesey to purchase them as well, thus stoking his insurrectionary fervor.

Vesey had been able to contrast the various conditions of bond-age in the Caribbean and South Carolina, likely giving him a unique perspective on the relativity of his own condition and that of his bonded brethren. While the majority of both South Carolina's and Charleston's populations were made up of the enslaved, some of the Negro population consisted of free Negroes who had fled what would become Haiti during the revolution that spanned from 1791 to 1803. Many such free Negro residents must have relayed tales of struggle and rebellion on the island as well.

Vesey was esteemed by many members of Charleston's majority-Negro population not only for his relative freedom, but also for his position of relative authority in the African Methodist Episcopal Church's "Bethel Circuit"—the first independent Negro denomination in the United States. One of the cofounders of the Charleston chapter of the Bethel Circuit, Vesey had resisted discrimination against Negro parishioners in the wider AME church by its white members. It was in this independent branch of the AME church that the independent carpenter is said to have culled coconspirators into his developing plot to overthrow slavery in Charleston.

———

WHENEVER I WALK INTO A SILENT ROOM, I SUBMIT TO THE PREEXISTING hush, try not to disturb anyone already there, do my best not to make a noise. And when I must disrupt the silence, I do so in a whisper, careful that the rush of breath over the reeds of my vocal cords does not emit a discordant sound. Yet the whisper is not only the sound of one seeking to obey the silence. The whisper is the medium of rumor. "In a country of silence," a *New York Times* journalist once wrote in 1974 about a military coup in Greece, "rumor is king." Gossip blossoms and proliferates like a wildfire or a rapidly accelerating disease. One endless game of telephone has begun, and distortion and exaggeration become the new elephant in the room.

———

AND WHAT WERE THE DETAILS OF VESEY'S PLOT? SIMILAR TO GABRIEL'S, the plan—reported to have included tens of thousands of the enslaved all along the coast of South Carolina—involved taking over and securing arms from the coastal city's arsenal, setting the city of Charleston on fire, seizing ships docked at the port and sailing them to Haiti, indiscriminately killing any and all whites who crossed their path. The insurrection was reportedly to commence on July 14 of 1822, the thirty-third anniversary of the storming of the Bastille (the fortress prison in Paris) by the masses. However, the July date was purportedly moved up to mid-June in order to avoid word spreading before the plot could be hatched.

This precaution proved moot. An enslaved man named Peter told his enslaver of overheard plans for the Vesey-led insurrection, and, thereafter, two enslaved men, George Wilson and Joe LaRoche, informed Charleston officials of the same. A secret city council meeting was convened, including South Carolina governor Thomas Bennett, who was also the commander in chief of the state militia. Though the secrecy was intended to allow officials and law enforcement to mobilize a defense without alarming white residents, this plot also proved moot, as murmurings of insurrection grew deafening all around the city.

Militia and patrols rounded up suspects, including Vesey, in the ensuing weeks, which—after brutal interrogations of the apprehended in a Charleston workhouse—culminated in a hasty trial conducted in secret. Vesey, in the end, was sentenced to death by hanging along with five other enslaved men. The arrests, court hearings, and hangings did not end there, however. Following a second trial round, a total of thirty-five people were executed and thirty-two were deported from the United States.

The executions did not immediately ease anxieties about further revolt. Thereafter, about 2,500 citizens (according to a woman's missive to a local newspaper) procured arms to protect their property and lives. "But," the woman also wrote, "it is a subject not to be mentioned and unless you hear of it elsewhere, say nothing about it."

———

DURING A GLOBAL PANDEMIC, THE FIRST WAVE OF WHICH HAD SHUTtered New York City and quarantined all its inhabitants, including myself, unable to lawfully leave home other than to carry out some essential task, I encountered a new sound. I was already generally familiar with sounds of silence—but there are different kinds of silence. This was a new silence that, due to my unfamiliarity with its tones and resonances, had imposed itself as a presence in my apartment.

In this revamped aural backdrop, the birds still chirped, unidentified insects chattered, and certain monotone machinery still droned in the distance, but there was another set of frequencies that asserted itself over the sound that I would typically ignore. Sirens blared and waned, rose and dipped, in between these background sounds, weaving a new silent tapestry. This new silence, of course, was not a metaphor for peace and stillness, but of emergency and death. Even so, within about a week of this new and constant sound, I became impressed by my ability to completely ignore it.

———

"OUR NIGHTS ARE SOMETIMES SPENT IN LISTENING TO NOISES," HERBERT Aptheker quoted in *Nat Turner's Slave Rebellion*, from a letter written by a gentleman in Virginia at the end of 1831 or the beginning of 1832. "A corn song, a hog call, has often been a subject of nervous terror, and a cat, in the dining room, will banish sleep for the night. There has been and still is a *panic* in all this country." This letter was written more than fifty years following the birth of the nation, and in the aftermath of a notorious slave insurrection, due to which the letter writer confessed: "I have not slept without anxiety in three months."

The man was responding to the news of Nat Turner, who with his scantily armed coconspirators, some drunk and many fatigued, was repressed after two days and nights in 1831 by white patrolmen reinforced by local militia and federal troops. Both literate and a religious fanatic, Turner had managed to wage a "successful" slave insurrection in Southampton, Virginia. The insurrection did not, of course, succeed in securing liberation for any of the enslaved, however, but was successful insofar as it was not suppressed before it ever got off the ground. On August 21, 1831, about a week after having interpreted a solar eclipse as an auspicious signal, Turner and his coconspirators rose up in their Southampton neighborhood and moved from house to house, killing the white slaveholding families who lived in each and liberating the enslaved they encountered to add to their insurrectionary band.

Armed only with whatever deadly instruments they were able to gather from the homesteads of the families they killed, Turner and his crew of sixty to eighty enslaved and free Negro men had planned to continue to an arsenal in the county of Jerusalem, where they would secure sufficient weaponry for their cause. The absence of slavery, of course, was not necessarily freedom, and it is not clear to what extent Turner and his cohorts imagined how—once their respective enslavers were slain and they roamed relatively free—they would proceed from there. What is clear, or at least has been documented, is that the Turner Rebellion lasted for two days and nights, resulting in the killing of anywhere from fifty-five to two hundred white citizens.

The revolt, then, represents the worst-case scenario of a slave insurrection—from the perspective of the white citizens who deathly feared them, that is. As Lacy K. Ford puts it in *Deliver Us from Evil: The Slavery Question in the Old South*, "[T]he true danger of insurrection was that some whites would likely lose their lives and others would see their property destroyed . . . before the white militia prevailed." The institution of slavery and the sanctity of the state that enforced it, by contrast, seemed impervious to insurrections, whether actual or threatened. In any event, Turner's revolt, quelled in part by the deployment of federal troops, is considered by some military historians to be the first invocation of the Insurrection Act.

⸻

THE MOST ODIOUS SILENCE IS COMPLICIT SILENCE, WHICH ABETS HARMFUL deeds with quiet observation. Silence laced with complicity is that of your classmates when the reprimand by your third-grade teacher was far too harsh compared to the purported offense. It is the silent rubbernecking of pedestrians who pass their eyes over someone being stopped and frisked on the sidewalk. In silence, voyeurs may be mildly sympathetic but are mostly self-satisfied, as if another's reproach reflects their relative obedience and lack of guilt. Perhaps this is why, in her poem "For Assata," Audre Lorde referred to the "vanities of silence," capturing, by definition, the often unjustified feeling of being pleased with oneself or one's situation, which is a subtle characteristic of complicit silence.

The "vanities of silence" capture the complicity, the secret agreement, whereby the silent ones vow to not question, investigate, challenge, or defend. If you are silent, the thinking goes, then you can continue to enjoy the attendant privileges of remaining so without having to acknowledge that they are, in fact, privileges. You just look about at "those less fortunate," the "wretched of the earth," and think, that's too bad, but that has nothing to do with you. Though not without its short-term rewards, this kind of silence is, in the end, suffocating. And as Lorde has also put it, your silence will not save you.

⸻

SOME HISTORIANS DIFFER AS TO THE UNDERLYING MOTIVE OF THE TURNER insurrection, with some pointing to the more obvious objective of liberation and others to mere plunder. However, what is clear is the practical impossibility of waging a successful slave insurrection. The ongoing irrational fear of slave insurrections notwithstanding, white citizens at the time generally enjoyed both safety in numbers and under law, according to which Negroes were subject to severe restriction, including being prohibited from owning any weaponry or joining any militia. While the revolutionaries who successfully fought to end their enslavement in Haiti outnumbered their enslavers, in the United States as a whole slave insurrections were doomed from the start by the mere fact of math and military might.

Turner himself, though, was hardly practical. He was a fanatic. Not necessarily because he was an avid reader of the Bible, but in large part due to his conviction that he had a direct line to God, whom Turner believed communicated with him in visions, including the ominous solar eclipse that signaled the ripe occasion for revolt. Perhaps Turner's otherworldly insistence on his mission, his reliance on divine assistance rather than material, strategic assessment, was the factor that set apart the "success" of his insurrection from the "failures" of his predecessors. Perhaps the will to actually undertake an insurrection is as irrational as the deep fear of the enslavers that one would actually succeed.

In the immediate aftermath of the rebellion, nearly fifty men were apprehended for conspiring with Turner, with anywhere from eleven to nineteen of them judicially executed. Turner himself, however, evaded capture until October 30, and was finally executed by hanging the following month. The relatively successful insurrection, then, finally came to an end.

Panic nonetheless ensued. And with this panic came a reign of terror over the Negro population in Virginia. "It appears safe to say," writes Aptheker in *Nat Turner's Slave Rebellion*, "that at least as many Negroes were killed without trial as whites had perished due to the Revolt and that probably the number in the former case was considerably more than in the latter."

The terror spread throughout other southern states, where further repressive laws were enacted to prevent insurrections and help quell white fears. Such official measures were as extreme as the underlying fear. As noted by the sleepless Virginia letter writer quoted above, with the elevation of fear, even the "silence" came to have a sound.

———

ALL THESE SILENCES—THE HEDGING, THE REFUSAL TO SPEAK, THE AVOID- ance of the obvious—they all forge a tacit arrangement. Silence is traded for security, albeit a false sense of it. This is because complicit silence is actually the sound of fear—or, at times, the background thrum of whispers creating fabulation from fear.

There are ways out of this agreement. Speaking of the wretched of the earth, in his book of that title, Frantz Fanon offered one way, when he wrote of the intellectual who "sheds all that calculating, all those strange silences, those ulterior motives, that devious thinking and secrecy as he gradually plunges deeper among the people."

———

JORDAN'S OBSERVATION IN *WHITE OVER BLACK* THAT THE MERE DISCUS- sion of slave insurrections was tantamount to inciting them is in keeping with one recurring theme that emerged from my reading on slave revolts—and that is the reluctance among white citizens to speak about them. News of actual slave conspiracies was fre- quently suppressed from publication, for fear that it would incite even more. Some historians have described local papers at the time as untrustworthy sources, rarely giving complete information on slave revolts. Virginia papers, for example, were described as having decided upon a "studied silence" on the subject. Meanwhile, white citizens engaged in muffled conversations about rumored and real revolts locally and abroad.

Publicly, however, white citizens remained silent, and they silenced each other. This is the kind of silence that threatens to thicken into a coat of denial. Muffled conversations notwithstanding, if one doesn't speak of the fear of insurrection, does the fear really exist?

This was not a rhetorical question. The enforced answer was "No." The silence was complicit, its own conspiracy, as if to keep secret—not just from the slaves themselves, but from their oppressors—that the slave's much feared humanity could not long be suppressed.

CHAPTER 3

A House Divided

As with each human being, a body politic is both singular and plural, seemingly indivisible and the sole representative of fragmented multitudes teeming within. Whenever someone experiences a discrepancy between two interpretations of the self—by observing some conflict among one's beliefs, behaviors, and/or attitudes—this person is said to be suffering from cognitive dissonance. By extension, perhaps, a body politic may also display symptoms of cognitive dissonance—the most glaring of which is the eruption of civil war.

———

ON APRIL 15, 1861, PRESIDENT ABRAHAM LINCOLN ISSUED A PROCLAMATION to authorize calling forth 75,000 militiamen, citing the obstruction of federal law in South Carolina, Georgia, Alabama, Florida, Mississippi, Louisiana, and Texas "by combinations too powerful to be suppressed by the ordinary course of judiciary proceedings or by the powers vested in the marshals by law." The president did so to suppress an insurrection at Fort Sumter in South Carolina. That this battle marked the start of the American Civil War is a widely accepted fact. The names of the main characters cast in this bloody saga are also well known, including, apart from Lincoln, Jefferson Davis, Robert E. Lee, and Ulysses S. Grant. As the conflict raged, figures like Frederick Douglass and William Lloyd Garrison continued to wage their own war of words against slavery, agitating for abolition through publications and oratory. To this day, enthusiasts reenact battles at their original sites, which, together with celebrated names and memorized dates, are strung together to form a detailed and incontrovertible timeline of the Civil War. However, *why* the Civil War actually occurred has been, over time, a matter of historical debate.

One theory emphasizes commerce, framing the Civil War as a regional contest over which form of economic production would prevail within the Republic—industrial manufacturing in the North or agricultural production in the South. That northern industry was fueled by free labor and the southern plantation by the yield of slave labor, under this theory, is incidental to the fundamental question of how the country's captains of commerce were to continue to reap their revenues. This view was put forth by historians Charles and Mary Beard, whose version of the Civil War was described by W. E. B. Du Bois as a "sweeping mechanistic interpretation." The Beards' calculus was purely economic, with issues of morality of little consequence.

Another theory highlights a sharp difference in regional opinion over states' rights, with officials of southern states both fiercely defending against unwanted federal intrusion into their local affairs and wielding representational power in Congress to use federal authority to enforce their local interests. Emphasizing the horizontal separation of powers between the federal and state governments, this theory frames certain key events leading up to the Civil War— including violent clashes over whether Kansas would be a slave or free state in 1859, the 1850 enactment of the Fugitive Slave Act federally enforcing the return of the enslaved who had escaped back to the states from which they had fled, and, of course, the penultimate secession crisis in the southern states that formed a newfound Confederacy, among others—as an inherent battle over the nature and utility of federalism, with slavery, again, somewhat incidental to this primary disagreement.

Yet another theory, of course, involved white fear of slave insurrection. The fear, again, was an undercurrent of personal and political activity—a fear of the *potential* for slave insurrections rather than *actual* insurrections themselves, which proved sporadic and easily suppressed whenever attempted, barely materializing beyond a notional conspiracy. And yet the potential for revenge from the person who lay suppressed within the property struck terror into the hearts of enslavers and other white citizens. As Virginia governor James McDowell once put it: "Was it the fear of Nat Turner, and his deluded, drunken handful of followers, which produced such effects? No, sir. It was the suspicion eternally attached to the slave himself—the suspicion that a Nat Turner might be in every family, that the same bloody deed might be acted over at any time and in any place."

What is clear, however, is that the Civil War was waged with the support of federal military intervention in order to preserve the Union. Whether the Union to be preserved was the mere political association of states with the same central government, or a psychic Union representing the alignment of the principles and practices of a nation that was supposed to be founded on "freedom," depends on the narrative deployed to connect the evident facts of this portion of U.S. history.

―――

COGNITIVE DISSONANCE GIVES RISE TO AN UNCOMFORTABLE PSYCHOLOGical state, an internal tug of war between, say, a belief and a behavior, each pulling at one's peace of mind from opposite directions. One might, say, purport to believe in God while regularly engaging in "sinful" behavior. The same person might also be inclined to rebuke anyone bold enough to point out this contradiction, rather than humbly admit fault and repent. Fractious multitudes swarm beneath the skin and swim behind the eyes. And yet their outward representative, the singular human, continually strains to maintain a consistent front.

The dissonance between two categories of cognition, if deemed sufficiently important to this person (i.e., critical to the idea such a person has of herself), arouses tension and turbulence within. The singular human in this predicament is like a person with each foot set on a different raft, striving to keep balance as the makeshift floats drift apart.

———

IN THE YEARS LEADING UP TO THE CIVIL WAR, ON FEBRUARY 11, 1856, PRESident Franklin Pierce issued a proclamation under the Insurrection Act ordering the dispersal of persons obstructing law and order in the state of Kansas. The reason for the proclamation, which was made at the request of territorial governor Andrew Reeder, was to quell factional violence in a conflict that came to be known as "Bleeding Kansas." The violence was incited by bands of so-called border ruffians who crossed state lines from Missouri to advocate for and intimidate Kansas residents into voting for slavery to be authorized within the state.

The Kansas-Nebraska Act, enacted two years prior, in 1854, had authorized settlement in the newly authorized territories that had been acquired from France via the Louisiana Purchase. Although an initial draft of the bill had been formally silent on whether slavery would be allowed in the territories, there was to be a tacit understanding that the precedent established under the Missouri Compromise of 1820—which, with the exception of Missouri, prohibited the expansion of slavery into territories above the 36° 30' circle of latitude that marked the United States—would apply. However, the Act's author, Illinois senator Stephen A. Douglas, succumbed to pressure applied by southern representatives to repeal the Missouri Compromise, and instead used the legislation as an opportunity to institute his preferred mode of determining the issue of slavery—namely, popular sovereignty. Where the framers emphasized states' rights to delegate the question of slavery to the existing individual states, the concept of popular sovereignty deferred the question of slavery within a newly established state to the vote of its white residents.

Where Douglas intended to establish a democratic solution to the ever-present slave problem, he instead effectively incited a bloody riot (which was presaged by the words of Lincoln himself, who in an 1855 letter referred to the Kansas-Nebraska Act "not as law, but as violence from the beginning"). Missouri, then a slaveholding state, bordered Kansas, and Missouri's resident enslavers had an interest in agitating for Kansas to become one too: if Kansas ended up a "free" state, they credibly feared that their property would have more incentive to flee across the border. Though southern representatives had successfully pushed the enactment of the Fugitive Slave Act in 1850, compelling federal enforcement of a given state's constitutional obligation to return enslaved persons who had escaped from their home state, the practical application of the law proved less dependable than hoped. Four years later, in May 1854, President Pierce ordered federal troops into Boston, Massachusetts, to suppress an interracial mob attempting to free one Anthony Burns, a fugitive who had escaped enslavement and whom Massachusetts authorities were aiming to return to the state of his enslaver. A guard was killed.

Given this recent history, Missouri enslavers had reason to fear the loss of their "property," and flooded out of Missouri into neighboring "Bleeding Kansas," voting illegally and engaging in vigilante violence to ensure that the new state would not become a haven for fugitives. Their immediate antagonists were abolitionists, including humanitarian associations and armed guerrilla groups. The most notorious among such armed bands was the one led by John Brown, a white man from Connecticut who arrived in Kansas in October 1855 to help defend the town of Lawrence, a de facto headquarters for free-state supporters.

In May 1856, about three months after the president invoked the Insurrection Act to deploy federal forces to suppress the domestic violence in Kansas, Brown headed a militant group, which included his sons, to launch a reprisal against proslavery vigilantes in Lawrence, killing five such men in what came to be known as the Pottawatomie Massacre. After being sheltered for a time by an interpreter for the Pottawatomie tribe named John Tecumseh Ottawa Jones, Brown left Kansas in September of that year.

———

THERE ARE NUMEROUS TACTICS AT ONE'S DISPOSAL TO REDUCE AND, HOPE-fully, eliminate cognitive dissonance and the discomfort it causes. If your actions do not align with a belief you hold, then you can reduce the importance of the belief by changing your attitude toward it. Perhaps the sanctity and sentience of all animal life is not exactly a high priority in the grand scheme of your complicated existence, you might decide as you bite into a chicken thigh. In other words, you can maintain your underlying belief that animals probably shouldn't be eaten, but change your attitude about the importance of that belief in order to engage in contradictory behavior without experiencing too much discomfort.

Another option would be to simply layer onto your mental palette additional cognitions that align with your apparent behavior and overshadow your discrepant belief. You could, for instance, emphasize your intense hunger, convince yourself of your body's need for protein, consider the feelings of your kind friend who has spent all afternoon roasting the chicken on which you are presently munching. You could, in other words, tip the cognitive scale in favor of your behavior, thus reducing the relative weight of the contradictory belief on your conscience.

All that said, you could, of course, just change your behavior and refuse the chicken. Yet behaviors tend to be as ingrained as one's beliefs, and are more difficult to change. One's *attitude* toward either, however, is much more malleable and therefore easier to shift. Given this inconvenient truth, shifting attitudes has proven much more expedient.

Whatever the mental strategy, cognitive dissonance is so uncomfortable that something must be done. The phenomenon is said to be a by-product of the human's innate desire to experience consistency. So, the move to reduce the tension that arises from the dissonance is not usually experienced as a conscious choice—like, say, deciding which fuel-efficient car to purchase. Rather, it is experienced as a primal urge, like some autonomic drive that prompts the generation of more consonant thoughts and the transformation of inconsistent ones in order to soothe inner turmoil.

———

ON OCTOBER 18, 1859, LOCAL VIRGINIA MILITIA TOGETHER WITH FEDERAL troops led by General Robert E. Lee seized upon John Brown and his twenty-odd cohorts, foiling the abolitionist's plot to break into the poorly guarded federal arsenal at Harpers Ferry, then arm and liberate the enslaved in the area. It was, actually, more of a divine mission than a plot, because John Brown's raid was not very well planned; he and his cohorts were easily cornered. Although Brown had a clear vision of abolition and retribution for enslavers, he was not at all practical about how to translate this revelation into a strategic battle plan.

Though a staunch abolitionist, Brown was not a man who cared for deliberate theory. Unlike members of the antislavery societies in New England, Brown did not express his opposition to slavery through publications and speeches. (However, Brown did help fund the printing, in a single pamphlet, of the "incendiary" appeal drafted by David Walker and the "Call to Rebellion" speech given by Henry

Highland Garnet—both of whom demanded the immediate abolition of slavery and prompted their fellow Negroes to do so, by any means necessary.) Brown also did not spend time debating whether immediacy or gradualism—the latter the preferred approach of the by-then-deceased Thomas Jefferson—was the optimal path for finally ending the peculiar institution. Brown was a man of action. And his belief in abolition was translated into swift and direct force, in the form of retributive violence.

Though fiercely religious, Brown did not leave the question of slavery in God's hands. His devout Christianity did not inspire meekness and patience; he did not emulate Jesus by turning the other cheek. Brown's religious temperament was, evidently, aligned with the Old Testament, where wrath rather than forgiveness was the mechanism for restoring divine order. As for divine intervention, Brown did not wait for some impersonal force to rectify the depravity of slavery, nor was he inclined to defer salvation to the afterlife. He assumed personal responsibility for avenging the enslavement of peoples of African descent.

At an 1858 convention in Ontario, one year before the failed raid at Harpers Ferry, Brown held meetings about his plans to institute a new government of freed slaves in the Appalachian Mountains. There he discussed the provisional constitution he had drafted, which called for the establishment of a new state within the United States where the enslaved would be liberated and treated equally with white people, both male and female. The constitution, which Brown's lawyer introduced at trial to support a defense of insanity, stated, among other things, that slavery was a "barbarous, unprovoked, and unjustifiable war of one portion of its citizens upon another portion," that was "in utter disregard and violation of those eternal and self-evident truths set forth in our Declaration of Independence." Among the justifications for the enumeration of rights in his provisional constitution, Brown cited the Supreme Court's 1857 Dred Scott decision, which infamously proclaimed that slaves "have no rights which the white man is bound to respect."

After attending the Ontario convention, Brown moved to act more viscerally: he launched an attack on a slaveholder in Missouri, killing him and freeing eleven of his slaves, whom he then helped ferry over the border to Canada.

———

STUDIES HAVE SHOWN THAT THE EXPERIENCE OF COGNITIVE DISSONANCE correlates with the relative freedom a given person has had to choose his or her actions or convictions. For example, if someone had a "free" choice in their behaviors, expressed beliefs, or attitudes, then, according to studies, if any of them conflicted, this person would experience dissonance. However, where there is no freedom of decision—when one's behaviors, beliefs, and attitudes are compelled by, for example, violence—there is no cognitive dissonance.

———

THERE IS AN ORIGIN STORY OF SORTS THAT, IN ADDITION TO BROWN'S devout Christianity, has served as the incident that incited his hatred of slavery. It is said that at the age of twelve, Brown witnessed a young black boy being savagely beaten with an iron shovel. Perhaps Brown suffered from cognitive dissonance, born from the observed discrepancy between his interpretation of the scriptures he sought to rigidly uphold and the practice of enslavement provided for in the very documents that founded the United States. If so, Brown sought to resolve the dissonance not only by redirecting his own behavior, but by compelling the behavior of those around him, with brute force.

———

IF, AS PSYCHOLOGICAL STUDIES SAY, THERE IS NO COGNITIVE DISSONANCE without the freedom to choose your behaviors, beliefs, or attitudes, then enslavers were the ones who largely suffered from it. The enslaved, having little to no freedom of decision, would, by logical extension, not experience this brand of inner tension.

———

"[W]HEN LINCOLN SEEMED TO THINK OF MATTERS REACHING AN 'EXTREME state,'" writes Gabor S. Boritt in *Why the Civil War Came*, "what came to mind was John Brown and not a horrendous Civil War." Also, when Lincoln remarked in 1855 that "there is no peaceful extinction of slavery in prospect for us," writes Boritt, "a tumultuous political war and not a military one was on his mind." Following Lincoln's election to president in 1860, Boritt suggests, his apparent blindness to the grave nature of the mounting conflict he was presiding over could be attributed to the psychoanalytic concept of avoidance, which refers to the mental effort expended by someone attempting to avoid dealing with a stressor. With this bend of mind, according to Boritt, Lincoln "could refuse to face dangerous realities and indulge in wishful thinking and behavior."

Is it too intrusive to surmise what might have been going through Lincoln's head? To consider not only his documented speech and actions, but to also hypothesize about the state of mind from which they arose? The answers to these questions are just as speculative as the psychoanalytic theory. What is clear, however, is that in the period preceding the Civil War, Lincoln foregrounded the sanctity of the Union and relegated the obvious tensions signaling disunion to the backdrop.

Lincoln, though, was not in complete denial. As of 1854, during his time as a member of the House of Representatives for the state of Illinois, Lincoln openly acknowledged the discrepancy between the freedoms the United States claimed to stand for and the institution of slavery. He was, as he made clear then, a staunch detractor of Stephen A. Douglas's popular sovereignty; instead he supported the

prohibition of slavery in any new territories. In line with such predispo-
sitions, Lincoln also opposed the overturning of the Missouri Compromise by the Douglas-drafted Kansas-Nebraska Act, which he mocked
as sanctioning "'the sacred right' of taking slaves to Nebraska."

In a speech given on October 16 in Peoria, Illinois, Lincoln further stated that "[a]t the framing and adoption of the Constitution,
[the founders] forbade to so much as mention the word 'slave' or 'slavery' in the whole instant." Of this glaring omission, Lincoln further
said, "the thing is hid away, in the Constitution, just as an afflicted
man hides a wen, or a cancer, which he dares not cut out at once, lest
he bleed to death; with the promise, nevertheless, that the cutting may
begin at the end of time."

So there is no doubt that Lincoln often verbalized his awareness
of dissonance—so much so that Douglas, his one-time political opponent for the Illinois Senate seat, tarred him as an abolitionist and
"Black Republican" who sought unequivocal freedom and equality
for Negroes. Of course, in one of Lincoln's most famous orations,
the "House Divided" speech delivered on June 16, 1858, prior to
his becoming president, he recited the oft-quoted statement that the
United States government "cannot endure permanently half-slave and
half-free." He predicted that the country would have "to become one
thing or all the other."

―――

THE ENSLAVER, PERHAPS, OBSERVED THE DISCREPANCY BETWEEN HIS
patriotic belief in "freedom" and his behavior of enslavement. Fortu-
nately, the enslaver would have had several options at his disposal to
reduce the dissonance and his attendant discomfort. The enslaver's
most expedient route would have been to convince himself that the
enslaved was not even human, only property, at best a savage or heathen. An enslaver who perceived himself as compassionate could have
emphasized his paternalistic care for the enslaved, whom he would

have considered childlike, lacking the capacity for making responsible "free" choices, like himself.

And so on. The justifications for dehumanizing enslaved peoples were, perhaps, not merely cynical ploys to marshal widespread support for a profitable institution. Maybe they were also a manifestation of a psychic urge to settle the dissonance within.

———

WHILE THE "HOUSE DIVIDED" SPEECH IS OFTEN HIGHLIGHTED AS A TESTAment to Lincoln's aspirations for a United States that would ultimately stand for freedom or nothing at all, the speech—together with many of his other public statements—can also be read as evidence of an attitude that he prioritized the "united" nature of the several states above all else. Lincoln's stated preference for a completely "free" nation notwithstanding, it is clear that he was more than willing to tolerate slavery in order to preserve the Union. While he surely acknowledged the root cause of the dissonance—that of being a free nation composed of enslaved peoples of African descent—the discrepancy between his stated belief in the ultimate entitlement of persons of all races to equality under the law and the observed reality within the United States, not only of slavery but of a contentious southern bloc, was tempered by an attitude that worked to lessen the importance of the freedom of Negroes.

———

WHITE CITIZENS WHO WERE NOT ENSLAVERS—WHO HAD RELATIVELY HIGH decision freedom but who were not, whether by choice or by circumstance, "masters"—might also have been prone to cognitive dissonance. Perhaps a patriotic belief in freedom would have been betrayed by the situation they found themselves in, whereby their fellow white citizens were enslavers. We have seen how John Brown dealt with this

kind of dissonance. But he was, of course, an anomaly. White abolitionists like William Lloyd Garrison, for their part, also aligned their
beliefs with their behavior, insofar as their behavior entailed public
advocacy rather than violent militancy. But again, the vocal minority
of abolitionists hardly represented the majority of the white citizenry.
Silence and complicity, instead, formed the norm.

IF ONE WERE TO, SAY, RADICALLY SIMPLIFY THE CIVIL WAR BY REPRESENT-
ing it as a violent contest between two discrepant cognitions, it would
not be so simple to represent the first as "proslavery" and the second
as "antislavery." Rather, it would be more precise to reframe the mind-
sets as "proslavery" and "not proslavery." Again, Lincoln's champion-
ing of "free" states was not abolitionist or antislavery in the absolute;
his stated aversion to slavery within a given state had to do with the
reality that the institution would effectively drive down wages for
poor whites—who, given the escalated price of the enslaved, could
scarcely hope to afford to one day become enslavers themselves, much
less compete with them.

WHAT HAS SOMETIMES BEEN TAKEN FOR LINCOLN'S PRIMARY INTENT TO
abolish slavery was, in fact, his intent to simply contain the institution.
Lincoln, as evidenced by his words, initially only politically endeav-
ored to limit the practice within defined borders. That he did so with
a hope for the gradual elimination of slavery through some inevitable
forward march of progress does not displace his primary interest in
preserving the Union.

Lincoln's vision of a "United" States did not picture a population
of free Negroes incorporated among the white citizenry. His preferred
method of resolving the dissonance, and thereby preserving Union,

in fact, was colonization—basically, sending liberated slaves back to
Africa. ("My first instinct would be to free all the slaves and send them
to Liberia," Lincoln stated in one of his 1858 debates against Douglas
for the Illinois Senate seat.) At best, he considered a future for the
enslaved in the United States whereby the government would "[f]ree
them all and keep them among us as underlings," although he admit-
ted this would not be his preference (or, perhaps, would continue to
be a source of internal discomfort).

As for the other change in behavior that would reduce the dissonance, that being to "[f]ree them all and make them politically
and socially our equals," Lincoln stated, "[m]y own feelings will not
admit of this, and if mine would, we well know that those of the
great mass of white people will not." Lincoln's vision of a house not
divided, of a "United" States, was, again, one in the interest of poor
white citizens—many of whom had newly immigrated from parts of
Europe, like Germany and Ireland.

Lincoln's proposed constitutional amendment exemplifies this
state of mind. Everyone is familiar with the codified Thirteenth
Amendment, which formally abolished slavery (except for prisoners)
after the Civil War. What is less widely known is the draft of what
is called the "Original Thirteenth Amendment," first conceived of in
late 1860 during the outgoing year of James Buchanan's presidency
by Senator William Seward—the representative of New York who
also favored the containment of slavery, an institution he prophesied
would give rise to an "irrepressible conflict" within the country—and
Representative Thomas Corwin of Ohio. Following the secession of
eleven southern states to form the Confederate States of America,
they drafted and proposed the constitutional amendment with the
hope of reconciling seemingly irreconcilable differences with the following prophylactic language: "No amendment shall be made to the
Constitution which will authorize or give to Congress the power to
abolish or interfere, within any State, with the domestic institutions

thereof, including that of persons held to labor or service by the laws of said State."

Again, neither the word "slave" nor "slavery" was mentioned in the proposed amendment, only "the domestic institutions" of a state. Lincoln referenced the Original Thirteenth Amendment some weeks before the Civil War broke out, in his inaugural address, stating that he had no objection to a permanent prohibition against federal intervention into the institution of slavery "being made express and irrevocable."

———

IF, PERHAPS, ONE VIEW OF THE CIVIL WAR IS A KIND OF VIOLENT MEANS OF resolving the cognitive dissonance of a body politic—the proslavery against the not proslavery—all the while acknowledging that, even while representing these two conflicting cognitions, each side suffered from its own form of cognitive dissonance, creating multiple internal bargains in order to resolve the root cause of their discomfort, then it makes sense that there are so many theories of the Civil War.

The ultimate source of disagreement over the "true" cause of the American Civil War, it seems, is a difference in opinion over the nature of the cognitive dissonance: different takes on what, in the end, was the greatest cause of discomfort for those driven to take arms against their fellow countrymen in order to restore consistency. The root cause of the dissonance—a nation that was, in Lincoln's words, "half-slave and half-free"—is obvious. As Lincoln also put it, slavery was "first introduced without law," as "[t]he oldest laws we found concerning it, are not laws introducing it, but regulating it, as an already existing thing." Slavery was self-evident, indisputable as to its existence, and tacitly acknowledged, albeit largely in silence.

Though enslavement conflicted with the purported national belief in freedom, the apparently prevailing attitude of political represen-tatives toward the barbarous practice tended to shift accordingly in order to accommodate the union of the several states. Slavery was relegated to the backdrop as white politicians noisily debated states' rights and avowedly pursued their region's economic interests— surface symptoms of the root cause of the cognitive dissonance.

This clash of cognitive dissonances could be what produced the copious verbiage about the relative importance and unimportance of economic systems and states' rights and labor rights and electoral politics and gradualism and containment and this and that, but only marginally on the fundamental morality of enslaving other human beings. In this light, reviewing all the various takes on the Civil War is like reading word salad. That is not to say that all these issues are unimportant, only that they seem like coping mechanisms for attempting to suppress the root cause of discomfort. Resolving this root cause, through abolition and equality, would have required a change in behavior among white citizens that was apparently too arduous to commit to on a collective basis; ultimately, it was a last resort.

So, it would be left to the Negroes finally enlisted by the Union army to behold the cognitive simplicity of fighting, to the death, for freedom.

═══

AS GABOR BORITT REPORTS, IN THE DAYS PRECEDING THE DISPATCH OF troops to Fort Sumter, on Good Friday, Lincoln's wife, Mary Todd, noted that "her husband had keeled over with sick headache for the first time in years." By April 2, writes Boritt, "Lincoln knew that the time may have come for those 'bloody bullets' which, for so long, he had promised would not be 'necessary.'" While there is no way to know what was going through Lincoln's head, it is in any event documented that he did, immediately prior to the Civil War—before ordering troops to battle against their fellow citizens—suffer from a splitting headache.

IRREPRESSIBLE CONFLICT

I never had much interest in history. The subject in and of itself was not the source of my disinclination. I was educated in a public school district in Suffolk County, Long Island, that was well-resourced and, for that reason, drew residents to purchase homes in qualifying neighborhoods to ensure their children could attend one of the primary or secondary schools encompassed by the district. I am not ungrateful, but the entire experience was an ordeal.

Much of the history I remember studying was presented under the moniker of "social studies," a catchall for certain fields of learning, including history and geography, that unlike, say, math or English, didn't neatly fit into any other discipline within the school's curricula. As the proverbial only-black-kid-in-my-class, I dreaded social studies class, in part because whenever the teacher would make mention of the word "slave" or "slavery," several of the white kids would turn to glance or outright stare at me. I would sit there at my desk, on the receiving end of these looks, and awkwardly pretend I wasn't being forced on display.

Whatever we were discussing at that given moment was clearly causing the white kids to feel uncomfortable, and their immediate response was to project that discomfort onto me. I didn't have the vocabulary at the time for this silent interaction laced with malevolence, but I remember how I felt—ashamed. I didn't know what I felt ashamed about, again, as I then lacked the words to name the source of my feelings. However, what was being made clear with the uttering of the word "slave" or "slavery," and the almost accusatory stares in my direction, was that my present-day being was directly associated with enslavement, a badge of inferiority that was mine, and mine alone, to carry.

Whenever slavery was discussed in those classrooms, not only could I count on the stares, but also the teacher's reassurance that "we," meaning all of us present-day beings learning "social studies" at that very moment, should not judge those historical enslavers by our contemporary morals. I never felt included in that "we," the balm of historical relativism, which seemed intended to soothe the potentially guilty consciences of the white kids, who managed to thereby distance themselves from the karma of any ancestral enslavers while pinning the burdens of slavery and the enslaved onto me. Historical relativism buttressed their sense of innocence, while their glares in my direction seemed to project some kind of guilt.

RECALLING PAULO FREIRE'S *PEDAGOGY OF THE OPPRESSED*, IF A FUNDA-mental precondition for being human is to be engaged in the endeavor to "name" the world and emerge from silence—or from having been silenced—then declaring one's own word was, for the enslaved, a form of liberation. Frederick Douglass, the fugitive slave turned grand orator and editor, emerged in the 1850s to speak against the construct that had maliciously defined him and all others of African descent in the United States. Having been taught to read and write by one of his "masters," Douglass broke the mold of his societal and legal definition and reinvented himself. "Throughout his life Douglass was acutely aware that one of the most important contributions he could make was to tell his own story," writes David Blight in *Frederick Douglass' Civil War*. "As the author of the autobiographies, he repeatedly re-created himself, linking the past with the present."

Though generally aligned with white abolitionists of the Northeast like William Lloyd Garrison, for whose Massachusetts antislavery organization he lectured in 1841, Douglass departed from them by choosing to engage with the political system to the extent that it reaped practical advancements for Negroes and did not rely solely on moral suasion to advance abolition. If violence was necessary to achieve that end, according to Douglass, then so be it. However, the imposition of federal power upon the several states was his stated preference for achieving abolition. The "word," of course, was Douglass's most deployed weapon in a slaveholding society, but his religious faith and belief in a "chain of events" that would emancipate the slaves by divine order did not at all dissuade him from advocating for violence, whether legal or extralegal.

As an internationally renowned author and speaker, Douglass did enjoy more freedom of choice, especially relative to any slave or other "free" Negro lacking such a platform within the United States. To the extent that he suffered from cognitive dissonance, perhaps it arose in his efforts to downplay the importance of certain ideals and moral commitments to immediate abolition in order to psychologically accommodate strategic political alliances, or compromises that effectively tolerated gradualism. However, as Douglass's speeches, editorials, and written works were, in effect, directed at a white audience, he made a sermon out of the muted slave's binary decision between freedom and death (even though the pursuit of the former could very well result in the latter). Douglass also made sure to rhetorically tie the fate of the enslaved to that of the white citizen: "No man can put a chain around the ankle of his fellow man without at last finding the other end fastened about his own neck." Either both would be saved or both would be damned.

In line with such rhetoric, Douglass was also a vocal proponent of the enlistment of Negroes into the Union army, and agitated for an end to the formal exclusion of Negro soldiers from service. The official exclusion of Negro soldiers was, ultimately, born from the will to preserve the Union under Lincoln's administration, which attempted to assuage representatives of the slaveholding Confederacy that the slave system would survive the end of the conflict. However, this sentiment changed by necessity, as the morale of white northern soldiers flagged and the Union was threatened with dissolution. As Blight writes in

Fredrick Douglass' Civil War: "Most northern whites did not accept the idea of black soldiers until the preservation of the Union required an assault on slavery itself, and, the impatience of abolitionists and the bitterness of black leaders notwithstanding, this would not occur until well into the second year of the war."

Given this reality, the Second Confiscation Act of 1862 was passed in July of that year, stating prior to the eventual Emancipation Proclamation that enslaved persons "shall forever be free of their servitude," and authorizing the employment of "persons of African descent . . . for the suppression of the rebellion." This second act was a departure from the first of the Confiscation Acts passed in 1861, under which enslaved persons were merely considered contraband of war. The Militia Act of 1862 was passed in the same month as the Second Confiscation Act, and for the first time authorized Negroes to serve in state militias. In this regard, the 1862 Militia Act overturned the Second Militia Act of 1792, which restricted militia service to white men.

―――

WHAT I REMEMBER LEARNING ABOUT THE CIVIL WAR, IN SHORT, WAS THAT it was a great American war fought "to end slavery." It was long, bloody, brothers against brothers, etc. Despite the barrage of names, places, and dates I was confronted with in my state-compelled study of history, I came away with what amounts to slogans, the kind that infiltrate and remain lodged in one's memory long after the details of the product that was being sold have faded from recollection.

Upon a closer reading, while it's clear that the Civil War did, effectively, end slavery, it is also clear that this goal did not drive the country to war in the first place. Yet I was taught, more or less, that northern brothers came to arms against their southern brothers because slavery was "wrong." While I can't pretend to remember the precise details I was taught, I am certain that the lessons impressed upon me the moral rectitude of white northerners.

———

BY A STROKE OF THE PEN, ON SEPTEMBER 22, 1862, LINCOLN ISSUED THE Emancipation Proclamation. In the course of around seven hundred words, he summarily declared that "all persons held as slaves within any State," including those then in rebellion, were "then, thenceforward, and forever free." The proclamation further stated that the federal government, backed by military and naval power, would "recognize and maintain the freedom of such persons." Within the proclamation's text Lincoln also enjoined "the people so declared to be free to abstain from all violence," unless in self-defense, and recommended that "they labor faithfully for reasonable wages." And so it was that the enslaved became technically eligible to become a "free" laborer.

———

BEYOND THE CONTEXT IN WHICH I WAS SUPPOSED TO BE LEARNING HIStory, the subject matter itself presented barriers to my early willingness to engage with it. My grade-school encounters with history consisted of names, dates, notable events, and geographical locations that I was compelled to memorize from textbooks and recite on test day, and which then, frankly, would promptly evaporate from my mind.

The textbook presentation of history as a simplified, sanitized list of chronological factoids largely devoid of narrative is, of course, intentional. The project of teaching history is inextricable from the project of imprinting students with a sense of nationalistic identity and patriotic fidelity. And this project, at its core, is paradoxical, as it is guided by a single, self-contradictory intention: to teach what happened in the past without really teaching what happened in the past. It is a mission that is, ultimately, impossible.

DOUGLASS, GIVEN HIS LEVEL OF PROMINENCE AND AUTONOMY, WAS AN archetype of the "free" Negro before the Negro—whether enslaved or fugitive or manumitted and afforded a "crude quasi freedom"— became universally legally free. Douglass liberated himself not only through his own physical escape but also by crafting his own story. His prominence, perhaps, gave rise to yet another form of cognitive dissonance among white citizens with hard-wired beliefs in Negro inferiority and subordination. For such white citizens, Douglass and all the "free" Negroes before him were walking oxymorons, discrepant figures whose very existence clashed with their beliefs and attitudes, triggering further efforts to continue to suppress those who were formerly property and newly legally free.

ONLY YEARS LATER DID I FIGURE OUT THAT JUST BECAUSE THE CIVIL WAR formally ended slavery did not mean that it was fought *in order* to end slavery. (As Frederick Douglass stated, "[T]he South was fighting to take slavery out of the Union and the North was fighting to keep slavery in the Union.") Only years later did I discover that the Union's enlistment of Negro soldiers in the war against the Confederacy was considered, by Union military officials, a necessary evil to counteract the flagging morale and defection among white soldiers. (As W. E. B. Du Bois writes in *Black Reconstruction in America*: "Freedom for the slave was the logical result of a crazy attempt to wage war in the midst of four million black slaves and trying all the while sublimely to ignore the interests of those slaves in the outcome of the fighting.") It was only years later that I found out the Emancipation Proclamation was, in essence, a utilitarian move to induce yet more enslaved peoples to flee from their "masters" and join Union ranks, a governmental offer made to consummate a civic transaction—military service in exchange for freedom. In fact, Lincoln's move to arm Negro soldiers and formally emancipate slaves during the Civil War was considered, by Confederate officials, as a move to incite insurrection.

———

AFTER THE CIVIL WAR, ON JULY 30, 1866, GENERAL ABSALOM BAIRD, COMmander of the postwar "department of Louisiana," dispatched federal troops in New Orleans to disperse a violent white mob that had descended upon and around the city's Mechanics' Institute, where Louisiana governor James Madison Wells was attempting to reconvene a constitutional convention. Although there is no record of the Insurrection Act being formally invoked in response to the New Orleans riot, the violent incident came to serve as justification for the more stringent federal administration of the South. Prior to the deployment, delegates had been invited to the constitutional convention to discuss Negro suffrage, disenfranchising Confederate rebels, and, in essence, overhauling the state government, which, under then-President Andrew Johnson's fairly lenient oversight during the initial period of postwar Reconstruction—known as Presidential Reconstruction— had come largely under the control of unrepentant former Confederate soldiers and officials.

During this postwar period, efforts to reincorporate former rebel states into the Union under the Johnson administration were, to the surprise of defeated southern officials, rigidly deferential to states' rights and lacked a commitment to civil and political equality for Negroes. As for freedmen, Johnson's belief was that they were mere extensions of their former enslavers and would, if enfranchised, vote accordingly. A member of the Republican Party, Johnson was loath to enfranchise yet more Democrats. So, Johnson's defense of states' rights and his paternalistic attitude toward newly freed Negroes were a departure from the presumed postwar intentions of Lincoln, who was assassinated on April 15, 1865, three days after voicing support for Negro suffrage.

Among the more notorious illustrations of Johnson's defense of states' rights during Presidential Reconstruction was his two-time veto of the Civil Rights Act of 1866, which had been passed by Congress to counteract the proliferation of "black codes" in the former rebel states by affirming that all "citizens"—defined for the first time as all persons born in the United States—were equal under the law, and making it illegal to deny the rights of citizenship to any person on account of race or color. However, this was proposed federal law; the black codes in former rebel states affirmed inequality. Abundant in number but repetitive in substance, the black codes technically recognized that the formerly enslaved were legally free while continuing to regulate their movement and labor through vagrancy and apprenticeship laws. Common vagrancy laws, for example, prohibited wandering about without proof of employment, thereby criminalizing those who left one place of work in search of preferable terms and wages. The transition from slave labor to contract labor, in essence, translated into the transformation of "slaves" into "servants," many of whom either served the same "masters" or ended up laboring in chain gangs or convict-leasing programs for having violated such codes by being found "idle" or "loitering."

The Civil Rights Act had become a key source of tension in New Orleans immediately prior to the 1866 riot. On July 21 of that year, Judge Edmund Abell, who presided over a criminal court in New Orleans, was arrested for violating certain provisions of the Civil Rights Act when he declared that it was unconstitutional and "aim[ed] at the striking down of the independence of the States, to sap the foundation of the republican government, to override the laws of the State, and to obliterate every trace of independence of the State judiciary, by disgraceful servile ends." Yet another allegation that prompted the judge's arrest was his objection to Governor Wells's reconvening of the state's constitutional convention.

The judge's arrest, as well as two other violent skirmishes among groups of whites and Negroes in that same month of July alone, contributed to an atmosphere where rumors of Negro uprisings spread like a brush fire. There were reports of secret societies conspiring to overthrow the state government and bands of Negroes abandoning their work to converge upon the city, as well as of a plan by one delegate "preparing a black insurrection if reconvening the convention failed." Even before the constitutional convention, a representative of the lieutenant governor consulted with President Johnson and military authorities in Louisiana on how to prepare for the planned meeting.

In line with his defense of states' rights, Johnson confirmed that he would not respond with federal military force unless in support of the wishes of local authorities. The lieutenant governor and mayor then consulted with General Baird, informing him that they intended to use state and local law enforcement to disperse the convention. While Baird too confirmed that he did not intend to send the military to interfere with what was, in his view, a state matter, he defended the right of the delegates to assemble without interference from the governor or mayor. Nonetheless, Baird assured them that if "you doubt the ability of your small force of police to control [the conventionists], you have in such case only to call upon me, and I will bring to your assistance not only the troops now present in the city, but if necessary the entire force it may be in my power to assemble."

On July 30, a procession of about one hundred Negroes was making its way toward the Mechanics' Institute, where the convention was scheduled to be held, marching as if in a parade, beating drums and waving a Union flag. A white crowd began to jeer at the group, with a few eventually launching a physical attack. Soon, a shot was fired in the direction of the marchers, which incited a melee that spilled beyond the street and into the Mechanics' Institute, where both Negro and white attendees were assembled. A riot ensued, with white mobs numbering at least one thousand people, including local police forces, shot at the procession, then rushed into the building and aimed fire at those who ran to take refuge inside. By the arrival of federal troops, more than thirty Negroes and three white men were killed and more than one hundred persons injured in the massacre.

The New Orleans riots highlighted, especially for the radical wing of the Republican Party, the failure of Presidential Reconstruction, and laid the foundation for the drafting and enactment of the Reconstruction Act of 1876, under which the former Confederate states, except Tennessee, were divided into five military districts, each administered by an officer of the army. Such an officer was empowered to use military force to "enable [him] to perform his duties and enforce his authority within the district to which he [was] assigned." Among such an officer's assigned duties were to "protect all persons in their rights of person and property, to suppress insurrection, disorder, and violence, and to punish, or cause to be punished, all disturbers of the public peace and criminals."

———

CONCURRENT WITH HISTORICAL ERASURE IS THE SELECTIVE IMPARTING of facts: omitting whatever is disruptive to the sanitized, nationalistic portrayal of history, while including and highlighting whatever bolsters it. I am particularly stubborn about filtering out and selectively ignoring anything that I can tell is being aggressively marketed to me. All those swan songs to freedom-fighting founding fathers I repeatedly came across in a variety of media were, time and again, deflected by my own self-protective willful ignorance. I just did not want to know.

Though I was repeatedly being "taught" *what* happened, *when* whatever happened, *who* did what and to *whom*, what was missing was *why*. Why were these things happening? Without this distinct perspective, without any narrative through line, I was simply unable to care about this so-called history. Any reckoning with the *why*, or any unavoidable facts, like the existence of "slaves" or "slavery," were mollified by historical relativism and that useful yet illusory notion of "progress," overshadowing a violent past with both the evidence and the promise of a bright future.

None of these observations are new. W. E. B. Du Bois himself, in the last chapter of *Black Reconstruction in America*, writes that history is propaganda, "lies agreed upon" that are characterized by "libel, innuendo, and silence," with respect to which "evil must be forgotten, distorted, and skimmed over." When Du Bois wrote *Black Reconstruction*, he was not merely recording history, but revising it. And he did so in the face of so many pernicious theories or "schools" of thought, including that of William Archibald Dunning of Columbia University, who interpreted the Reconstruction period as a grand mistake, when "radical" northerners interfered with southern affairs, using federal military power as mortal blackmail, while inept Negroes were elevated to political power they were not equipped to wield.

In fact, Du Bois presented the paper that would become *Black Reconstruction* at a 1909 meeting of the American Historical Association, which Dunning himself attended. Despite the paper's gracious reception at the meeting, it did not influence contemporary scholarship on Reconstruction. As David Levering Lewis noted in the introduction to a 1998 edition of *Black Reconstruction*, "African American scholars were not silent, only unheard or dismissed by the white academy." During the twentieth century and beyond, historians have continued to challenge such renderings, connecting the lines between names, places, and dates with narratives that expose biases and dispel persistent myths.

So it is, then, that in my reading and relearning of history, time has no meaning, and the true definition of history—that is, any history that is actually worth learning—is "news." It remains the case that all that is considered news isn't inherently new, but only new to the one who has no knowledge of it. The conciliatory notion of "progress" notwithstanding, current events often are not new, but merely reincarnated versions of history.

CHAPTER 4

They Will Bring a Mob Against You

As anyone who peruses a thesaurus well knows, words with approximate definitions have different connotations. In America's English, "people" has a patriotic ring, bringing to mind those citizens imbued with freedom. The "people," in the U.S. Constitution, is that group of persons for whom the government exists, by whom it has been established, and whom it comprises (albeit via a cadre of elected representatives). The "people," in this context, are invested with the right to direct the priorities of their government, as well as the duty to repel overreaching governmental authority. The actions of the "people," whether intended to be aligned with the aims of government or in opposition to the government's perceived excesses, are ultimately branded as loyal—if not to the government as presently constituted, then to the ideal of government the "people" fervently desire to uphold.

However, the "masses," a word that more or less has the same meaning as the "people," has an ominous tone. The "masses," as typically used, does not simply refer to a large group of persons. Unlike the "people," the "masses" are not some orderly bunch, dutifully engaging in their civic duties and primarily peaceful—unless, that is, they are pushed too far by an unruly government. The "masses" do form part of the body politic, but as a dormant gene, a sleeping menace the government forever fears will be stirred into activity.

That is one interpretation of the "masses." Another casts a positive spin on the word. From this other perspective, the "masses" represent latent potential, an untapped force akin to unexplored oil reserves. The "masses," yes, are dormant, but they are awaiting the right combination of cultivation and inspiration to be awakened into revolutionary action. The "masses," unlike the "people," are not represented by the government. The "masses," by contrast, are managed or even suppressed by the government.

Where no government is possible without the "people," the "masses" pose a threat to the government's survival.

THE CROWD

Gustave Le Bon was among those who heralded the study of crowd psychology with his work *The Crowd: A Study of the Popular Mind*—a guidebook of sorts for coming to terms with the mentality of the mob. Published in 1895, the book diagnoses the crude mentality of crowd behavior, detailing the crowd's irrationality, credulity, groupthink, and overall threat to "civilization." What Le Bon calls the "crowd" represents "the disappearance of the conscious personality, the predominance of the unconscious personality, the turning of feelings and ideas in an identical direction by means of suggestion and contagion, the tendency to immediately transform the suggested ideas into acts [. . .]." Individuality is subsumed by the crowd, an anonymous and hypnotized mob that Le Bon has said follows only one rule: "the Law of Mental Unity." The crowd is not just a multiplicity of persons. The crowd thinks and acts as one.

The crowd, according to Le Bon, possesses a collective mind and behaves as if under a trance, having succumbed to some propaganda that has spread among its members like a contagion. Crowd members are thereby compelled to commit acts as a group that might very well contradict each individual's professed code of conduct.

Le Bon's crowd is also prone to "impulsiveness, irritability, incapacity to reason, the absence of judgment and of the critical spirit, the exaggeration of sentiments [. . .]." As for the sentiments expressed by the crowd, they are at once simple and exaggerated, often displaying "intolerance and fanaticism." What in one individual would amount to a stewing resentment, explodes, in a crowd, into "furious hatred."

Assuming power according to its number, the crowd is formed of those who, once assembled, embody a new hubris. As a crowd, individuals amass a collective gumption to, say, murder, pillage, or storm a palace. The crowd is no assembly of citizens. That would imply order. The crowd is an assembled horror akin to Frankenstein, which implies disorder, and, most importantly, fear.

For Le Bon, "civilization"—perhaps the cultural traits, traditions, and mores of a mass of people—is the manifestation of a noble heritage bequeathed from generation to generation on account of what he calls "race." This "race" has a particular definition in Le Bon's study of the crowd. It refers to something like ethnicity or the kind of cultural identity formed through the continued adoption and transfer of established practices and values among a culturally homogeneous group, and it is not merely a matter of phenotype. Le Bon's "race" in 1895 is likely the present day's "nationality."

Inherent in "race," Le Bon says in *The Crowd*, is a certain genius that is distorted and undermined by the technocratic monopoly that an established State comes to assume over the rules that govern society conduct. Where "race" provides those persons who share one cultural identity a common ground (from which the customs of an advanced civilization may thrive), the State artificially cobbles together an amalgam of peoples under the rubric of law and creates a false sense of commonality among individuals who are fundamentally isolated. From such alienated persons, from this heterogeneous group, according to Le Bon, the formation of a crowd becomes a palpable threat. Le Bon discusses this kind of heterogeneous crowd almost exclusively; he mentions the homogeneous crowd only briefly, in examples of "sects," "castes," and "classes." However, he designates the homogeneous crowd as relatively superior to the heterogeneous one, stating that "the inferior characteristics of crowds are the less accentuated in proportion as the spirit of the race is strong."

———

THE RECONSTRUCTION ERA IS OFTEN BROKEN DOWN BY HISTORIANS INTO two phases, the lax Presidential Reconstruction administered by Andrew Johnson, and Radical Reconstruction ushered in at the behest of northern Radical Republicans via the Reconstruction Acts. However, the period of Reconstruction overseen by Johnson's immediate successor, President Ulysses S. Grant, might represent a third phase of Reconstruction, where the form of Radical Reconstruction initially authorized under the Reconstruction Acts became more zealous, as lawmakers used federal military power against violent white mobs who resisted Republican political power and the incorporation of Negro freedmen into the citizenry—a period that could very easily be described as a resurgence of military conflict waged in spite of the purported peace during the postwar era.

The Enforcement Acts—of May 31, 1870, February 28, 1871, and April 20, 1871—authorized federal enforcement of the Fourteenth and Fifteenth Amendments, ratified in 1868 and 1870 respectively. With the formal establishment of Negro suffrage under the Fifteenth Amendment came the expansion of the Republican Party's political dominance of former Confederate states, where freedmen exercised their newfound rights in large numbers. Where Radical Republicans might have intended the Enforcement Acts to realize the new constitutional commitment to equality by enforcing Negro suffrage, other members of the party considered voting freedmen to be crucial to their strategy to increase and consolidate Republican representation across all levels of government. In other words, among Republican politicians—including those carpetbaggers from the North who contended in southern elections, and white southerners who were called scalawags for doing the same—the institution of Negro suffrage ushered in a dual perception of freedmen as both ends in and of themselves and a means to electoral power.

All three Enforcement Acts authorized federal marshals to summon the "posse comitatus" to help enforce their provisions. Also, the Enforcement Act of May 1870 among other things specifically authorized the president to deploy federal armed forces and the state militia to protect the right of newly enfranchised freedmen to vote, imposing fines and criminal penalties on those who discriminated against, intimidated, or otherwise frustrated the ability of any citizen who sought to exercise his voting rights. The act further gave federal courts jurisdiction over Enforcement Act crimes, as well as authorized federal marshals to apprehend anyone suspected of committing them.

The Enforcement Acts of February and April 1871 were enacted to combat the vigilante violence of the Ku Klux Klan, which is particularly evident in the fact that the Enforcement Act of April 1871 is also referred to as the Ku Klux Klan Act. Established in Pulaski, Tennessee, in 1867, the nominal social club for white former Confederate soldiers soon proliferated into a multistate secret society that, by the late 1860s and early 1870s, was regularly targeting and terrorizing Negroes who were bold enough to exercise their nascent rights as citizens in the defeated South.

While the Enforcement Act of February 1871 provided for the federal supervision of elections, the April 1871 act specifically outlines the criminal violations of those who "shall conspire together, or go in disguise upon the public highway or upon the premises of another for the purpose [. . .] of depriving any person or any class of persons of the equal protection of the laws. . . ." Also notable is the fact that the Enforcement Act of April 1871 tracks the language in the

Insurrection Act almost verbatim, authorizing the president to deploy federal armed forces and call forth state militia in order to suppress "insurrection" or "rebellion." Unlike the Insurrection Act, the April 1871 act specified the paramilitary terrorism of the Ku Klux Klan as an instance of "insurrection" warranting federal military intervention.

Southern objections to federal military intervention were not solely rooted in abstract principles of federalism, but also arose from the embodiment of those engaged in such intervention. The proportion of Negro troops increased after the Civil War, as many of their white counterparts who had been enlisted from the conflict's start began to roll off service at the expiration of their respective term limits. Once authorized to enlist in 1862, Negro soldiers comprised about 10 percent of Union troops during the war. "But by the last quarter of 1865, blacks made up about one third of the occupation army," as Nicholas Johnson explains in *Negroes and the Gun*. "Many Southerners took this as a deliberate Union insult."

———

IF THE CROWD IS VULNERABLE TO SUGGESTION—TO HAVING ITS COLLEC-tive unconscious tapped into and its drives channeled into unified action—then who, exactly, is doing the hypnotizing? Le Bon puts forth a charismatic leader who, through his projection of strength and confidence, can transform a mere group of individuals into a crowd at his command. Such a charismatic leader can, perhaps, also transform a government of laws into a government of men. Yet, as Le Bon suggests, this charismatic leader alone may not have the influence to muster a crowd. Though largely parroting the repetitive slogans of a strongman, the crowd also tends to be formed by members primed to defend their long-standing beliefs. The crowd whisperer must simply echo such beliefs through a megaphone, restating the deeply held convictions of his or her mesmerized audience in order to pull it under his thrall.

The crowd, as Le Bon says, is inherently conservative, and seeks to either preserve the present or reinstate the conditions of the past. Only the crowd's erratic violence might cause its members to be mischaracterized as revolutionary instead of what they actually are, which is reactionary. "It is precisely crowds that cling most tenaciously to traditional ideas and oppose their being changed with the most obstinacy," Le Bon writes. The crowd does not usher in the new, but, instead, clears the way for the reinstatement of the old. And such beliefs, once finally implanted in the crowd, are difficult to uproot, and can only "be changed at the cost of violent revolutions." As Le Bon also writes, "The beginning of a revolution is in reality the end of a belief."

The crowd, finally, is not some distinct group of Others inherently disposed to riotous behavior. Rather, members of the crowd include any hypothetical individual, regardless of Le Bon's "race" or any other creed. The final message of the crowd theory Le Bon advanced was that no person is immune from becoming a part of the crowd. Le Bon's crowd psychology eliminated the sense of remove that so-called ordinary, civilized, and law-abiding persons might have felt when they observed crowds with contempt and horror. The crowd, then, is not just an amalgamated monster, but also a mirror. The "people," in the end, are always a potential "crowd." The "people" are always a potential "mob" or would-be "masses."

Mapping this crowd theory onto the United States, it's clear that white citizens were originally defined as the "people," and Negroes—whether enslaved or relatively free—originally interpreted and regulated as a "crowd." However, with the formal incorporation of Negroes into the citizenry, and as part of the "people," a contingent of white society emerged as the "masses," when they reasserted their dominance through violence.

———

THROUGHOUT HIS TWO-TERM PRESIDENCY, BEGINNING IN 1869 AND ENDING in 1877, Ulysses S. Grant made seven proclamations regarding the restoration of "law and order" in Arkansas, Mississippi, South Carolina, and Arkansas. The first, issued on March 24, 1871, pursuant to the Insurrection Act, was made at the request of South Carolina governor Robert Scott, who pleaded for federal troops to help put down the campaign of brutal violence led by the paramilitary Klan within the state, typically carried out via nighttime raids against Negro residents. Among the Klan's victims in March of that year were members of a Negro militia that served as guardsmen to help enforce the civic engagement of freedmen in York County. However, militia members were also reportedly unapologetic about their specific role as defenders against the Klan. As told in Matthew Pearl's vivid recounting of this period in his essay "K Troop: The Story of the Eradication of the Original Ku Klux Klan," the militia also "swore to avenge the Klan's growing list of misdeeds and murders, to become a kind of counter-Klan force."

On March 6, 1871, Klansmen descended upon the home of one Negro militiaman named Jim Williams. The leader of this particular troop of Klansmen was prominent York County physician Dr. J. Rufus Bratton, who served as a Confederate army surgeon during the Civil War. They eventually found Williams, after prying up the floorboards in his house, and absconded with him over the cries of his wife and children. The Klansmen soon picked out a pine tree for Williams's hanging. "Williams agreed to climb up by his own power to the branch from which they would drop him," writes Pearl, "but when they were ready to finish the job, he grabbed onto a tree limb and would not let go. One of Bratton's subordinates, Bob Caldwell, hacked at Williams's fingers with a knife until he dropped."

By the time Scott made a request of President Grant for federal intervention, he had been forced to disband South Carolina's own state militia because they had been outmanned by Klansmen, a fact that gives rise to the plausibility that several such Klansmen may very well have been South Carolina militiamen in disguise. After honoring Scott's request, President Grant signed the Ku Klux Klan Act into law on April 20, 1871. Thereafter in 1871 the president made five additional proclamations under the Ku Klux Klan Act. The first, made in May, was a general pronouncement promising to enforce the Fourteenth Amendment. The May proclamation referred to "combinations of lawless and disaffected persons in certain localities," and vowed "to exhaust the powers thus vested in the Executive whenever and wherever it shall become necessary to do so for the purpose of securing to all citizens of the United States the peaceful enjoyment of the rights guaranteed to them by the Constitution and laws."

The following two proclamations, made in October, once again responded to Klan violence in South Carolina, the first regarding "unlawful combinations" in the counties of York, Spartanburg, Marion, Chester, Laurens, Newberry, Fairfield, Lancaster, and Chesterfield, and the second suspending the writ of habeas corpus in these counties, therefore allowing any suspected Klansmen to be arrested and held without charge. Another pair of similar proclamations were made in November, the first ordering the dispersal of Klan "combinations" and the second suspending habeas corpus once again. After federal troops were dispatched to these counties starting in October, writes Eric Foner in *Reconstruction*, approximately two thousand Klansmen fled the state of South Carolina.

———————

THE KU KLUX KLAN IS OFTEN ASSOCIATED WITH POOR AND UNEDUCATED white ruffians. Yet the Klan was founded by learned southern "gentlemen"—a small cadre of Confederate veterans in Pulaski, Tennessee, who started what was, for all expressed intents, a social club. Then only known as the Ku-Klux, the founders even drafted an elaborate charter for the group, which they called a "prescript." This prescript, however, did not establish what exactly the group's actual purpose was, and instead set forth a procedural manual of operations. As Elaine Frantz Parsons writes in her close examination of the Klan's founding in *Ku-Klux: The Birth of the Klan during Reconstruction*, the Ku-Klux was intended to be well organized, hierarchical, and even formally deferential to governmental law. As stated in the Ku-Klux prescript preamble: "We recognize our relations to the United States government and acknowledge the supremacy of its laws." At its establishment, the would-be terrorist organization made a point to associate its founding with the U.S. government and submit the activities that it did not expressly set forth to the rule of law.

Having arisen amid the military occupation of former Confederate states and with the growing organization and political prominence of freedmen, when societal norms were experiencing a seismic shift, the Klan provided those who joined its ranks a sense of safety in numbers and a newfound social status. The Klan, postwar, was perhaps a desperate bid to remake a sense of self and of meaning—a new identity fashioned in stealth, as among the Klan's official rules was secrecy. Its members were forbidden from disclosing who was in the organization and what activities they engaged in.

———

ON MAY 22, 1873, PRESIDENT GRANT MADE A PROCLAMATION UNDER THE Enforcement Act with regard to "certain turbulent and disorderly persons [who] have combined together with force and arms to resist the laws and constituted authorities" of the state of Louisiana, and cited his authority to call forth the militia and employ federal troops "in all cases of insurrection in any State or of obstruction to the laws thereof." Such turbulent and disorderly persons, as stated in Grant's proclamation, were contesting the rule of Republican Louisiana governor William P. Kellogg, a carpetbagger from Illinois, who they insisted was not duly elected in the state's 1872 gubernatorial contest. Following the highly contested election, both Kellogg and his Democratic contester, John McEnery, claimed victory, and, for a time, each presided over a divided state government. Although a federal court found that Kellogg was duly elected and ordered his Republican-led representatives to govern, Kellogg's Democratic opponents considered the order to be unwarranted federal intervention into state affairs and moved to take matters into their own hands: a militia led by McEnery unsuccessfully attempted to take over the state arsenal, then the New Orleans police department.

Grant's proclamation was made about a month after the bloodiest conflict in this electoral battle erupted on Easter Sunday of 1873, an event that historian Eric Foner in *Reconstruction* called "the most dramatic example of anarchy that reigned throughout much of rural Louisiana." On April 13, 1873, in what came to be known as the Colfax Massacre, one hundred and fifty Negroes and three white men were killed when a makeshift militia of white men, most of whom were Confederate veterans, raided a courthouse in a newly established parish, which for the previous six weeks had been occupied by Negro militiamen aiming to prevent Democrats from taking over the local parish government. The Confederate veterans involved in the massacre were associated with the White League—a paramilitary group organized to intimidate freedmen from voting and exercising other civic rights.

As LeeAnna Keith writes in *The Colfax Massacre: The Untold Story of Black Power, White Terror, and the Death of Reconstruction*, rumors circulated among whites that "the seizure of the Colfax courthouse was the first step in a war of conquest to eradicate the white race." Among other things, the armed Negro men who took over the courthouse were said to be planning to kill all white men, take over their property, and make wives of their women. In the end, the militia surrounded the courthouse and—by shooting cannon fodder, they set the roof on fire, then stormed the building—descended upon its defenders, eventually capturing those they did not kill. The captors later executed the Negro prisoners who didn't manage to escape.

SO, IF KLAN MEMBERS WERE REQUIRED TO REMAIN ANONYMOUS, WHAT
would be the newfound sense of identity the group could offer to
those who joined it? As the Klan proliferated throughout the South
and became notorious for its deadly terrorist acts, the answer to this
question became clear: it allowed white men to reenact their formally
state-sanctioned roles as authorized purveyors of violence against
Negroes. In the antebellum South, the line between public and private acts of violence intended to enforce slavery was blurred, as, with
respect to slaves and free Negroes, all white persons were effectively
authorized by law to surveil Negroes and thereby enforce slave codes.
As Parsons writes:

> While it had always been a gentlemen's prerogative and duty
> to use violence against his inferiors when necessary, the pre-
> rogative had been mediated by two key institutions: the private
> one of slave ownership, and the public one of gentlemanly, even
> chivalric military service. Neither institution had survived the
> war. The Ku-Klux, by creating spaces set apart from ordinary
> life through spectacle and disguise, offered an insecure sub-
> stitute for these occasions of "civilized" gentlemanly violence.

Upon emancipation, and the effective transition of the formerly
enslaved into "servants" notwithstanding, the state and its official
agents usurped the effective right of white citizens to engage in private
acts of violence against Negroes during the antebellum period. The
Klan then formed and illicitly reassumed this erstwhile right.

"It is well known that the Ku-Klux frequently claimed to be ghosts
of the Confederate dead," Parsons also writes. In her examination of
the testimony by surviving victims of and witnesses to Klan attacks,
she recounts how—with their faces masked and bodies cloaked in

full regalia—Klan members often posed as ghosts and spirits. If energy can never die but merely changes form, then, again, the Klan channeled what had been state-sanctioned private violence against Negroes into vigilante violence.

———————

GRANT'S USE OF FEDERAL POWER IN LOUISIANA UNDER THE ENFORCEMENT Acts was contested in *U.S. v. Cruikshank*, in which the Supreme Court ultimately overturned the convictions of white insurgents involved in the massacre and prosecuted for committing federal crimes. The Court held that the defendants were wrongly convicted of depriving massacre victims of their constitutional rights because the Bill of Rights, including the postwar amendments, only applied to states and not private actors—therefore, it was unconstitutional to prosecute the defendants under the Enforcement Acts. The ruling effectively paralyzed federal efforts to protect Negroes from the Ku Klux Klan and other white supremacist groups across the South by suspending the writ of habeas corpus and prosecuting members for violating constitutional rights.

The Supreme Court ruling also made Grant less willing to invoke the Enforcement Acts, as evidenced by his hesitancy to intervene in what is known as the Brooks-Baxter War, an armed conflict between Republican factions in Arkansas, with one supporting Joseph Brooks in his attempt to overthrow the administration of state governor Elisha Baxter following a gubernatorial race marred by stuffed ballot boxes. After Baxter was eventually pronounced the victor, Brooks and a band of armed men dragged Baxter out of the Arkansas Capitol building, demanding that he relinquish his seat. Subsequently, Baxter and Brooks each mobilized militia forces made up of Negro men and waged an armed battle. Having been criticized for using the federal military intervention to settle the gubernatorial dispute in Louisiana in 1872, Grant waited for about a month after Brooks seized office to make a proclamation commanding "all turbulent and disorderly persons to disperse" and authorizing federal troops to help restore Baxter to his elected seat.

———

THE KLAN COSTUMES—WHETHER THE WELL-KNOWN WHITE GHOST-LIKE sheets and coned headgear, or the lesser-recognized female cross-dress or blackface—were, in part, intended to theatrically incarnate a legally banished paradigm. It is true that the costumes were meant to disguise Klan members, who kept their identities secret. However, secrecy, again, might not have been merely a cover for Klan members' criminal activity. Ordained by the Ku-Klux's original prescript, some time before the group spread and ventured into terrorist activity, the secrecy might have served another, albeit less obvious, function.

———

ON SEPTEMBER 15, 1874, PRESIDENT GRANT ISSUED ANOTHER PROCLAMA-tion under the Enforcement Act stating that "turbulent and disorderly persons have combined together with force and arms to overthrow the State government of Louisiana and to resist the laws and constituted authorities of said State." The day before the proclamation was issued, a coup was successfully launched against Louisiana's Republican-led government by the White League. Once again, supporters of former gubernatorial candidate Democrat John McEnery attempted to rein-stall him and oust Republican governor William Kellogg. In a conflict known as the Battle of Liberty Place, White League members defeated Louisiana's state militia in the streets of New Orleans, and occupied the statehouse and armory for three days, until federal troops were dispatched to restore Kellogg's government.

———

LIKE THOSE OF NASCENT AND SELF-STYLED SUPERHEROES, PARSONS suggests, Klansmen's costumes might have represented the attempt of such postwar white men to visually express their dual identities, whether as both "gentleman" and vigilante, or as both master and subservient. As masked vigilantes, the Klansmen were attempting to reclaim their prewar entitlements, thereby, in effect, liberating their inner slave by enforcing the subservience of Negroes through terrorist violence.

ON DECEMBER 21, 1874, PRESIDENT GRANT MADE A PROCLAMATION UNDER the Enforcement Act authorizing federal military intervention in Mississippi, stating "that several of the legally elected officers of Warren County [. . .] are prevented from executing the duties of their respective offices by force and violence." Earlier that year, Republican politicians had been newly elected to some offices in the Negro-majority county. However, in November Democrats came to control the House of Representatives in Congress for the first time since the Civil War, further emboldening white supremacist terror groups as federal will and power to intervene in southern affairs waned.

Members of the White League then found their opportunity to intimidate elected Negro officials in the county, forcing them to resign, including the Negro sheriff Peter Crosby. Mississippi governor Adelbert Ames called forth the Warren County militia to combat the White League and suggested that Sheriff Crosby assemble a posse of men to help put down the paramilitary group. In response, hundreds of armed Negro men marched toward Vicksburg and were eventually fired upon by the white supremacist militia and forced to flee. In what is known as the Vicksburg Massacre, at least seventy-five and perhaps three hundred Negro men were killed.

IN SOME DOCUMENTED CASES, SEPARATION BETWEEN EACH OF A KLANS-man's identities was rigidly maintained. Parsons recounts the story of a freedwoman named Martha Hendricks, who fled with her baby from Klansmen who were attacking her husband. Mrs. Hendricks sought shelter at the house of her white neighbor, one Mrs. Grogan, who reluctantly allowed her inside. As Hendricks waited in a room with her baby, Grogan's toddler son eventually remarked that his father was one of the Klansmen attacking Hendricks's husband next door. Eventually, Mr. Grogan returned to his own house and, having reassumed his gentlemanly repose, took it upon himself to assure Hendricks that her husband had managed to escape the Klan attackers.

ON OCTOBER 17, 1876, PRESIDENT GRANT ISSUED A PROCLAMATION UNDER the Enforcement Act declaring that "insurrection and domestic violence exist in several counties of the State of South Carolina." More specifically, the proclamation cited "certain combinations of men against law [. . .] known as 'rifle clubs,' who ride up and down by day and night in arms, murdering some peaceable citizens and intimidating others [. . .]." In the month leading up to the proclamation, conflicts arose between armed Negroes and members of "rifle clubs"—groups of armed white men who, under the thin guise of affiliation through "benign" civic associations, intimidated Negro voters and planned attacks on their state governments.

In one incident, known as the Ellenton Riot, rifle club members from Georgia and South Carolina, joined by hundreds of armed white men, roamed through the town of Ellenton to intimidate Negro voters, warning them that they would be whipped or killed if they did not vote Democrat. In the wake of this terror campaign, up to one hundred Negroes were killed. On the day of Grant's proclamation, six members of the Red Shirts, a white supremacist paramilitary force active in South Carolina, were ambushed by two Negro men, who killed one of the Red Shirts.

The most notorious of such incidents, however, had occurred

months earlier, in July 1876, in Hamburg, South Carolina. A town with mostly Negro inhabitants near the Georgia border, Hamburg was the site of an armed conflict in the summer of 1875 between Negro militiamen and the Red Shirts. After a confrontation broke out between two armed white men and members of the Negro militia company marching through Hamburg in celebration of the Fourth of July, the militia and white rifle companies that formed part of the Red Shirts got into a gun battle.

Benjamin Ginsberg quoted Red Shirts leader Ben Tillman in *Moses of South Carolina: A Jewish Scalawag during Radical Reconstruction*: "The leading white men of [the nearby town of] Edgefield had determined to seize the first opportunity that the negroes might offer them to provoke a riot and teach the negroes a lesson [. . .] by killing as many of them as was justifiable." With the arrival of more armed white forces, the Negro militiamen were outnumbered and barricaded themselves in a house, which they soon fled once it was bombarded by shrapnel. "After several hours the white paramilitaries began to execute their captives," writes Ginsberg, "shooting them through the head, one by one." Although a number of white men involved in the massacre faced criminal charges at the state level, none were brought to trial.

———

GROWING CONCERNS IN THE FORMER CONFEDERACY OVER FEDERAL MILItary intervention were leveraged in resolving the hotly contested presidential election in favor of Republican candidate Rutherford B. Hayes. Among the terms of the Compromise of 1877—an unwritten pact made between the political factions to settle the 1876 presidential election—was an agreement by southern Democrats to recognize Hayes as the victor of the election over Democrat Samuel Tilden in return for, among other things, removing all remaining federal troops from the former Confederate states.

The removal of federal troops from the South constituted the end of Radical Reconstruction, and was codified in the Posse Comitatus Act of 1878 passed the following year. The Posse Comitatus Act heralded a legal end to the Reconstruction era by formally prohibiting the domestic deployment of federal troops to enforce the law—that is, unless otherwise authorized by the Constitution or Congress. From then on, the Insurrection Act endured as an exception to this general rule.

WHITE RIOT

I was stalking down a busy sidewalk one morning when I diverged to enter one of those souvenir shops that for whatever reason also sell a variety of portable electronic devices. I strode inside, single-minded in my pursuit to replace the flimsy white headphones I had lost. I ♥ New York T-shirts, Lady Liberty statuettes, and snow globes encasing the city skyline blurred in my peripheral vision. I quickened my steps. As much as I needed to be in there, I desperately wanted to get out.

Then I halted—or, rather, I didn't consciously decide to stop, but was arrested, awestruck by a display in the middle of the store. I stood there staring at figurine after figurine of Donald Trump. Oversized heads with tufts of blond hair swept across furrowed brows; long straight creases for mouths with slight bottom lips protruded into pouts; blue eyes, almost eclipsed by painted black pupils, signified gazes as intense as they were vacant. All of these big heads atop small bodies clothed in navy blue suits, white shirts, and red ties. Some of the little arms were raised, giving a thumbs up. Some of the big heads wore MAGA hats.

The display didn't end there. Donald Trump baseballs. Donald Trump mugs. Donald Trump shot glasses. Donald Trump pencils. Donald Trump pens. Donald Trump playing cards. Donald Trump mints (to "Make Your Breath Great Again!"). Donald Trump bottle-openers. Donald Trump chocolate bars ("Contains: Milk and soy. May contain wheat, peanuts, and tree nuts"). Donald Trump refrigerator magnets—one set arrayed like a redbrick wall up and down one side of a rotating metal display, each tile announcing the full MAGA slogan in white letters.

Presumably these shops carry similar paraphernalia for every presidential administration. I wouldn't know because I'd never paid attention before. But that morning, these grotesque knickknacks triggered, all at once, the rage and shock I'd been suppressing in order to function on a daily basis. I imagined some tourist idly browsing, turning each Trump souvenir over in her hands, considering which one to gift to her nephew. Somehow this image—both terribly and terrifyingly normal, as Hannah Arendt put it—induced more disgust than the hollering throngs at Trump's rallies.

———

THE POSSE COMITATUS ACT OF 1878—"POSSE COMITATUS" REFERRED TO the federal government's authority to call forth the state militia or deploy federal troops—might have heralded the end of the Reconstruction era, but it did not bring an end to the posse. The concept is a holdover of English origin that empowers governing officials to call forth armed civilians to enforce the law. In the United States—most notably in the antebellum South and, later, throughout the western territories—the posse comitatus was a group of civilians deputized by local authorities to help deter and capture outlaws. Prior to the development of more organized police forces funded by the government, the posse comitatus—composed, at the time, of able-bodied white male citizens, for whom such service was compulsory—was a fundamental resource for local authorities to maintain law and order.

Depictions of the posse in popular entertainment are legion in Western films, where the local sheriff or lawman, like Wyatt Earp, is often depicted rallying bands of armed civilians to help corral their lawless adversaries. However, the posse was also called forth during the antebellum period to enforce the slave system. The Fugitive Slave

Act of 1850, for example, authorized federal marshals to summon civilians to help enforce the return of fugitive slaves. Specifically, the 1850 act stated that "all good citizens are hereby commanded to aid and assist in the prompt and efficient execution of this law." Such civilians, in the United States, were, for the most part, white citizens, who—prior to the postwar change in law that formally incorporated freedmen as part of the citizenry—effectively enjoyed the express and generalized authority to oversee and police Negroes.

After the Civil War, the fledgling emergence of Negroes as citizens was enforced by a forbidding military presence in the former Confederate states. The threat of violence effectively administered the newfound emancipation of Negroes under the Thirteenth Amendment, the Fourteenth Amendment's formal entitlements to equal protection under the law, and the prohibition on federal and state governments from denying *all* male citizens the right to vote on account of "race, color, or previous condition of servitude" under the Fifteenth Amendment.

With the withdrawal of federal troops from the former Confederate states after the Civil War, the posse, in theory, should have been ready, willing, and able to step in to enforce the newfound rights of freedmen. However, the postwar era saw the resurgence of a new kind of posse, composed of white vigilantes who enforced the old racial order through extralegal violence.

ACTUALLY, THE THRONGS AT TRUMP RALLIES WERE NOT ALWAYS HOLLERing. It's true that they intermittently booed, or chanted "U.S.A.!," "We Love You!," or "Lock Her Up!" on cue, like a live studio audience dutifully responding to prompts by some off-camera hype man. As it turned out (after I forced myself to watch a few of these recorded conventions), the crowd was often surprisingly rapt, respectfully silent as Trump commanded their attention from behind a podium, which he'd grip at each side like a steering wheel. Whatever unruliness I had projected onto them was not being reflected back to me on my laptop screen. Yes, the atmosphere channeled a sports arena, what with the coordinated chanting, the dominant red color scheme of the MAGA baseball caps, the slogan-ridden insignia rallygoers wore on their bodies and placards. Yet, as clamorous they were, shouts were organized, subject to direction. And Trump himself was their hype man.

And what was he hyping? To the "loyal, hard-working American patriots" at a Make America Great Again rally held in Tucson, Arizona, he longed for the "old-fashioned days," and promised, among other things, that for the crowd's vote, "we" would "support our police," "protect our Second Amendment," and "defend our borders." He proclaimed that no one has ever done what "we have done," or "accomplished what we have accomplished" in the prior four years. Again and again, Trump deployed the majestic plural, the royal "we," to pronounce how his official actions would translate into the crowd's safety, prosperity, and realization of the American Dream.

WHITE MOB VIOLENCE, OF COURSE, WAS NOT SOLELY EXACTED UPON Negroes. President Grover Cleveland issued two proclamations under the Insurrection Act in response to the organized expulsion of Chinese laborers from Washington State in the mid-1880s. Amid an economic downturn that hit the Northwest Pacific region, Chinese residents— who had largely migrated to help build the region's transcontinental railroad—became scapegoats for anxious white laborers who blamed Chinese workers for driving down wages and, thereby, posing unfair competition for available work. A wave of propaganda campaigns by members and sympathizers of the Knights of Labor, a labor union, recommended expulsion of Chinese laborers, a strategy that gained significant public support.

As Carlos A. Schwantes discusses in his article "Protest in a Promised Land: Unemployment, Disinheritance, and the Origin of Labor

Militancy in the Pacific Northwest, 1885–1886," the discontent of such white laborers was crystallized into "a crude ideology of disinheritance," where the scapegoating of Chinese laborers advanced by the Knights of Labor was intertwined with rhetoric "that implicitly recognized the American dream of economic plenty and social advance for all honest toilers." Rhetoric of white entitlement coincided with the dehumanization of Chinese laborers, who—as Schwantes cites from the *Daily Call,* a Seattle periodical that was popular among the white underemployed—were referred to as "treacherous, almond-eyed sons of Confucius," "[c]hattering, round-mouth lepers," and "yellow heathen." Such sentiments were also expressed in the rallying cries of white laborers, as Schwantes further notes:

> "The Chinese must go!" was an utterance heard frequently in Pacific Northwest communities in September and October 1885. Residents discussed little else but expulsion. Daily they grew ever more excited—or anxious. It was "War! War! War!" screamed an advertisement for Seattle's great IXL clothing store, which catered to a mass market.

The first proclamation under the Insurrection Act, issued on November 7, 1885, concerned the move by white mobs incited by the Knights of Labor to threaten and intimidate Chinese residents into leaving Tacoma, Washington. On November 3 of that year—a few weeks after three Chinese laborers were murdered and masked men torched quarters where thirty-seven Chinese workers resided—some two hundred Chinese persons were ordered to pack, escorted by Knights of Labor supporters to a Northern Pacific railway station, and forced to leave the state on a train to Portland, Oregon. President Cleveland's proclamation, which was made at the request of the territorial governor of Washington, stated "that by reason of unlawful obstructions and combinations and the assemblage of evil-disposed persons" it had become impracticable to enforce the law to suppress mob violence without federal assistance. However, such "evil-disposed people," having completed their mission, notes Schwantes, wondered what federal troops would do when they reached Tacoma: " 'What insurrection?' asked perpetrators as they returned peaceably to their homes . . . 'How will they manage to put down a people who are not in rebellion?' 'Let them come,' said the calm minded. 'We shall be glad to see them. It will give the boys a change.' "

THE PORTRAIT OF THE FUTURE TRUMP PAINTED FOR HIS CROWD WAS NOT always utopian. There was an alternative future that could very well unfold—that is, if his opponent were voted into office. Whereas the promise of abundance and security were to be shared among the plural "we"—the "people"—the mortal threat posed by an alternative Democratic dystopia was to be suffered by the crowd and the crowd alone. Trump, as he often pointed out, didn't even have a dog in that fight. He wasn't even a politician. He was just taking a break from his *real* life to provide a sorely needed public service—to help out. As Trump warned, the Democrats would "bury you in regulations," "dismantle your police department," "dissolve your borders," "destroy your suburbs," and "surrender your jobs to China." Whether the bogeymen were looters, rioters, radical socialists, or even the Chinese virus, the "you" of the crowd, according to Trump, was on the verge of being subsumed by some faceless, ubiquitous enemy—the "masses."

PRESIDENT CLEVELAND'S SECOND PROCLAMATION, WHICH WAS ALSO MADE at the request of Washington's territorial governor, also cited "evil-disposed persons" whose unlawful obstructions and combinations made it impracticable to enforce the law. Issued on February 9, 1886, the proclamation responded to a riot that erupted in Seattle after a white mob largely composed of local members and sympathizers of the Knights of Labor attempted to expel Chinese laborers using what they called the "Tacoma Method," which had prompted Cleveland's prior invocation of the act.

On February 7, the mob marauded through Seattle's Chinese neighborhood and threatened residents to "encourage" them to depart on a steamship leaving that afternoon. After plans were made to postpone the expulsion to the following day, the intended departure was further disrupted by violent clashes between Knight supporters and white residents who sought to put a stop to the scheme. The ship ultimately departed with nearly two hundred Chinese people on board, but, thereafter, the opposing parties clashed when Knights of Labor supporters tried to escort the remaining Chinese laborers off the dock to await the next ship, leaving five wounded and one person dead.

———

AS FAR BACK AS 2016, AT THE RALLIES PRECEDING TRUMP'S PRESIDENTIAL term, the actual violence at such events was directed at protesters, those present who openly decried the xenophobic principles underlying the spectacle. "I love the old days," said Trump at one such rally in Nevada, as a black protester who had been punched by a white male was being dragged out of the event. "You know what they used to do with guys like that in a place like this . . . they'd be carried out in a stretcher." Cheers from Trump's audience are then heard rising in the background.

———

ON JULY 8, 1894, PRESIDENT GROVER CLEVELAND MADE ANOTHER PROCLA-mation under the Insurrection Act to warn persons engaged "with such unlawful obstructions, combinations, and assemblages" in the state of Illinois "to disperse and retire peaceably to their respective abodes on or before 12 o'clock noon on the 9th day of July instant."

The incident that triggered this proclamation was the Pullman Strike in Chicago, involving employees of the Pullman Palace Car Company who went on strike after the railroad car manufacturer reduced wages and made drastic cuts to its workforce in response to a global economic downturn. The Pullman Company not only manufactured railway cars but also operated its signature sleeping car on railways across the United States, which were exclusively manned by male Negro porters as per the preference of company head George Pullman, who believed that the formerly enslaved would make the best servants for the cars' elite white customers. In June, after the Pullman Company refused to bargain with the American Railway Union, which represented the striking employees, the union organized a boycott by its members against handling any Pullman cars until the company agreed to arbitration. The American Railway Union, headed by Eugene V. Debs, only represented white workers and excluded Negro membership, making it convenient for the Pullman Company to hire Negro strikebreakers to resume work while the labor conflict ensued.

Despite the American Railway Union's representation being limited to white workers, union representatives deployed rhetoric that compared the plight of Pullman laborers to enslavement. "In response to critics who maintained that the strikers had mounted a 'rebellion' and 'insurrection' as threatening as the Civil War," writes Carl Smith in *Urban Disorder and the Shape of Belief: The Great Chicago Fire, the Haymarket Bomb, and the Model Town of Pullman*, "labor spokesmen revived the argument the anarchists had made in calling their cause the liberation of a subject people from bondage." Smith further quotes labor activist William Burns, who stated that Pullman workers were "reduced to a condition of slavery beneath that of the black slave of the South," who were provided food and shelter while "the white slave of Pullman was forced to work for wages entirely inadequate to furnish a sufficient amount of food to keep body and soul together."

After Attorney General Richard Olney claimed that the strike unlawfully obstructed interstate commerce, a federal court issued an injunction on July 2 enjoining the American Railway Union from interfering with railroad traffic. A few days later, a mob defied the injunction and attempted to obstruct a train being guarded by the state militia. After soldiers and the mob clashed, four rioters died and several on both sides were wounded. President Cleveland dispatched federal troops into Chicago despite the objection of Governor John Altgeld, who opposed federal military intervention to disband the strike. The formerly peaceful strike erupted into violence, as crowds of strikers began to riot and damage property throughout the city. By July 18, armed forces had broken the strike and were ordered by the attorney general to evacuate.

WHAT WITH THE CHEERFUL COLOR COORDINATION OF REDS, WHITES, AND blues, as well as the rapt reverence of the participants, what I was witnessing, when forcing myself to watch a Trump rally, was not an actual mob. The unruly violence that is characteristic of the mob does not erupt amid the unanimously aligned and abstract "we." Mob violence erupts in direct confrontation with the mob's imagined adversary, with the Other. So, what I was watching was not a full-blown mob, but a would-be mob.

While Trump is ultimately his own hype man, his congregations were also a prep rally of sorts. Trump was merely the opening act. He created a mood, warmed up the crowd. The Trump rally was not the main event.

HOME OF THE RELATIVELY FREE

There was a meeting, my father told me, among a concerned group of white neighbors who were conspiring to devise how, exactly, they were going to remove the black families from our neighborhood. My father only found out because one of the neighbors who had been invited to the meeting warned him. Although I heard this anecdote several times growing up, I never knew the details of the expulsion plan or who else, specifically, was involved. For all I knew, any of those neighbors were my elementary school classmates' parents. I might have played tag on their lawns, or have been briefly inside their houses to check out their kids' new Barbie dolls. All I recall is that our three-person family of West African descent—as well as three families from Jamaica and one African American family—represented all that the white meeting holders had been hoping to flee from. We, according to the whistleblower who confessed their plot, would bring their home values down.

Whenever hearing this quip as my father told and retold it from time to time, I don't ever remember feeling surprise or dismay. By the time I had sufficient conscious awareness to file the anecdote in my long-term memory, I had no discernible reaction. I now figure my lack of surprise had to do with the fact that this reported conspiracy was entirely consistent with the behavior to which I had apparently already adapted.

My parents moved to the United States from Sierra Leone in the early seventies as college graduates, by then adults. Whenever I overheard them discuss some racist affront one of them had suffered—from the quotidian to the egregious—I would sense the same high intensity of offense and bewilderment. Whether micro or macro, the very same violations that had already become unremarkable and expected aspects of my daily existence were, to them, inflicting fresh wounds with every swipe. I never remembered a time before I became accustomed to my hostile environment. Like the document of the first encounter of white settlers from the perspective of indigenous peoples, the record of any initial shock, in my mind, is sparse if not nonexistent. It wasn't the superficial differences, like our clashing accents or their dismay at my appetite for fast food, that set me apart the most from my parents, but this quality I have seemingly always had of being relatively inured to racism.

We were living, after all, on Long Island—that elongated land mass that serves as a coda to the boroughs of Brooklyn and Queens. Having grown up there, I found it interesting that many New York City transplants didn't know much about Long Island apart from the celebrity-laden Hamptons at the tail end of it. They would simply leapfrog over the site of my formative years to the fancy beaches, kind of like people who like to tell me all about how they have traveled to Africa and only talk about the safaris.

Long Island, after all, is the adopted home of what some like to call "ethnic whites." This refers to white people whose descendants didn't disembark from the *Mayflower* or otherwise exist outside of that other catchall, "White Anglo-Saxon Protestant." They are usually Catholic and originally Irish or Italian or Polish and/or a combination of two or more of these nationalities. In my experience, they were also white Jewish residents who technically didn't fit any of these categories. A more accurate description of the people I was raised around would probably be that they subscribed to "ethnic whiteness," because the "ethnic white" identity was the hegemonic one to which it seemed everyone assimilated regardless of their actual background.

If I were being facetious I would say that everyone I grew up around was loud, angry, loved pizza, and aggressively celebrated St. Patrick's Day. However, if I were trying to be sociologically precise, I would say that they had adopted a negative identity that—aside from hyperbolic attachments to certain ethnic artifacts—was exclusively defined by who was excluded. It's an age-old story, how ethnic whites who immigrated to the United States after their British or Germanic predecessors were barred from meaningfully participating in the economy and, in effect, relegated to a social status not much higher than that assigned to black people. The exclusionary signs on shops and other businesses reading "No Irish Need Apply" or "No Italians Allowed" have been well documented. That such newcomers were legally white was all they could hang their hat on, and represented both a low rung and coveted jumping-off point on the socioeconomic ladder they aimed to climb.

The lore of Ellis Island and the tired, huddled masses who arrived to the United States is not my history. My ancestral introduction to the situations called the "United States" and "Long Island" was marked by the year 1965, when the Immigration and Naturalization Act eliminated the prior quotas put in place in the 1920s. From that point on, skill rather than nationality would serve as the requisite bar for, or barrier to, entry to the United States. So, not only did one have to be the model immigrant, but by widely shared implication it would also be prudent to ascribe to whiteness, which, as always, had required performative demonstrations that one was not black. This is an old story, one explored at length, for example, by Noel Ignatiev in *How the Irish Became White*, which considers the central question of how Irish immigrants arriving in the eighteenth century relinquished both the deep resentment of caste, English oppression, and the abolitionist rhetoric of Catholic priests in their home country of Ireland to align themselves with white American racism against black people in the United States. Then again, this is all ancient history, but it was definitely news to my parents.

─────

THE "MILITIA," IN THE UNITED STATES, WAS INITIALLY AN ARMED FORCE OF white male citizens and/or subjects organized at the local or state level and sanctioned to do battle at the command of a governmental authority—at first by English colonial officers, then, after independence, at the direction of territorial, state, or, in exceptional circumstances (such as under the Insurrection Act), federal officials. The militiaman, under colonial and subsequent state law, did not voluntarily enlist, but was automatically conscripted if he was white and male and able-bodied within a given age range set forth in a relevant statute.

A 1738 colonial law of Virginia, for example, authorized the compulsory enlistment of "all free male persons, above the age of one and twenty years," providing, however, that "free mulattos, Negro [*sic*], or Indians, as are or shall be listed, as aforesaid, shall appear without arms," relegating them to serving as drummers or trumpeters or "in such other servile labor as they are directed to perform." The proviso here, that nonwhite men should not be armed, is aligned with the insurrectionary threat that Negroes, both free and enslaved, and indigenous peoples posed to the security of the colonial territory-cum-state. The armed citizen-soldier was, by definition, a white man.

THERE IS A SAYING THAT IN THE NORTH, A BLACK PERSON COULD GO AS high as he wanted as long as he didn't get too close, and that in the South, he could get as close as he wanted as long as he didn't get too high. This was a pithy way of highlighting the relative penchant white northerners had for physical segregation, Jim Crow notwithstanding. Despite southern hysterics over maintaining a "way of life" through racial segregation, the legacy of black enslavement, then servitude, was said to have inculcated in white southerners a kind of intimacy with African Americans through sheer proximity that was not historically present in the North, where residential segregation was a de facto rule. This difference between the two regions was a matter of degree and not absolute, of course, but the saying periodically comes to mind when I think of Long Island as the place where, as a black person, you can neither get too close nor too high. In this way, Long Island has always represented, to me, the worst aspects of the racist South and the racist North.

WITHIN THE PREVAILING NARRATIVE OF U.S. MILITARY HISTORY, THE MILItia is understood to be disorganized, poorly equipped, and fairly ineffective, especially in comparison to their trained counterparts who comprised the British armed forces that helped fight the French in pre-independence wars, such as the French and Indian War. The militia, further, is distinct from those organized squadrons composed of full-time colonial military troops, known as "rangers," who regularly patrolled and fought on the frontier lands that bordered white settlements and indigenous territories, as well as provincial troops raised by British authorities to engage in other distinct military operations and wars, often against other European-led forces. As evident from many of the colonial and state militia laws, militia members were required to procure their own arms, although they were also permitted to rely on certain resources of their local arsenals. Given this relative lack of training and reliable access to munitions, it was not until militia members joined the ranks of the Continental Army during the Revolutionary War that they were afforded, in the prevailing narrative of U.S. military history, more credibility as an effective armed force.

However, this prevailing narrative often overlooks the role colonial militia played in defending and, indeed, expanding the territory of white settlers during the pre-independence era. John Grenier discusses this period extensively in *The First Way of War: American War Making on the Frontier*, where he extensively details the rules of engagement—or, in fact, the lack thereof—that colonial armies employed in their battles with indigenous tribes. Such colonial militia engaged in extirpative warfare—or, as it is now termed, unlimited warfare—waging battles against indigenous peoples characterized by indiscriminate killing or the slaughter of noncombatants, and the destruction of agricultural resources.

In *The First Way of War*, Grenier quotes an indignant letter Thomas Jefferson sent in July 1779 to British army officer William Phillips, defending his decision not to intervene on behalf of a British lieutenant governor named Henry Hamilton—a prisoner of war who was shackled in irons while confined in a prison. In response to

Phillips's request that Hamilton be paroled or exchanged for another POW, in accordance with established custom, Jefferson cited Hamilton's wartime strategies in defense of his refusal. "The known rule of warfare with the Indian Savages is an indiscriminate butchery of men women and children," Jefferson wrote. "In the execution of that undertaking he associates small parties of whites under his immediate command with large parties of the Savages, & sends them to act, not against our Forts or armies in the field, but farming settlements on our frontiers," he continued. "Governor Hamilton then is himself the butcher of men women and children." While unlimited warfare— what Grenier has called the "first way of war" within the United States—was appropriate for the "Savages," according to Jefferson, it was a grave affront to the dignity of white settlers.

———

GROWING UP IN SUFFOLK COUNTY, MY ONLY ENCOUNTER WITH INDIGENOUS peoples was through the names of various towns or institutions. In my school district alone—an amalgam of five elementary schools, two junior high schools, and one high school—children in kindergarten through sixth grade might have attended Arrowhead or Minnesauke or Nassakeag or Setauket. If my parents or I wanted to cut our commute to the city by half an hour or so, we would take the train in from the Long Island Railroad station at Ronkonkoma. If resigned to a longer ride, we would take a local train and intermittently make stops at Syosset and Mineola before eventually arriving at Penn Station. I remember my mother driving to shop at a boutique in Commack. I also recall competing in track meets against students from Shoream, as well as giving a pitiful performance in the scrub round of a basketball game against a rival team from Wyandanch. Aside from such names, certain other legacies were apparent. My high school lacrosse team was among the highest ranked in the country. The game of lacrosse was originated by indigenous tribes in the Northeast.

The routine presence of indigenous monikers was, I suppose, intended as a form of commemoration, but my experience of these names always highlighted their erasure as human presences. Among the history that I did not learn in grade school was how indigenous peoples on Long Island were massacred by Dutch settlers. Though I was vaguely aware of dubious land purchases, where indigenous leaders who did not have any notion of private property inadvertently exchanged large swaths of land with the Dutch for items like knives or cloth, I was not, for example, aware of Governor Kieft's War—named after William Kieft, a Dutch governor of the then-province. In a series of raids carried out between 1640 and 1645, Dutch settlers killed more than one thousand indigenous residents in brutal battles characterized by beheading and burning indigenous people alive, as well as murdering young children.

I never met an indigenous person during my sixteen years growing up on Long Island. So I was surprised to discover that according to census estimates just under 1 percent—0.6 percent to be exact—of census respondents on Long Island identified as "American Indian and Alaska Native alone." Out of an estimated population of 1,476,601 Suffolk County respondents, the number of people who identified as "American Indian and Alaska Native alone" would, according to my rough math, total about 8,860 people. Even so, that number to me seems astronomically high. I'm very familiar with certain white classmates or neighbors periodically boasting "Indian" ancestry as a kind of exotic accent to their racial identity, but I never encountered anyone who identified as "American Indian alone."

There are two surviving reservations on Long Island whose residents likely account for the census numbers quoted above. Yet even as they contend for federal recognition or to preserve what has survived of their languages, such struggles are ensconced in a thick fog of silence, amid which appropriated names of towns and schools and highways and lakes stand firm like gravestones.

THOUGH THE MILITIA IN COLONIAL AMERICA WAS INITIALLY INTENDED TO
repel "foreign" enemies, such as indigenous peoples and European
adversaries like the French and the Spanish, the military organization came to play a significant role in the enforcement of slave codes
and the overall prevention and suppression of slave insurrections. As
Sally E. Hadden writes in *Slave Patrols: Law and Violence in Virginia and the Carolinas*, the legally mandated participation of white
male citizens in the surveillance of enslaved Negroes, as well as the
capture and return of fugitives, in the form of organized so-called
patrols were, upon their inception, closely linked with already formed
militias. Though, as Hadden discusses, the inception of slave patrols
differed from colony to colony, the members of slave patrols at the
time largely overlapped with members of militia—to the extent that
those designated to enlist in the militia would attempt to shirk their
duties by claiming pressing patrol duties. As early as 1727, Virginia
officials enacted a law to authorize the deployment of the militia to
patrol slaves, which, as Hadden writes, constituted the colony's first
slave patrol. Thereby, militia commanders would be authorized to call
forth "as many white men as they believed were needed to patrol" from
time to time. Regardless of the composition of their membership, it
was common practice even prior to independence for slave patrols to
be the first line of defense against slave insurrection, and the militia
the second if patrollers failed in their suppression efforts.

The routine deployment of the militia to repel indigenous invasions and suppress slave insurrections provides additional and under-
explored context to the Second Amendment right to bear arms. "A
well-regulated Militia," the amendment reads, "being necessary to
the security of a free State, the right of the people to keep and bear
Arms, shall not be infringed." As Roxanne Dunbar-Ortiz discusses in
Loaded: A Disarming History of the Second Amendment, jurists, gun-

control advocates, and gun enthusiasts have long debated whether this constitutional right was intended to be conferred upon each individual citizen or was instead conditioned upon the widespread conscription of citizens into militia of the several states. As the state militia has been eclipsed by the National Guard, gun-control advocates would argue, the right to bear arms enumerated in the Second Amendment would therefore be obsolete. Meanwhile, gun enthusiasts, including members of current-day right-wing militias, continue to defend their Second Amendment right as an individual one—a right that Dunbar-Ortiz contends is an outgrowth of the history of the United States "that has entitled white nationalism, racialized dominance, and social control through violence."

THE ABIDING MYTH OF THE UNITED STATES IS THE AMERICAN DREAM, YET for every group within this country's borders, this dream has distinct subplots. I was not raised to envisage the African American dream, that dream deferred which is pursued nonetheless through faith in a higher power, or willpower, and resilience and determination to become at least twice as good. My dream, the mirage that I was lulled into, also emphasized hard work, but dangled the false promise that such work naturally would be rewarded roughly in correspondence to my talent and efforts. In other words I was entranced into believing in meritocracy. This is the subplot called the Immigrant Dream, in which a cornucopia of opportunity is ripe for the picking by anyone who is hungry enough to sow their harvest.

I sometimes think that my awakening from this dream would have been far less jarring if someone had pulled me aside and had "the talk." Perhaps then I could have been more lucid in an African American dream, the dream within the American Dream that is also the most prevalent hallucination so many white Americans suffer from. Borrowing from Toni Morrison's remark about the nature of paradises and utopias, the (white) American Dream is "designed by who is not there, by the people who are not allowed in." The dream of inclusion by way of exclusion was never mine, but it was the one many ethnic whites I grew up around were sleepwalking in, and—when our dreamscapes overlapped—it was the one in which they dutifully reminded me I did not belong.

Census numbers apparently corroborate my feelings: approximately 84 percent of the population in Suffolk County, Long Island, identifies as white, with about 66 percent of those respondents considering themselves to be "white alone" (i.e., not "Hispanic" or "Latino"), and the remaining 20-odd percent categorizing themselves as "Hispanic" or "Latino." While just over 4 percent of census respondents identified as "Asian alone," nearly 9 percent of Suffolk County's population identified as black. In the zip code where I grew up, the present black population is calculated at 1.6 percent of the total residing population.

Now, I'm aware that the tiny number of black residents in my neighborhood at the time of the meeting of those conspiring about how to drive us from our homes did not necessarily correspond to the overall percentage of black people in Suffolk County. But I am also aware that our abstraction was not numerical. Our statistical presence was not at issue, only our perceived presence. Our families were indistinguishable to the white meeting attendees who were seeking to evict us. In their eyes, we were not distinct people with particular backgrounds and occupations, or humble and hardworking residents also striving to attain the American Dream. We were, instead, synonymous with poor exterior paint quality or power lines or a highway or an unsightly yard or anything else that risks lowering home values. Our relative freedom within the American Dream, apparently, had historically emancipated persons of African descent transformed from being designated as property into personal threats to property value. Ironically, though, the black families in the neighborhood often traded anecdotes about how the quotidian improvements they would make to their homes would breed resentment in white neighbors, who seemed to not want to be outdone by black people.

———

THE MILITIA ACT OF 1903, ALSO KNOWN AS THE DICK ACT, EFFECTIVELY reconfigured the "militia" into the National Guard—an organized reserve force that serves at the will of the state governor unless called forth into federal service by the president. The 1903 act is also notable for dividing the militia into two different classes: first, the organized militia, consisting of the National Guard and the naval militia (a component of state military reserve forces that include current and former members of the Navy, Marine Corps, and Coast Guard), and second, the unorganized militia.

The unorganized militia, under the 1903 act, is not defined by what it actually is, but rather by what it is not, namely "the members of the militia who are not members of the National Guard or the Naval Militia." Though both the organized and unorganized militia are bracketed by age (seventeen to forty-five years old), the catchall statutory definition of the unorganized militia has certainly cast a wide net. Accordingly, gun enthusiasts have tried to argue their way into this authorized category, and therefore enshrine their private military-like activities within the limits of the law.

As recently as 2017, a gun enthusiast named John Cutonilli brought a pro se action against the state of Maryland to challenge the state's Firearm Safety Act of 2013, claiming among other things that it violated his constitutional rights under the Second Amendment. Cutonilli argued that the Firearm Safety Act curtailed his right to purchase assault weapons and the "large-capacity magazines" he desired to obtain in order to arm himself as a member of the unorganized militia, which may be called into service by the governor of Maryland or the president. Inclined to dismiss the case entirely, the district court ultimately ordered that Cutonilli show cause why his case should not be dismissed, having found that his "hypothetical" claim of membership in an unorganized militia was not protected by the Second Amendment.

In the Cutonilli decision, the district court cited the 2008 Supreme Court case *District of Columbia v. Heller*, which held that the Second Amendment did in fact protect an individual right to bear arms that was unrelated to membership in a well-regulated militia and, instead, realized the natural right of self-defense. Though the district court here relied on *Heller* to maintain that Cutonilli's claimed membership in the unorganized militia was insufficient due to his reliance on a collective rather than individual right of self-defense, the *Cutonilli* decision and several others like it are, effectively, only rhetorical denial of the gun enthusiast. By legal interpretation, at least, *Heller* redrew the map of authorized self-defense for the gun enthusiast, redefining the threshold of self-defense from that of "country" to "home." As the majority held in *Heller*, "whatever else [the Second Amendment] leaves to future evalua-tion, it surely elevates above all other interests the right of law-abiding, responsible citizens to use arms in defense of hearth and home."

———

OUR SUBURBAN PLOT WAS A LOGICAL EXTENSION OF LEVITTOWN, THE VERY first suburb established after World War II, which largely accommo-dated veterans eligible for federal housing loans administered under the G. I. Bill. Negro veterans were systematically denied access to such loans, as well as to Levittown, since the developer found it profitable to bar prospective Negro buyers from purchasing property in order to lure and secure white house hunters. Like Levittown, our suburb was a font of uniformity. The homes only varied between two stock models, a one-story ranch or a two-story house, each with an assortment of structural and ornamental options available to mix and match on the chosen pro-totype like add-ons to a potato-head doll. Some homes had basements and others did not; driveways could sit before either one- or two-story car garages; some houses had brick fronts and others shingles, and yet others some form of siding. The houses were all different, but essentially the same. All the labrynthine streets in our development began with the letter *M*, adding even more confusion to visitors who would attempt to drive home and lose themselves in the neighborhood that slid past the car windows like repeating cells of the background of a cartoon.

The dream of white flight was not only the house, the yard, and the 2.5 cars and children. It was an oasis of homogeneity, in which only the most minor of differences—say, an artfully hedged shrub or a cement rather than tar driveway—would make any one of the suburb's inhabitants distinguishable from another.

ON JUNE 21, 1943, PRESIDENT FRANKLIN DELANO ROOSEVELT ISSUED A proclamation under the Insurrection Act "directing Detroit rioters to disperse." Roosevelt made this proclamation at the request of then-governor of Michigan Harry Kelly, resulting in the dispatch of around six thousand federal troops to patrol the streets of Detroit and enforce an imposed curfew. The inciting incident—which escalated into a three-day brawl that left thirty-four people dead, more than six hundred injured, and about two million dollars in property damage—occurred on the Saturday evening of June 19, 1943, at the Eastwood Amusement Park, where a group of young white men harassed two black men. The following Sunday evening, on an island off the coast of Detroit called Belle Isle, the same two black men were set upon by another group of whites, who had decided to avenge the altercation from the previous night.

This confrontation then spread, coopting larger groups of black and white day-trippers as the melee continued across the bridge connecting the island to the city of Detroit. By late that evening, several hundred people were embroiled in the racially divided fighting, which had been fueled by the dissemination of false rumors—of a white mob having thrown a black mother and child into the Detroit river, a story that circulated among black residents, and of black men raping white women, broadcast among white residents. In the meantime, white and black crowds marauded through the streets of Detroit, attacking each other and, by early the following morning, looting city storefronts.

After the federal cavalry was called in, the riot was calmed and the damage assessed. Where city and state commissions reviewed the data and concluded that the riot was caused by Negro youths and "outside agitators" who had recently migrated to Detroit, the NAACP issued a report drafted by Walter White and Thurgood Marshall, which painted a more nuanced portrait. Citing the recent influx of migrants to the city, a hub of the World War II manufacturing economy— half a million people in the three years preceding the riot—as well as fierce competition for lucrative jobs in federally funded wartime factories, the NAACP report detailed the long-brewing dissension between black and white Detroiters. Of those who partook in this Great Migration from parts of the South, about forty to fifty thousand at the time were Negro migrants. Roosevelt's executive orders barring racial discrimination with respect to federal jobs were scarcely enforced, contributing to an environment where the KKK proliferated and influenced local unions to resist the employment of black laborers—who, given their surplus in a discriminatory labor force, often occupied the position of scabs willing to work during strikes.

While the conclusions of city and state riot commissioners relied upon data showing that black residents made up the majority of police arrests, they overlooked reports that police officers themselves had been involved in the riots—often dissolving into the white mob, and shooting and beating black rioters themselves, ignoring white laypersons who were doing the same. In support of this proposition, the NAACP report cites an emblematic photograph in the *Detroit Free Press*, which depicted an elderly Negro being restrained by two police officers as two other policemen stand by mounted on horseback. "In the meantime," reads the report, "a white rioter strikes the helpless Negro full in the face with no indication on the part of any of the four policemen of any effort to protect the Negro." Further, where news reports publicized many identifiable images of white rioters engaged in violence and other unlawful activity, according to the report, "few if any, of them have even been arrested." Negroes, by contrast, bore the brunt of the harm, consisting of twenty-five of the thirty-four dead and the large majority of those wounded.

═══════

ISN'T IT OBVIOUS THAT–DESPITE MY RACIAL SINGULARITY ON LONG ISLAND as a "raisin in the milk"—I, together with any other black person in this majority-white country, have been ritually regarded as indivisible from "black people," that mythical monolithic group? Even my acknowledged individuality was oft perceived, by my white neighbors and friends, in relation to the millions of persons of African descent whom it would be impossible for anyone to know on a case-by-case basis. It's an age-old song a with familiar refrain: "But you're not like the rest of them . . ." This phenomenon is, frankly, so boring that it's not worth discussing at the level of specific examples, which would be endless. It's enough to simply state that whiteness bestows the one deemed to possess it with individuality, and blackness with a kind of sameness, qualities that are seen to conform across an entire group.

But, I suppose, this too depends on the one doing the seeing. "They even know the color of their eyes . . ." was the punch line of sorts from an anecdote shared by my father. He was quoting one of his fellow Sierra Leonean expatriates who was, back then, most likely to reside in the New York tristate area or in and around the District of Columbia. My father's friend was talking about one of his children, commenting on the child's uncanny ability to distinguish among his white classmates down to the most minor of details.

This quip stuck with me. It is because this predicament of presumed sameness among black, rather than white, people was so commonplace that my father's recitation was funny. Role reversal is a comedic device.

———

BEFORE THE CIVIL WAR, THE LAW HAD FRAMED NEGROES AS POTENTIAL insurgents, ever on the brink of a full-scale insurrection. But for the prescribed duty of white citizens to oversee the movements of Negroes, and the effective authority to engage in acts of violence against them, the prosperity, security, and very survival of the nascent Republic would be in peril. Negroes, prewar, were not part of the "people," then defined as white citizens. Negroes, however, were perceived to possess the collective potential to emerge as the "masses."

When, with the stroke of an official pen, Negroes were formally incorporated into the citizenry, brought under the definitional umbrella of the "people," the previously authorized role of white citizens to help suppress the Negro masses—whether as an enslaver or overseer or surveiller or patrolman or part of the posse or militia—was no longer licit. Suddenly, by law, the posse and militia could be called forth specifically to help enforce the very newfound entitlements that, prior to their constitutional enshrinement, such parties had been called upon to prohibit.

Like a deep furrow imprinted over time in hard stone by the persistent flow of rushing water, the suppression of Negroes by white citizens was, by this time, a habitual practice. The formality of Negro citizenship was, indeed, as tenuous as the formal duty of a larger white society to protect it. The law had changed, but the habitual practice had not. Alas, as Negroes were formally incorporated into the "people," a battalion of white citizens was simultaneously transformed into the "masses."

Part II

TIME LOOP

CHAPTER 5

Turn to Him the Other Cheek

One way to end a recurring nightmare—to disrupt the pervasive pattern of, say, frantically running away from some faceless monster until falling off a tall precipice—is to awaken within the dream. If a recurring nightmare is a subconscious vista, where scenes and characters are psychic manifestations of the dreamer's deep-rooted fears, then the dreamer who does not awaken within the nightmare risks remaining a mere captive to her dreamtime surroundings and becoming, once again, a casualty of the menaces that lurk there. If the dreamer becomes lucid in the nightmare, however, she has an opportunity to stop running, overcome her fear, and confront her would-be captor. In this way, she can change the narrative trajectory of the dream and, hopefully, never experience that particular nightmare again.

———

THE FAMOUS "I HAVE A DREAM" SPEECH GIVEN BY DR. MARTIN LUTHER King, delivered during the March on Washington in 1963, is often celebrated for its refrain, in which King orates the contents of his "dream" that is "deeply rooted in the American Dream." Much less

attention is drawn to the beginning half of the speech, which recounts
the nature of America's recurring nightmare:

> But one hundred years later, the Negro still is not free; one
> hundred years later, the life of the Negro is still sadly crippled
> by the manacles of segregation and the chains of discrimina-
> tion; one hundred years later, the Negro lives on a lonely island
> of poverty in the midst of a vast ocean of material prosperity;
> one hundred years later, the Negro is still languished [sic] in
> the corners of American society and finds himself in exile in
> his own land.

A recurring nightmare is demoralizing, not at all aspirational like
King's dream. In the nightmare, "freedom" is forever elusive; in King's
dream, "freedom" rings from every mountaintop. In this sense, King's
dream is comparable to the formal equality afforded to Negro citizens
under the law. If, as Robert Cover writes in "Violence and the Word,"
"[l]aw is the projection of an imagined future upon reality," then King's
dream—that dream that seeks to be included within the walled-off
vista of the American Dream—projects a similar vision.

However, absent federal military enforcement during the all-too-
brief respite that was Reconstruction—or, in other words, absent
violence and its threat—the equality of Negroes enumerated by the
Thirteenth, Fourteenth, and Fifteenth amendments became as ephem-
eral as any dream. Violence, however, endured. Though violence and
its threat became untethered from federal military enforcement of
the fledgling constitutional rights of freedmen, violence and its threat
continued to be wielded by ardent defenders of "states' rights." White
paramilitary groups like the Ku Klux Klan, initially suppressed during
the administration of Ulysses S. Grant, rebounded in the 1920s and
again in the 1950s, exercising violence through extralegal terroristic
means like intimidation and lynching. But threat of violence was also

effectively embedded in state laws passed to circumvent the spirit of the Civil War amendments.

Abundant in number but repetitive in substance, Jim Crow laws erected visible and invisible borders between white and Negro patrons in public facilities, so far as, according to the Supreme Court ruling in *Plessy v. Ferguson*, such facilities were "separate but equal." Overall, Jim Crow laws were effective in maintaining separateness but not equality, as such accommodations reflected the second-class citizenship relegated to Negro citizens. As the new incarnation of the black codes, and the slave codes before them, Jim Crow laws were part of the recurring nightmare that civil rights protesters strove to wake up from.

———

ON SEPTEMBER 23, 1957, FOLLOWING FAILED TALKS WITH ARKANSAS GOVernor Orval Faubus over allowing Negro students to enter Little Rock's all-white Central High School, President Dwight D. Eisenhower issued a proclamation under the Insurrection Act to enforce the school's desegregation. In a statement justifying the federal deployment of troops, Eisenhower stated that "mob violence cannot be allowed to override the decisions of our courts." The ultimate court decision Eisenhower was referring to was the landmark 1954 Supreme Court ruling *Brown v. Board of Education of Topeka*, which held that state laws mandating racially segregated public schools were unconstitutional. The day after Eisenhower made this statement, he federalized the entire Arkansas National Guard, placing it under his command, and deployed the 101st Airborne Division of the U.S. Army to stand by and shield Negro students from the wrath of white mobs as they walked into the high school.

Earlier that month, Faubus had ordered his state National Guard to form a blockade around Central High School to prevent Negro students from entering. Though the obvious effect of Faubus's deployment was to thwart the school's desegregation, the governor's expressed intention was to deter what he maintained was an imminent threat of violence. Faubus claimed he was responding to rumors that both resident whites and Negroes were arming themselves in preparation for a showdown over desegregation. Faubus's claim, however, has proven a dubious one, backed by little evidence—that is, apart from the governor's insistence that he had received credible reports of a sharp increase in gun purchases in the state. Nonetheless, Faubus never publicly deviated from his justification for calling forth the National Guard, which, as he expressed in his speech, was "to protect the lives and property of citizens." In fact, when Faubus announced his decision to call forth state troops in a September 2 televised address, he insisted that the state-commandeered troops would "act not as segregationists or integrationists, but as soldiers called to active duty to carry out their assigned tasks"; such state troops, he maintained, would serve as neutral defenders of the "peace."

THE WORD "PEACE" IS NEGATIVELY DEFINED. "PEACE," TECHNICALLY, refers to "freedom from disturbance" or absence of war. So, by the word's very definition, there is no telling what "peace" actually *is*, only what it is *not*. "Peace," then, is a vacuum, a void waiting to be filled by man-made projections. In that light, what is understood to constitute "peace" is a byproduct of the social contract—that theoretical pact between the State and its subjects whereby the governed relinquish some of their "freedoms" in exchange for the semblance of security provided by the government. Under this contract, so it is said, laws offer those governed by them a sense of stability and control, the ability to predict outcomes of commonplace conflicts. Laws, effectively, help construct the status quo—that familiar social landscape founded on established rules and precedent, often considered to be peaceful, no matter how violent it actually may be.

So, what is understood as "peace" in practice is actually referring to "order." The word "order," unlike "peace," is positively defined by what it *is* rather than by what it is *not*. The prevailing understanding of "order," especially when coupled with "law," is "a state in which the laws and rules regulating the public behavior of members of a community are observed and authority is obeyed." Another definition, though, is "a particular social, political, or economic system." When this particular social, political, or economic system is buttressed by a set of laws enforced by violence and its threat, then this "order" is a mandated status quo.

So it follows that to maintain the "peace" is no different from maintaining "law and order"—that age-old refrain of politicians, capturing in a pithy slogan the willingness to deploy violence and its threat to secure the existing state of affairs, and, at the same time, masking the violence inherent in such state, as the term projects the menace of violence on those who dare to disrupt it.

"Law and order," after all, has a much more palatable ring to it than "law and violence."

REGARDLESS OF WHETHER THE WORDS OF SOUTHERN POLITICIANS—WHEN seemingly hesitant or hostile toward desegregation—were truly heartfelt or merely paying lip service, appeasing a white segregationist base was certainly politically advantageous. Historians have generally interpreted Faubus's effective defiance of federally mandated desegregation as a strategic move to consolidate political support among a white electorate that was vehement about upholding "the southern way of life." The differences between Faubus's first and second terms as governor of Arkansas corroborate this theory. When Faubus was first elected governor in 1955, he did so as a moderate Democrat who even supported the entry of Negroes into the leadership of the state's party ranks in his first term. However, upon confronting rumors that he was a "Communist," as well as a contender for his second-term seat who was a staunch segregationist, Faubus ramped up his racial rhetoric in order to fend off any threat to his continued leadership.

Faubus's mixed motives aside, the military spectacle he authorized was a bold show of state defiance against what was mandated by the highest court in the federal judiciary and, thereby, supposed to be legally inevitable. Though the 1954 *Brown* ruling was technically the supreme law of the land, it carried little tangible effect absent practical mechanisms for enforcement. In a subsequent ruling in 1955 (often called *Brown II*), the Supreme Court relegated the implementation of its 1954 decision to the states, declining to specify deadlines or any other criteria for effecting desegregation apart from declaring that it be carried out with "all deliberate speed." This "speed" turned out to be incredibly slow, moving at a crawl's pace if at all across the South, where state officials either advised their constituents of the need for a gradual approach to desegregation or brazenly obstructed any concerted movement in that direction.

———

IT MAKES SENSE THAT ANOTHER DEFINITION OF "ORDER" IS "THE ARRANGE-ment or disposition of people, or things, in relation to each other according to a particular sequence, pattern, or method." This particular definition of "order" not only refers to the fact that a given structure exists, but also to a kind of classification or regularized and regimented template pursuant to which behavior is modeled. This sense of "order," in other words, implies hierarchy—where one or another thing comes first, and yet another second, and so on. To maintain the "peace," in this light, is in a way synonymous with maintaining this hierarchical sense of "order."

———

UPON OBTAINING A SECOND TERM, FAUBUS FOLLOWED HIS SEGREGATION-ist rhetoric with action. For one, he supported a 1956 amendment to the Arkansas state constitution that attempted to enshrine the doctrine of interposition, pursuant to which a state assumes the authority to prevent the federal government from enforcing law or otherwise taking action that the state deems unconstitutional. Adopted by the Arkansas state legislature on November 6, 1956, the amendment authorized "interposing the sovereignty of the State of Arkansas to end the nullification of these and all deliberate, palpable, and dangerous invasions of, or encroachments upon, the rights and powers not delegated to the United States." (Though intended to establish a legal basis for state officials to oppose the implementation of *Brown,* the amendment itself was unconstitutional because it violated the supremacy clause, which binds lower courts to enforce Supreme Court decisions.)

Also, in February 1957 a State Sovereignty Commission was established by the state legislature to "protect the sovereignty of Arkansas [. . .] from encroachment by the federal government." The commission, which included the governor of the state as an ex officio member, was granted investigatory powers to help prevent federal intervention into state affairs. In short, by the time Faubus called forth the National Guard to Central High School, any talk about safeguarding states' rights was not simply grandstanding, but backed by institutional, if not technically legal, support.

THERE IS ANOTHER MEANING OF THE WORD "ORDER," WHICH MAKES THE term "law and order" a tautology: that is, "an authoritative command, direction, or instruction." In tandem with "order" as a command, yet another meaning of the word "order" implies obedience—meaning "a state in which the laws and rules regulating the public behavior of members of a community are observed and authority is obeyed." And "order," in this sense, does not only imply the banal sort compelled by violence or the threat of violence. "Order" in this other sense imparts obedience inspired by a kind of devotion, recalling yet another definition of the word "order" that refers to a society of monks, priests, nuns, or some other members of a disciplined community living according to certain religious and social regulations. Members of such orders often take solemn vows and are fervent in complying with their promise to fulfill them.

———

THE BATTLE OVER "DESEGREGATION" IN LITTLE ROCK, ARKANSAS—ALL THE political wrangling that eventually escalated to the point of state and federal deployments of troops—was, specifically, about the enrollment of only nine Negro students. Nicknamed the "Little Rock Nine," Minniejean Brown, Elizabeth Eckford, Ernest Green, Thelma Mothershed, Melba Pattillo, Gloria Ray, Terrence Roberts, Jefferson Thomas, and Carlotta Walls were the nine teenagers recruited by the Arkansas chapter of the NAACP to attend Central High School as part of the local school board's plans for "gradual" desegregation. The students were not only selected for their good grades, but also for their demeanor and their potential to keep their composure under stress— qualities the students were asked to cultivate in intensive counseling sessions during the weeks preceding the start of the school year. Eckford, in particular, has since become emblematic of the ability to maintain her poise: she was photographed in a black-and-white dress, clutching her notebooks to her chest with one arm, her face inscrutable behind sunglasses as a hostile crowd of white men and women mill behind her, one white girl's expression caught mid-scream and contorted into a snarl.

———

"MORAL JUJITSU" IS WHAT AUTHOR RICHARD GREGG CALLED THE PRACTICE of maintaining one's composure in the face of brutality and malice in *The Power of Non-Violence*, a primer assigned in workshops held by social justice organizations for civil rights protesters in the 1960s. Typical of martial arts disciplines, jujitsu is the practice of specified techniques that are aimed at using the force of one's opponent against them. Instead of directly attacking an opponent with one's own force, a jujitsu battle may be won, for example, by darting out of the way of a challenger who lunges in one's direction and thereby making way for the opponent to slam him- or herself on the floor. In keeping with this metaphor, while nonviolent protesters always risk bodily harm and even death, their state-sanctioned attackers inevitably display their own violence, thereby toppling their legitimacy in front of their watching audiences.

———

THE ICONIC PHOTOS OF ECKFORD WERE TAKEN ON SEPTEMBER 4, 1957, TWO days after Faubus announced the deployment of the National Guard that denied her and the other eight students' entry. Brought to bear by the national and international media attention from such dramatic images, Eisenhower soon met with Faubus, who removed the National Guard but, in a continued show of defiance, left the local police at the site to patrol the area. Eckford and the rest of the Little Rock Nine moved to enter Central High School again on September 23, thereby prompting a white mob of around one thousand members to surround the school and erupt into a riot. When Eisenhower dispatched federal troops to Little Rock the following day, Faubus referred to such intervention as "the military occupation of Arkansas."

Indeed, when the nine students were permitted to attend classes thanks to such federal enforcement, they were each initially assigned an individual soldier to walk them to and from classes. "The troops did not, however, mean the end of harassment," recalled Melba Pattillo, one of the nine. "It meant the declaration of war."

———

NONVIOLENT RESISTANCE ULTIMATELY IS POLITICAL THEATER. IN THE case of civil rights activists, the audience included spectators of the domestic and international media. Keen to break a news story, broadcast and newspaper journalists reporting on nonviolent protesters could be counted on to document the ensuing violent drama for public consumption. Such viewership, then, would force the hand of the federal government to intervene in a conflict that representative officials would have rather stayed out of in the name of respecting states' rights. In the case of the civil rights movement, any success of the peaceful tactics of nonviolent resistance did not only rely on summoning the violence of state and nonstate actors for worldwide display: it also depended on the compulsion of the federal government deploying the military to enforce constitutional rights.

———

ON SEPTEMBER 30, 1962, PRESIDENT JOHN F. KENNEDY ISSUED A PROCLAMA-tion under the Insurrection Act ordering persons obstructing the enforcement of federal court-ordered desegregation to "cease and desist therefrom and to disperse and retire peaceably forthwith." Soon afterward, Kennedy dispatched about 23,000 federal troops to the University of Mississippi to enforce the right of James Meredith, a Negro Air Force veteran, to register at the all-white school. Despite his great reluctance to do so, Kennedy invoked the Insurrection Act following the administration's failure to persuade governor Ross Barnett to stand down and allow Meredith to enroll in the Oxford, Mississippi–based university known as "Ole Miss." In a televised statement justifying federal military intervention, Kennedy stated: "[I]n a government of laws and not of men, no man, however prominent or powerful, and no mob however unruly or boisterous, is entitled to defy a court of law."

On the prior day, September 29, Kennedy had held talks with Barnett in a bid to secure his participation in a staged scenario where, supposedly without the governor's knowledge, Meredith would be "secretly" registered at the university from an outpost in Jackson, thereby allowing the governor to save face in front of his white segregationist base. During this conversation—among several conducted during the course of three public confrontations where Barnett and other state officials blocked Meredith from registering at the university—Barnett agreed to the scheme. But while challenging the Jim Crow system was, ultimately, a matter of life or death for civil rights activists, for state officials like Ross Barnett maintaining a show of defying desegregation was just as important as actually defying desegregation, if not more so. Barnett truly did believe in the separation of the Negro and white races; however, as with any politician, his chances for reelection would depend far less on his actual beliefs than in the perception of his beliefs among his desired electorate. So, following his appearance at an Ole Miss football game, where he addressed a stadium full of cheering spectators and declared his fidelity to the state's "customs" and "heritage," Barnett called the president to renege on the plan. Soon thereafter, Kennedy signed an executive order under the Insurrection Act authorizing the deployment of troops.

———

TO AWAKEN WITHIN THE RECURRING NIGHTMARE IS NOT ONLY TO WATCH all that had seemed solid in one's surrounding melt into the psychic airs of the dreamscape, it is to also realize that you are a character within the dream—that you are a mere performer within the subconscious stage of your own mind. When living within the recurring nightmare that is history, a similar sensibility might strike those on the world stage, on which they make a conscious decision whether to simply *be*—to respond authentically to what arises in the field of life—or to *appear* to be.

To simply be is to relinquish control over the effects of one's actions, to allow events to unfold as they may, without regard to the consequences. To *appear* is to calculate one's actions, which are premeditated and orchestrated to inspire a specific outcome. Whether the motives behind one's actions are pure or performed, the consequences—in the dreamlike field of "real" life—can be nonetheless deadly. As French theorist Jean Baudrillard writes in *Simulacra and Simulation,* someone who stages a holdup with a fake gun has nonetheless set up a scenario into which law enforcement will eventually charge with weapons drawn.

———

BARNETT AND THE KENNEDY ADMINISTRATION WERE NOT THE ONLY CONscious players in this political theater. In step with the tactics devised by leaders of the civil rights movement, Meredith was also a calculated actor, as he was well aware that his mere intention to become the first Negro student at Ole Miss would incite a political impasse between federal law and state resistance to desegregation that eventually would force the state of Mississippi's hand. "We felt that we could count on the racists of the South to create a crisis," Meredith later stated, "so that the federal government would be compelled to enforce the law." Meredith has described his second attempt to register at the university, when, while flanked by white federal officials, Barnett had asked "Which one of you is Meredith?" After Barnett uttered this question, Meredith recalled, both he and Barnett "could barely keep [themselves] frcm bursting out in laughter."

Fundamentally, what differentiates political theater from actual theater is the violence and the threat of violence that all political dramas foretell. After yet a third thwarted attempt to register by Meredith, and Barnett's reversal on his commitment to make a show of deference to federal marshals as rumors circulated that Meredith was once again attempting to register, a white mob descended upon Ole

Miss's administrative building with bricks, bottles, and Molotov cocktails, which they aimed at the federal marshals. The violent outburst left two people dead and one hundred and twenty-two people injured. On October 1, 1962, the morning after Kennedy sent troops to disband the mob, Meredith successfully registered at Ole Miss.

Although a last resort, the dispatch of federal troops to Mississippi was, especially in hindsight, inevitable under the circumstances. During Barnett's inauguration as Mississippi governor in 1960, he pledged to "maintain segregation in Mississippi at all costs." True to his word, Barnett was an active member of Mississippi's State Sovereignty Committee, serving not only as an ex officio member, but also administering the committee's speaker's bureau, which conducted a nationwide public relations campaign to spread the state's prosegregation message. The propaganda campaign contended that Mississippi's Negro residents not only preferred segregation, but were in fact making socioeconomic "progress" within the existing social system, and trumpeted the merits of "states' rights" and "home rule."

Mississippi's State Sovereignty Committee was influential in popularizing the conflation of civil rights activism with Communist "subversion," coopting the language of the flagging McCarthyist inquisitions of the 1950s to associate the civil rights movement with a foreign plot to "divide and conquer" the United States. The investigatory powers of the committee were dedicated to unearthing and disrupting such "plots" by working to smear and discredit local civil rights activists as "outside agitators."

———

PROPAGANDA IS A NATURAL OUTGROWTH OF PERFORMANCE. JUST AS PERformers do not act for the sake of any given action but to influence their audience, with propaganda information is not disseminated for its own sake but to advance an agenda. If what we call "facts" are each individual stars, and narrative is the through line that connects them to reflect an overall meaning, then propaganda is not necessarily false in all its elements. Propaganda, rather, is consciously crafted to disseminate a particular meaning behind otherwise disparate events. Like a dreamer who awakens within the dream, the propagandist aims to direct the general understanding of events in his interests.

For the segregationist propagandist, for example, the defense of states' rights is a deeply held belief that reflects a devotion to the principle of federalism—that abstract and racially neutral doctrine of the founders, who sought to establish a vertical balance of power between state and federal governments. And like the carpetbaggers and scalawags before them, such propaganda transformed civil rights activists into "outside agitators" who dared to challenge "home rule" and disturb the "peace"—which is essentially maintained when all those within the dream stay asleep, or at least pretend to be.

ABOUT TWO WEEKS BEFORE PRESIDENT KENNEDY DEPLOYED FEDERAL troops to Mississippi, in a September 13 address broadcast on television and radio Barnett cited the powers relegated to the several states under the Tenth Amendment and denounced "an ambitious federal government, employing naked and arbitrary power, [which] has decided to deny us the right of self-determination in the conduct of the affairs of our sovereign state." Calling supporters of desegregation agitators and troublemakers "pouring across our borders," Barnett claimed that the "federal government teamed up with a motley array of un-American pressure groups against us." In the end, Barnett assured his constituency that he would do all in his power to prevent desegregation and rallied a posse of sorts by "call[ing] on every public official and every private citizen of our great state to join [him]."

Resistance to desegregation, of course, was not confined to the State Sovereignty Committee or to the governor's official pronouncements. Among other influential groups was Mississippi's local Citizens' Council, a white supremacist organization whose membership was composed of prominent local white citizens, including business, law enforcement, and other civic leaders. The Council was the first of several established in southern states following the *Brown* decision to collectively oppose desegregation and any other organized challenges to Jim Crow. Though the Council had the imprimatur of legitimacy, its membership ranks were known to overlap with those of the Ku Klux Klan, which defended segregation with extralegal terrorist violence.

The state of Mississippi is, of course, where white men had brutally beaten and killed Emmett Till in 1955; where the head of the state NAACP, Medgar Evers, would be shot dead in front of his home in 1963; and where three civil rights workers named Michael Schwerner, Andrew Goodman, and James Chaney would be lynched two years later. And these are merely the highly publicized incidents that have continued to resonate across the decades, overshadowing the many lynchings in the state and the rest of the South that savagely delivered a message through bloodshed. White segregationists aimed to preserve the Mississippi way of life through terrorist violence.

VIOLENCE, WHEN UNTETHERED FROM LAW, MAY NOT ENFORCE ORDER IN the sense of the word referring to "a state in which the laws and rules regulating the public behavior of members of a community are observed and authority is obeyed." But it has worked, and does work, to enforce order in the sense of "a particular social, political, or economic system"—in the case of southern segregationists, "home rule" or their "way of life." Echoing that antebellum debate over whether immediate action or gradualism was the preferred approach to upending the South's unconstitutional and hierarchical sense of "order," the formal mandate of "all deliberate speed" was, in practice, deliberately slow. Negroes submitting themselves as test subjects to fulfill the letter of the law attempted to compel legal "order" over the established social "order," and in doing so, both subjected themselves to violence and its threat and, through the spectacle they created, compelled the federal government to wield violence and its threat in their favor.

———

IN 1963 PRESIDENT KENNEDY ISSUED TWO PROCLAMATIONS UNDER THE Insurrection Act: the first in June of that year to compel the entry of two Negro students into the all-white University of Alabama, and the second in September to enforce the enrollment of fourteen Negro teenagers in the all-white Tuskegee High School in Huntsville. In both instances Kennedy overrode the bold obstinance of George Wallace, the Alabama governor who rose to national prominence for his sensational opposition to desegregation.

At least two hundred Negro students had applied to attend the University of Alabama following the 1954 *Brown* decision, but it would not be until 1963, due to a federal district court order, that the university would be forced to enroll three Negro applicants— Vivian Malone, James Hood, and Dave McGlathery. On June 11, federal marshals and U.S. deputy attorney general Nicholas Katzenbach escorted Malone and Hood to the university campus, where, surrounded by Alabama state troopers, Wallace was awaiting their arrival to make his infamous "stand in the schoolhouse door" and block their entry. Wallace refused to defer to the federal court order, which Katzenbach cited as he confronted Wallace with the federal marshals. Instead, Wallace took the opportunity to formally address the assembled crowd and hovering news media, announcing: "The unwelcomed, unwanted, unwarranted and force-induced intrusion upon the campus of the University of Alabama today of the might of the central government offers frightful example of the oppression of the rights, privileges and sovereignty of this state by officers of the federal government." Wallace further recited the Tenth Amendment of the Constitution, then stated that his "action seeks to avoid having state sovereignty sacrificed on the altar of political expediency."

Kennedy subsequently federalized the Alabama National Guard under his command and deployed them to the university in order to compel the enrollment of Malone and Hood. Wallace stood down later the same day, when the general of the state National Guard requested that he do so. Thereafter, the National Guard continued to stand by under Kennedy's authority in order to forestall any violent retribution from Alabama's sizable contingent of the Ku Klux Klan.

Wallace's posturing at the University of Alabama did turn out to be favorable for his self-promotion, as his office received thousands of letters and telegrams from across the country thanking him for his courage. His performance, and the federal military intervention that disrupted it, also prompted sweeping changes in law. Shortly after Wallace's "stand," Kennedy proposed the bill for what, under Lyndon B. Johnson, would eventually become the Civil Rights Act of 1964, which, among other things, prohibited discrimination on the basis of race, color, religion, or national origin in public accommodations engaged in interstate commerce, such as hotels, motels, restaurants, and theaters, and, further, specifically established federal powers to enforce the desegregation of public schools.

Political theater, however, often has deadly consequences. The governor's words have also been condemned for inciting violence, most notoriously with the bombing of the Sixteenth Street Baptist Church in Birmingham, Alabama, which killed four young girls. Though the bombing by the Ku Klux Klan took place on September 15, 1963, about three months following Wallace's "stand," some historians have interpreted the terrorist act to be a result of the turbulent atmosphere riled up by the governor's bombast.

Although far less theatrical than Wallace's staged defiance at the University of Alabama, before the Sixteenth Street bombing Wallace ordered the state National Guard to block the federal-court-ordered entry of Negro students into Huntsville's all-white Tuskegee High School. On the same day, Kennedy simply federalized the Alabama National Guard under his command and ordered them to return to their stations.

———

DISTURBING THE "PEACE" IS THE CORE MISSION OF NONVIOLENT TACTI-cians. "Nonviolent direct action seeks to create such a crisis and foster such a tension that a community which has constantly refused to negotiate is forced to confront the issue," wrote Dr. King in his famous 1963 "Letter from Birmingham Jail." "It seeks so to dramatize the issue that it can no longer be ignored." The crisis King sought to help bring about was the spectacle of violence waged by state authorities against civil rights activists for the mere offense of positioning their bodies where the authorities told them not to. The protesters were not directly opposing the extralegal lynching, intimidation, and overall terrorism employed by the Ku Klux Klan, white mobs, and other vigilantes. These elements hardly could be negotiated with, and any civil rights demonstrations would have at most an indirect effect on their unauthorized violence. Rather, civil rights activists were opposing the law itself by drawing forth and spotlighting the violence inherent in enforcing an unjust order.

Of course, not all civil rights activists submitted to this tactic. Not Stokely Carmichael. Not Malcolm X. And neither did Robert F. Williams, the Marine veteran turned NAACP representative who also asserted his right of self-defense. As Truman Nelson wrote in the introduction to Williams's autobiography, *Negroes with Guns*, "[h]e was not born to be a punching bag to test the longevity of the Southern whites' desire to beat him."

Becoming lucid in this dreamscape, nonviolent civil rights activists for their part chose to confront segregationists with their mere presence and take control of the narrative by forcing the hand of the federal government to deploy violence in favor of their formal rights.

———

ON MARCH 20, 1965, PRESIDENT LYNDON B. JOHNSON ISSUED A PROCLAMA-tion under the Insurrection Act to order the dispersal of persons obstructing the right, secured via federal court order, of civil rights protesters to march from Selma to Montgomery in Alabama. Hundreds of protesters had first set out to march days earlier, on March 7, in honor of slain civil rights activist Jimmie Lee Jackson, whom Alabama state troopers had clubbed and fatally shot the prior month in the town of Marion during an otherwise peaceful voting rights demonstration. On their way to Montgomery that day, Selma marchers were faced with a wall of Alabama state troopers on the Edmund Pettus Bridge, some towering on horseback, along with the local sheriff and his posse of white civilians. A number of white residents gathered nearby to watch the spectacle, some waving Confederate flags as if at a parade. The state troopers ordered the marchers to disperse; the protesters refused.

———

NONVIOLENT PROTEST INVOLVES PLACING ONE'S BODY WHERE, BY LAW, IT is not authorized to be, then refusing to obey orders to remove one's body to some amenable position. This was the self-possessed dare of Rosa Parks, who calmly refused to give up her seat on a public transport bus to a white man, the quiet taunting of young Freedom Riders who sat in white sections of segregated lunch counters and patiently awaited their menus, the solemn enticement of civil rights demonstrators who congregated on city hall steps or marched in solidarity over the objection of southern state and local officials. Nonviolent demonstrators are sirens. With their mere presence, they tantalize enforcers of law to injure, maim, or even kill them.

IN A VIOLENT, TELEVISED CONFRONTATION THAT CAME TO BE KNOWN AS "Bloody Sunday," the state troopers, as well as the sheriff and his posse, charged the protesters on the bridge, descending upon them with billy clubs and tear gas, and even trampling marchers under the feet of horses. In the face of this vicious attack, protesters, including would-be House of Representatives member John Lewis, ceded ground and backed away from the bridge—which was named after a former Democratic Alabama senator and Confederate veteran who also happened to be a Grand Wizard of the Ku Klux Klan—but they did not fight back against their aggressors. The march was thereby dispersed, and about fifty people, including Lewis, were hospitalized.

NONVIOLENCE MAKES A BATTLEGROUND OF THE BODY IN PROTEST OF A violent system. "Putting your body on the line"—the practice of which helped to galvanize a movement that, after twenty-six years of resistance led by Mohandas Gandhi, culminated in the independence of India from Great Britain in 1947—is a tenet of nonviolent direct action. The nonviolent body is neither weapon nor shield, but often a willing sacrifice. You cannot deploy this tactic spontaneously. If the will to survive is an instinct, then the willingness to sacrifice oneself requires practice. To put your body on the line involves cultivating the ability to lessen the fear of pain and the pain of fear—two primal drives of the survival instinct. Dr. King referred to such preparation as self-purification, a process involving discipline and self-inquiry, repeatedly asking oneself: "Are you able to accept blows without retaliating?" "Are you able to endure the ordeal of jail?"

WHAT MIGHT HAVE SEEMED LIKE THE LOSS OF A BATTLE, HOWEVER, WAS transformed into tactical victory, because the events of Bloody Sunday were broadcast throughout the world. Nationally, the violent attacks interrupted one television station's regularly scheduled programming, which happened to be a program called "Judgment at Nuremberg," based on the Holocaust of World War II. The juxtaposition was too stark, and the cognitive dissonance could not hold. In his article summarizing Bloody Sunday, journalist Christopher Klein recited a quote from a Selma shopkeeper who was interviewed by the *Washington Star:* "Everybody knows it's going on, but they try to pretend they don't see it. I saw 'Judgment at Nuremberg' on the Late Show the other night and I thought it fits right in; it's just like Selma."

MEASURED IN THEIR MOVEMENTS AND PRACTICED IN REFRAINING FROM any physical retaliation, nonviolent tacticians passively submitted to billy club blows, police-dog bites, and fire hoses. In this manner, they were displaying the stark contrast between their meek and reserved demeanor and the violence of state agents who brutalized them. The more excessive such violence was, the vaster the disparity between the retribution of state agents and the innocuous behavior that induced it. This spectacle was the crisis King cited in his Birmingham letter. Such crises were not, in fact, caused by civil rights protesters, but protesters brought attention to the ongoing crisis—what King called a *negative* peace, which he defined as "the absence of tension." Richard Gregg also notes as much in the *The Power of Non-Violence*, when he writes that "[p]eace imposed by violence is not psychological peace but a suppressed conflict."

DR. KING, WHO HAD BEEN SUPPORTING THE ORGANIZING EFFORTS OF THE
Student Nonviolent Coordinating Committee (SNCC) in Selma since
January, attempted to lead another march two days after Bloody Sunday but decided to turn the protesters around in lieu of a federal court
order authorizing their demonstration. Governor Wallace, of course,
was loath to help enforce the court order that civil rights activists ultimately secured. After Wallace made a televised refusal to use the Alabama National Guard to enforce the order, President Johnson issued the
Insurrection Act proclamation, which stated Wallace had "advised me
that the state is unable and refuses to provide for the safety and welfare,
among others, of the plaintiffs and members of the class they represent."

"THE PRESENCE OF JUSTICE" IS DR. KING'S DEFINITION OF POSITIVE PEACE.
The civil rights movement attempted to fill the vacuum that is "peace"
with a kind of justice that transformed the relationship among white
and Negro citizens, upending the segregated status quo. In King's
"Letter from Birmingham Jail," written while he was detained after
defying a court injunction to refrain from "parading, demonstrating,
boycotting, trespassing and picketing," he cites Austrian-born theolo-
gian Martin Buber. Buber is well known for establishing two primary
modes of existence, one he termed "I-it," designating the relationship
between a subject and an object—the latter of which would be passive, a mere instrument under the subject's control—and "I-thou,"
which refers to a relationship between two subjects characterized by
reciprocity and mutual respect.

For King, the "presence of justice," a positive definition of "peace,"
would involve the transformation of the relation between white and
Negro citizens from "I-it" to "I-thou." Progress notwithstanding, this

desired shift obviously recalls the Negro citizen's challenge of over-coming prior legal status as property.

———

THE JOHNSON ADMINISTRATION NOTABLY FRAMED THE DEPLOYMENT OF federal troops to safely escort marching civil rights protesters as a "request" from Wallace, even though, in keeping with character, Wallace had refused the president's advice to deploy National Guard troops to do the same at the state level. The circumstances of the request highlight the controversial nature of federal military interven-tion because, as is clear from White House transcripts of conversa-tions after Bloody Sunday and before the proclamation was ultimately made, President Johnson had communicated a strong preference for Wallace to protect the marchers with the state's National Guard, a strategy Wallace resisted in a deft political move to appear defiant before his anti-desegregationist base. In essence, then, Wallace's request was an official recharacterization of his unwillingness to act, one that Johnson was sure to make clear in a press statement that emphasized his reluctance to proclaim an "insurrection":

> It is not a welcome duty for the Federal Government to ever assume a state government's own responsibility for assuring the protection of citizens in the exercise of their constitutional rights. It has been rare in our history for the Governor and the Legislature of a sovereign state to decline to exercise their responsibility and to request that duty be assumed by the Fed-eral Government. Governor Wallace and the Legislature of the State of Alabama have now done this.

Even so, spurred by Bloody Sunday, and even before invoking the Insurrection Act, President Johnson introduced voting rights leg-islation in Congress on March 15, 1965. In doing so, Johnson gave a speech in support of the Selma protesters. "At times history and fate meet at a single time in a single space and shape a turning point in man's unending search for freedom," Johnson stated. He continued, recalling the American Revolutionary war: "So it was at Lexington and Concord. So it was a century ago at Appomattox. So it was last week in Selma, Alabama." In other words, he deployed rhetoric aligning black civil rights protesters with revolutionary "patriots" as a prelude to supporting the implementation of voting rights—which ultimately became the Voting Rights Act of 1965; among other things, it prohibited local and state governments from passing any voting law that would result in racial discrimination.

Two days after the voting rights bill was introduced, and the day after Johnson made a proclamation under the Insurrection Act, civil rights protesters completed the march from Selma to Montgomery under the protection of approximately two thousand U.S. Army troops and nineteen hundred federalized members of the Alabama National Guard. At the march's denouement, Dr. King made his famous "How Long, Not Long" speech, which amplified the recurring American nightmare over the American Dream:

> I know you are asking today, "How long will it take?" Somebody's asking, "How long will prejudice blind the visions of men, darken their understanding, and drive bright-eyed wisdom from her sacred throne?" Somebody's asking, "When will wounded justice, lying prostrate on the streets of Selma and Birmingham and communities all over the South, be lifted from this dust of shame to reign supreme among the children of men?" Somebody's asking, "When will the radiant star of hope be plunged against the nocturnal bosom of this lonely night, plucked from weary souls with chains of fear and the manacles of death? How long will justice be crucified, and truth bear it?

I ONCE HAD A DREAM THAT I WAS PLAYING MONOPOLY WITH THREE friends. The four of us sat on the carpeted floor of some living room, each commanding one side of the large, square board. I crouched and watched as each of the players—all of whom, incidentally or not, were white male friends of mine—rolled the dice and moved their small metal avatars around the board in turn, then collected property or paid their fines accordingly. Someone handed me the dice when it was my turn.

As I shook the two cubes in my cupped palm, I immediately noticed something was off. I opened my hand to find two small, roughly cubic balls of red clay. In vain, I turned my palm over and plopped the clay onto the board, after which my fellow players simultaneously began to advise me on how to roll the dice because I was clearly doing it wrong. I scanned their faces for a brief moment, then stood up from the game, grabbed a book, and went to lie down on a nearby sofa to read. As my eyes slid over the pages, I could feel their awkward silence in my periphery.

CHAPTER 6

Eye for an Eye

Anger is always abetted by an origin story. Yes, some perceived threat causes a person pain, thereby giving rise to anger to camouflage such pain. Then, such a person directs her ire toward the external provocateur. But anger is also always initially directed by the meaning made of a given situation. Anger, in other words, casts blame. The story fabricated to justify anger is like carrier fluid, suspending both "victim" and "perpetrator" in their fabulated roles. Just as there are different kinds of anger, there will be competing narratives bandied about to justify or denounce it.

I might decide that I am justified in sharply rebuking someone who I feel has disrespected me, but the person on the receiving end of my reprimand might call me aggressive, recasting him- or herself as a victim of my bullying. I might also perceive another person's venting about some unfairness as a tantrum, and see that person's moral claim to righteousness as egocentric complaining. Even someone's expressed annoyance at a nuisance can be magnified by the observer into some menacing aggression, overshadowing whatever the stated reason for the anger.

The gaslighting—the inflation and minimizing, the transference and projection—all of these don't only come into play when raging at the interpersonal level. They are also factors when crafting a story of collective rage. And the name fastened to the expression of collective rage tells its own story, each one casting its own victims and perpetrators.

———

ON JULY 24, 1967, PRESIDENT LYNDON B. JOHNSON MADE A PROCLAMATION under the Insurrection Act regarding "the conditions of domestic violence and disorder" in the city of Detroit. In the predominantly black area of Virginia Park the prior day, local law enforcement raided an unlicensed after-hours club hosted at the office of a local civil rights group, then arrested more than eighty patrons they found inside. While awaiting transport outside the club, the police and detainees drew the attention of onlookers, whose number continued to grow. The gathered crowd, however, did not disperse when law enforcement left with their arrestees, and instead started looting an adjacent store.

Thereafter, looting and arson spread rapidly throughout the city, prompting governor George Romney to call forth the state National Guard at the request of Mayor Jerome Cavanaugh. The riots nonetheless continued to escalate, and Romney requested that Johnson also supply federal troops, which the president granted in the form of 4,700 paratroopers from the 82nd and 101st Airborne Divisions. The federal deployment, though, was begrudging on the part of both Romney and Johnson, because the governor, due to his own presidential aspirations, was loath to admit the riots in the city had intensified to a level beyond his control. Johnson, meanwhile, remained generally averse to federal intervention of any kind. Accordingly, in a public address responding to his deployment of federal troops, Johnson noted that the action was taken with the "greatest regret" and assured that "[p]illage, looting, murder, and arson have nothing to do with civil rights," but were "criminal conduct."

———

ANGER CAN TAKE DIFFERENT FORMS. ANNOYANCE IS THE PETTY KIND, IRRI-tation at a minor disturbance. A tantrum is the immature kind, a self-centered outburst at not getting one's whims fulfilled. Justifiable anger is the righteous kind, the moral outrage generated by some injustice. And aggression is yet another, the expressed anger of a bully who seeks to distract himself from deep-seated feelings of inadequacy by attempting to dominate others. Similarly, the words used to describe collective expressions of rage imply whether the anger that underlies them is well-founded or unwarranted.

A "riot," for example, means a "violent disturbance of the peace," and implies that those who collectively vent their anger in this way are perpetrators. The much-feared violence associated with so-called race riots—the kind associated with mostly black rioters in cities as opposed to white mobs wherever they may roam—is generally directed at property, not necessarily people. So, within the narrative constructed around such race riots, "peace" has come to mean the sanctity of private property, which remains undisturbed when peace reigns. Property is the victim preyed upon by rioters, who perpetrate crimes ranging from theft to vandalism to arson. The race rioter, then, becomes synonymous with the looter and with the flamethrower. And the cavalry that is called forth to restore "peace and order" is, essentially, on a mission to protect private property.

———

AFTER FIVE DAYS WITH THE PRESENCE OF FEDERAL TROOPS, THE DETROIT riot subsided, leaving forty-three people dead, over one thousand injured, and more than two thousand buildings destroyed. The riot was, in the end, the most violent and destructive in "the long hot summer" of 1967, when riots broke out in fifteen cities across the United States. The riot was also the city's largest since 1943, which also involved federal military intervention. By 1967 there was a greater population of black Americans in Detroit than fourteen years before, on account of successive waves of migration from the South into northern cities. And, as with the conditions leading up to the Detroit riots of 1943, many black residents still suffered from the collective burden of shortages of affordable housing—exacerbated by redlining and restrictive covenants that maintained racial segregation—as well as underemployment, as the city's famed automotive industry was already in decline, with many existing factories moving jobs out of the city into the suburbs.

Such underlying causes were set forth in a report subsequently provided by the National Advisory Commission on Civil Disorders (the Kerner Commission) appointed by Johnson to investigate the rash of riots that started in 1965 and erupted during 1967's long, hot summer. That the riots under study followed the legislative successes of the civil rights movement—the Civil Rights Act of 1964 and the Voting Rights Act of 1965—is a testament to the fact that, in the case of race-related reform, changes in the law did not immediately translate into societal progress. The Kerner Commission's report offered scholarly support for this lived reality, stating in its oft-quoted summary:

> Disorder did not erupt as a result of a single "triggering" or "precipitating" incident. Instead, it was generated out of an increasingly disturbed social atmosphere, in which typically a series of tension-heightening incidents over a period of weeks or months became linked in the minds of many in the Negro community with a reservoir of underlying grievances.

WHETHER CAUSED BY REJECTION, LOSS, INJURY, OR THE RISK OF ANY OF
these, the sense of having been aggrieved or finding oneself in danger gives rise, first and foremost, to pain. Anger, in this way, is
deceptive. The accelerated heart rate, the tensed muscles, the quickened breath—all common effects of cortisol and adrenaline cours-
ing through the body—arise seemingly on cue in direct response to
some external provocation. The physiological effects of anger may
feel like immediate feedback to an actual or perceived threat. However, say psychologists, anger is a secondary emotion. Anger does not,
as it might seem, spontaneously arise in response to external stimuli.
Anger rather emerges from a primary feeling of pain, physical or
emotional, that was initially triggered by such stimuli. Anger is the
second domino in the chain of emotional arousal.

So it is pain, then, and not the external stimulus itself, that sparks
anger—a transition that can seem to occur so quickly the physiological switch can lurk below the level of one's awareness. And yet one's
experience of pain cannot be seen or touched, and may be prone to
dismissal or even denial.

AN EMPHASIS ON SYSTEMIC CAUSES THAT UNDERLIE RIOTS WAS A DEPARTURE
from the narrative that proliferated among white Americans at the
time. A 1967 poll cited by Lindsey Lupo in *Flak-Catchers: One
Hundred Years of Riot Commission Politics in America,* for example, "showed that more often than not, whites believed the riots to
be caused by 'outside agitation,' 'Communist backing,' or 'minority
radicals' rather than by the 'socioeconomic circumstances confronting blacks.'" Such widespread beliefs were not reflected in the Kerner
Commission report, which in its summary warned that the United

States "is moving toward two societies, one black, one white—separate and unequal." To the extent any blame was placed, the report's summary targeted "white racism."

That said, as Lupo discussed in *Flak-Catchers*, the riots might have represented growing impatience among some black Americans with the tactics of nonviolence. As a growing countermovement emphasized the right to self-defense, "many insurgents ultimately came openly to espouse violent insurrections as a viable tactic in the ongoing struggle."

———

ANGER IS A DEFENSE MECHANISM. ANGER HELPS THE ONE SUFFERING FROM it to summon sufficient energy to protect the Self by confronting the Other. Anger, also, distracts from the feeling of pain that underlies it, thereby transforming a sense of helplessness into control and vulnerability into power. Anger draws a border—not only between self and other, but also between what is acceptable and unacceptable, tolerable and intolerable, desirable and undesirable.

The word "rebellion" recasts collective demonstrations of anger as a defensive reaction. Similar to its close cousins "uprising" and "revolt," "rebellion" shifts the moral authority to "rebels" courageous enough to openly defy some unjust authority. However, a rebellion—by definition an "open, armed, and usually unsuccessful defiance of, or resistance to, an established government"—is typically doomed from its spirited start. That is unlike a "revolution," which refers to the forcible overthrow of a government or social order in favor of a new system. Revolutionaries, then, are always victorious; their revolutions only correctly labeled as such once their battles have been won (and they have gained the power to make and enforce law against would-be rebels and rioters). While there is some distant hope that today's rioters might become tomorrow's revolutionaries, amid this miraculous transformation the rioter's anger also transitions from a feeling that is, at best, questionable into one that is justified.

ON APRIL 5, 1968, AMID RIOTS THAT BROKE OUT FOLLOWING MARTIN
Luther King's assassination, President Johnson issued a proclamation under the Insurrection Act declaring the need to restore "law
and order" due to the "conditions of domestic violence and disorder" in the District of Columbia. Johnson soon dispatched about
one thousand National Guardsmen and over eleven thousand federal
troops to quell the rash of looting and arson in the district. However, Johnson, as U.S. president, technically did not have to invoke
the Insurrection Act in order to federalize the D.C. National Guard
or deploy federal troops in the District of Columbia, because the
district is not a state and, rather, is subject to direct federal administration. Unlike the states, where—except in certain events specified by Congress—the governor is the commander in chief of the
state National Guard, in the District of Columbia the president is
the Guard's immediate commander and does not have to submit to
the same protocols established to maintain the separation of power
between the state and federal government.

Regardless of Johnson's lawful authority in this regard, and the
widespread riots that erupted across the country following King's
murder, he was reportedly very reluctant to deploy federal troops in
the District of Columbia, just as he was to do so in any of the states.
Johnson was a strong adherent of federalism and respected the power
of state officials to exercise their authority over local matters—a stance
that, accordingly, made the Texas native generally opposed to federal
intervention in state affairs, especially the military kind. Johnson, as
Clay Risen discusses in *A Nation on Fire: America in the Wake of
the King Assassination*, had not only refused to "send anything but
indirect assistance to the California National Guard" in response to
the 1965 Watts riots; he also "resisted, for too long, the need to send
troops to Detroit" amid the 1967 riots in the city.

Johnson's reticence notwithstanding, after discussions with Mayor Walter E. Washington, the president ultimately did decide to deploy federal troops under the close advice of Cyrus Vance, his former secretary of defense, who had devised a federal riot-response plan during the Detroit riots of 1967. In line with Vance's plan, federal troops deployed would use the minimum amount of force necessary to restore law and order; they would not fire any weapons unless required to save a life. As Risen writes, federal troops in the district carried written rules of engagement to help reinforce this intention, for example stating "I will not load or fire a weapon except when authorized by an officer in person to," and "I will not discuss or pass on rumors about this operation."

Although these rules of engagement were meant to deter any injuries or fatalities meted out by federal troops—whose foreboding presence was broadcast far and wide through media outlets—Vance's approach nonetheless left an unfavorable impression in the minds of white suburban spectators, a number of whom had fled the District of Columbia for Maryland and Virginia when the riots first flared. "A recurrent image from the riots," writes Risen of the D.C. riots, "recounted in newspaper reports and beamed into suburban homes on the nightly news, was of police officers standing by while rioters went wild."

This impression was likely aggravated by the presence of Stokely Carmichael in the District of Columbia, where he was living at the time, when he heard word of King's death. A civil rights activist who converted from the kind of nonviolent civil disobedience characterized by SNCC to a proponent of armed self-defense, Carmichael, as chronicled by Peniel Joseph in *Stokely: A Life*, had launched into action as a "rare guerrilla general," instructing his SNCC comrades to inform local businesses that King had been killed and trying to persuade black residents to remain calm. Carmichael's media representation, however, amplified his already inflammatory reputation as a "violent" agitator. During a press conference after King's death, a journalist asked him if he was "declaring war on white America." Carmichael, later highlighting the need for black Americans to arm themselves with guns, responded: "White America has declared war on black people."

WAR LEGALLY DECLARED BY THE STATE IS A DE JURE ONE, BUT DE FACTO wars still exist. If enslavement itself was a de facto declaration of war, then the advances made in the United States with respect to civil rights of black Americans did not result in a total ceasefire. In *Women, Race & Class*, Angela Davis writes of "the widespread violence and terror suffered by Black people in the South," who, she states, were "engaged in an actual war for liberation." Of the 1965 Watts riots and the police brutality they decried, Eldridge Cleaver writes in *Soul on Ice*: "From one end of the country to the other, the new war cry is raised." In *Stokely Speaks*, Carmichael insists: "As the racist police escalate the war in our communities against black people, we reserve the right to self-defense and maximum retaliation." In a doctoral dissertation titled *War Against the Panthers: A Study of Repression in America*, Huey P. Newton describes, among other things, the counterintelligence program the Federal Bureau of Investigation initiated under J. Edgar Hoover that violently targeted the Black Panthers under the guise of an initiative to fight crime.

Emphasizing the warlike nature of "order" and "peace," such statements recast those who fight the status quo—whether through urban uprisings against police brutality, or through their assertion of Black Power—from perceived aggressors into the transgressed. Such counternarratives were waged in the hopes of undermining the prevailing one at the time, in which calls for black equality were heard as demands for black dominance, and insistence on black self-defense interpreted as an offensive measure.

———

ON APRIL 7, 1968, JOHNSON MADE A PROCLAMATION UNDER THE INSURREC-tion Act regarding "conditions of domestic violence and disorder" in the city of Chicago, commanding that "all persons engaged in such acts of violence cease and desist therefrom" and "disperse and retire peaceably forthwith." Before Johnson issued this proclamation, Chicago mayor Richard Daley had already requested about six thousand National Guard troops from Illinois lieutenant governor Samuel Shapiro on account of property damage and arson in the city following King's assassination.

As Risen recounted in *A Nation on Fire*, the riotous atmosphere in Chicago was aggressive while that in Washington, D.C., was described as carnivalesque. In Chicago, "[r]ioters set up several roadblocks, and as white drivers slowed down to make their way through, they were harassed, some even pulled out of their cars and beaten." Daley soon determined that federal assistance would be necessary to quell the riots, and made a formal request of Johnson to provide it.

In line with Johnson's overall reluctance to engage in federal intervention, a transcript of his phone call with Daley reveals that the president had put forth a condition: state officials must make a formal finding that they had been unable to "take care of the situation," despite having exhausted all of the state's resources in an effort to do so. Such a finding, according to Johnson, would ensure the record of events would show that federal military intervention was "at the insistence of local officials." Johnson also effectively reprimanded Daley for not contacting him sooner, citing headlines from local D.C. newspapers such as "Too Little, Too Late: Long Stretches of the Capitol Laid to Waste." However, under the Insurrection Act, Johnson had from the beginning the unilateral authority to deploy federal troops to a given state, as Kennedy and Eisenhower had done to enforce school desegregation. Just as Governor Wallace's and Governor Barnett's defiance against federal intervention had been, in some respects, performative, so was Johnson's direction that Illinois state officials make a formal request for federal troops. Johnson's irritation on his phone call with Daley was not necessarily born from his unwillingness to dispatch any troops, but from his unwillingness to be perceived as prone to do so. It was important to Johnson that his domestic deployment of troops be viewed as a last resort.

Although then-governor of Illinois Samuel Shapiro had been out of town during the Chicago riots, it was nonetheless fitting that Daley, rather than the lieutenant governor, was particularly active in discussions with the Johnson administration. A powerhouse of Chicago's Democratic political machine and chairman of the Cook County Democratic Party Central Committee, the mayor was a force for any presidential hopeful to contend with in garnering support during the Democratic primaries. Daley's core base was constituted from the working-class white "ethnic" communities of Chicago, including the Irish-American constituency of which he was part.

Following successive waves of the great migration of black Americans from the South to northern cities, the Daley machine was not primed to cater to the expanding population of black voters. Under the moniker of "urban renewal," public housing blocks were erected in mostly black neighborhoods and, thereafter, composed of mostly black residents, effectively exacerbating housing segregation in an already racially segregated city. Consistent with usual practice, racial segregation coincided with stark socioeconomic disparity, with higher incidents of underemployment and poverty also concentrated in the areas where black residents lived. Daley hardly came across as sensitive to such issues. During a press conference held in the aftermath of the riots, Daley made a point of taking a tough stance on disorder, stating that he had told the superintendent of police "very emphatically and very definitely that an order be issued by him immediately to shoot to kill any arsonist or anyone with a Molotov cocktail in his hand, because they're potential murderers, and to shoot to maim or cripple anyone looting." Thereafter, he received thousands of letters and telegrams from supporters congratulating him on his remarks.

———

A NUMBER OF WHITE "RIOTS" NOTED IN THE HISTORICAL RECORD ARE NOT called riots at all, but "rebellions." The Whiskey Rebellion. Shays' Rebellion. Bacon's Rebellion. Though a "rebellion" implies sure defeat, the word also connotes that the efforts of the rebel were valiant and the challenged authority unjust. Well aware of the various connotations carried by such terms, some commentators have attempted to wage a war of words, revising categories of unrest in order to recast victims and perpetrators. In this way, the 1965 uprisings in Watts were rebranded from "riots" to "rebellions."

At the same time, the word "riot" has been deemed, by some moral revisionists, to be too mild to describe the violent events that took place—with, for example, the "Colfax Riot" later referred to as the "Colfax Massacre." In the same vein, after a white mob descended upon the Tulsa County Courthouse in 1921—an event that spiraled into a tense standoff with bands of black residents and resulted in three hundred people killed and about ten thousand black residents left homeless—what was initially referred to as a "riot" was later called the "Tulsa Massacre." "Massacre," here, is a precise description of the violence that disturbed the peace—brutal killings of a large group of individuals.

There are few nouns at hand to describe the responsive military deployments of the state to suppress "riots" or "rebellions." The value-neutral word "intervention" comes to mind; when federal military deployments have been made to protect the civil rights of black Americans, they are in some way analogous to the kind of humanitarian intervention ostensibly made to enforce human rights abroad. Domestic insurrectionists like George Wallace, however, could be counted on to characterize any such intervention as an oppressive "interference" or being subject to an unwarranted "foreign invasion."

The federal military "intervention" made in response to so-called race riots, by contrast, has not been described by as many conflicting words. Nonetheless, even as times change and "progress" continues to be made, old conventions remain ingrained. Changes in law might have formally freed black Americans from the coterminous status of property, but the mission to suppress the human in order to protect the property is indelible.

SLOW TO ANGER

My anger has never erupted in a flash. There is nothing sudden or unexpected about my anger. My anger, rather, is monitored by an always-on system, like the kind that regulates the temperature of a room. I am always aware of my anger, on behalf of which another part of me consistently scans my environs to detect when my anger may switch from something unseen and subtle into something that is readily apparent to everyone else. But the thermostat for allowing my anger to break through the surface is set very high. I know that any inkling of anger I express, no matter what elicited it, will be overblown and misconstrued. My righteous anger is always susceptible to being reinterpreted as a tantrum, my irritation as aggression.

I know that expressed anger sets boundaries and repressed anger relinquishes them, rendering me porous and immaterial to external threats. At the same time, I know that I express my anger—my organic self-defense mechanism—at my own risk. There is no earthly justice handed down to quell my anger, only some form of punishment that is inevitably directed away from the root cause of my ire and back in my direction. Perversely, repressing my anger has become its own form of self-defense.

———

ON APRIL 7, 1968, PRESIDENT JOHNSON ISSUED A PROCLAMATION UNDER the Insurrection Act concerning the "domestic violence and disorder" that were "obstructing the execution of the laws of the United States, including the protection of federal property in and about the City of Baltimore." Pursuant to a subsequent executive order, Johnson deployed about five thousand troops from the 18th Airborne Corps to the state and federalized the National Guard. Maryland governor Spiro Agnew had already called up the state National Guard to assist the local law enforcement in subduing riots sparked by King's assassination. Before the rioting began in Baltimore, the emphasis of law enforcement was on policing the border in order to ensure the unrest in the District did not spill over into Maryland suburbs.

When under state command, the Maryland riot response was not subject to the Vance-dictated rules of engagement that emphasized saving lives. In *A Nation on Fire*, Risen includes a scene that illustrates this difference: a strip mall stands in flames within a few blocks of hundreds of people looting other stores. "Across the street, in Maryland," Risen writes, "a line of policemen armed with dogs, gas, shotguns, and rifles stoically watched the conflagration, on guard for any spillover rioting." Further, state troopers had permission from County Commissioner Gladys Spellman to shoot any looter who crossed the state line.

As the riots continued, federal and state law enforcement was further supplemented by self-appointed posses, including a group of white business leaders Risen interviewed. As one Frank Bressler from the Maryland suburb of Parkland Heights reported: "We decided since most of us, or many of us, were ex-military, people were going to set up a military type defense in Baltimore to protect this type of area, to keep this from happening here." Although such a group was bolstered by their military training, they were not, in fact, operating under any governmental authority or rules of engagement other than, as Risen describes, the mounting fears among whites that "the nation's blacks were a problem, a collective threat. No longer a moral problem, they were now a domestic security concern."

Once the Maryland National Guard was federalized and no longer under state command, they, together with other Army troops, would have been subject to federal, as opposed to state-administered, rules of engagement. However, Maryland governor Agnew rose to national prominence thanks to his representation in the media as a tough responder during the riots. As recounted by Alex Csicsek in "Spiro T. Agnew and the Burning of Baltimore," the governor emphasized personal responsibility over systemic causes in laying blame for the riot, stating in one of his executive orders issued during the time that riots were "caused in all too many cases by evil men and not evil conditions." Baltimore had experienced a sudden expansion of its black population, coinciding with a backlash from the city's white working-class constituency that begrudged new competition for already dwindling industrial jobs. Statistically, however, black Baltimore residents were not advancing socioeconomically in comparison to whites, who viewed them as competition, because they were, among other things, less likely to own their own homes and more likely to live in low-quality housing.

ANOTHER WAY TO DESCRIBE MY ANGER WOULD BE TO QUOTE JAMES BALDwin, who said in a 1961 interview that "[t]o be a Negro in this country and to be relatively conscious is to be in a state of rage almost all of the time." This quip is well known, and has been so oft repeated as to become a meme. What is less often repeated are Baldwin's following remarks: "And part of the rage is this: It isn't only what is happening to you. But it's what's happening all around you and all of the time in the face of the most extraordinary and criminal indifference, indifference of most white people in this country and their ignorance."

Here, Baldwin captures not only my perpetual state of anger, but names the negative "peace" in which it is stoked, the abnormal norm that incites it. He also captures the abstract and diffuse target for this constant state of rage. How do I focus my anger on "what's happening all around" me or on the "indifference of most white people in this country"? What would that even mean? This is the conundrum is expressed by "the Man," slang that personifies the entirety of a system and the squadrons of people who consciously and unconsciously reinforce it. At least through the use of words, there would be a focus for this anger. A name for the target.

NONETHELESS, AGNEW'S POST-RIOT GRANDSTANDING EFFECTIVELY TRADED on white resentment by squarely laying blame for the riots on the black community. In a public speech given on April 11, a few days after the riots were quieted, Agnew had local "leaders" of the black community to his Baltimore office for an event, which he opportunistically used to stand firm on his commitment to "law and order." At this event, reports Csicsek, Agnew took to the stage with an entourage that included a National Guard commander in fatigues, blamed the black leaders present for failing to stop the riot, and accused them of refusing to confront their militant counterparts for fear of being "stung by insinuations that you were Mr. Charlie's boy, by epithets like 'Uncle Tom.'"

Also following the riots, Agnew established May 1 statewide as "Law Day USA," and vowed "to those few who loot and burn we shall show no sympathy, nor will we tolerate those few who would take the law into their own hands." Indeed, Agnew's law-and-order rhetoric ended up drawing the attention of presidential hopeful Richard Nixon, who eventually chose the governor to be the vice-presidential candidate on his ticket—a strategic move to fend off his rival George

Wallace, who was leveraging his own legacy as Alabama governor in vying for the presidential seat.

FIGHTING WORDS

Unbridled anger is my illicit fantasy. It is one that I indulge in, here and there, whenever I come across one of those smartphone-filmed videos of some racist harasser being pummeled by his erstwhile victim. In one a white woman in a black-and-white striped dress approaches a young couple, a man and a woman, standing before the cashier at a convenience store and orders them to leave. An off-camera voice—the man apparently taping the altercation—provides context for the viewer, stating that the woman in the black-and-white dress had just told them to go back to their country. One of the couple—a young woman in a pink strapless top—then advises her aggressor that she is Native American and therefore from this country, whereas the woman in the black-and-white dress is not. The situation escalates, involving the woman in the black-and-white dress confronting the person taping the fiasco, then returning to the couple and prodding the young man standing with the woman in the pink strapless top on the shoulder.

DESPITE THE PRESENCE OF U.S. ARMY OFFICIALS ON THE GROUND, THE Insurrection Act was not invoked in response to the 1973 occupation of Wounded Knee, South Dakota, by about two hundred members of the Oglala Lakota (also known as Sioux) and some armed members of the American Indian Movement (AIM)—a civil rights group organized to fight for the self-determination of indigenous peoples in the United States. The U.S. Army personnel were dispatched to the site to observe and report on the occupation and advise the Department of Defense on whether President Richard Nixon should formally deploy federal troops. However, no such action was taken during the seventy-one-day standoff.

———

"DID SHE JUST TOUCH YOU?" THE WOMAN IN THE PINK STRAPLESS TOP RHE-torically asks her companion. "That's assault. You guys know that, right?" She asks of the silent cashier and the recording commentator.

The woman in the black-and-white dress further demands to know where the woman in the pink top is from, stepping very close to her and sniping in her face, "[Y]ou're going back to Mexico." As the woman in the black-and-white dress turns around, the woman in the pink top swats the other woman's shoulder blade with the back of her hand. Not until the woman in the black-and-white dress turns around and grabs and pushes the woman in the pink top does the woman in the pink top swing back around and slap her in the face.

———

THE ACTIVISTS ARRIVED AT THE TOWN OF WOUNDED KNEE ON FEBRUARY 27, 1973, to demand that various U.S. treaties be honored and to challenge the authority of Sioux tribal president Dick Wilson, who was notorious for corruption, patronage, and suppressing dissent with a private militia called the Guardians of the Oglala Nation (GOONs). The location of this armed protest was no coincidence. Wounded Knee, of course, is also the site of the 1890 massacre of about three hundred Lakota people by a U.S. Army regiment triggered by fears of white settlers witnessing some Lakota engaged in a ceremonial dance. AIM members and other activists selected the historic site to further dramatize their demands of federal agencies. Once there, until they were arrested they exchanged gunfire with surrounding federal law enforcement officers, which included FBI agents and federal marshals.

———

THE SATISFACTION I GET FROM WATCHING THESE MELODRAMATIC REVENGE dramas is more than schadenfreude. They rescript all of those racist encounters that involve aggressions, both micro and macro, in which I would either brush off my antagonizers or silently absorb their insults. During the extended period of time that usually elapses between the initial provocation by a racist aggressor and the ultimate blows, I can identify with the anger that is always present and controlled, poised and alert like the head of a coiled snake aiming, if necessary, to strike. By viewing videos like these, I vicariously reestablish my boundaries, take pleasure by proxy in these sporadic displays of self-defense.

———

SOME OF THE ARRESTED DEFENDANTS OF THE WOUNDED KNEE EVENT would later argue in federal court that, among other things, federal military officers were improperly engaged in civilian law enforcement activities in violation of the Posse Comitatus Act, which prohibits the domestic deployment of federal troops to enforce the law. In this way, some defendants argued, their search, seizure, and arrest by federal military officers was unlawful. The Insurrection Act, however, is among the surviving exceptions to this general prohibition. Opinions of federal courts considering whether the Posse Comitatus Act was violated in relation to the Wounded Knee occupation cited the fact that the president had not invoked the Insurrection Act as part of their analyses.

In the end, such federal court opinions articulated the difference between active and passive law enforcement, stating that, absent an invocation of the Insurrection Act, federal military officers were authorized to provide passive assistance to state and local law enforcement, such as supplies, equipment, or advice. But such officers were prohibited from engaging in active law enforcement—such as search, seizure, and arrest—without a formally declared "insurrection."

———

FOR ME, THE HEIGHTENED TENSION IN THESE SMARTPHONE-CAPTURED minidramas also clarifies the nature of racist anger. The boundary I see the racist aggressor attempting to enforce is geographical, not personal. The racist aggressors in these videos are not enforcing a boundary that encapsulates their very personhood, like being injured or abused. Instead, the racist aggressors are enforcing the boundary of some imagined territory, whether it is a neighborhood or an office building or the entire country. *You don't belong here* is the rallying cry of the racist aggressor. The mere presence of the other person represents the external threat to the racist aggressor's personhood. The exclusion and expulsion of said target is the action taken to resolve the racist aggressor's anger.

What is true at individual levels indicates a larger truth expressed at the level of the collective. Yes, the anger of the race (read: black) rioter is directed at the "system," and any property destruction or theft levels the playing field by either symbolically asserting power against institutions or making a crude attempt to redistribute wealth. Meanwhile, the anger of the white mob targets those who cross socioeconomic boundaries, delineated by physical or civic spaces where its members believe only they may enter.

CHAPTER 7

Disaster upon Disaster

W hen a massive hurricane, earthquake, or explosion rips off the veil of "order," the essence of human nature is exposed. The primordial or pre-law human. The apocryphal being who lived not under the rule of law but in the state of nature, where, according to Hobbes, persons were engaged in a "war of all against all" and lived in "continual fear, and danger of violent death." The self-centered and fundamentally antisocial being who resolves all disputes with violence. Absent a semblance of order, according to this theory, citizens of civil society are susceptible to regressing into a barbaric state of chaos, in which every man is for himself. Even absent outright violence the war of all against all in this pre-law state is always being waged, as everyone in the state of nature is always on guard, standing by to defend himself and his property from every other person, who is, by definition, a presumptive threat.

———

ON SEPTEMBER 20, 1989, PRESIDENT GEORGE H. W. BUSH ISSUED A PROCLA-mation under the Insurrection Act after having "been informed that conditions of domestic violence and disorder exist in and about the Virgin Islands endangering life and property and obstructing execution of the laws." The proclamation was referring to widespread looting and sporadic violence in the U.S. Virgin Island of St. Croix after Hurricane Hugo had made landfall three days earlier. U.S. Virgin Islands territorial governor Alexander Farrelly had by then already deployed the local National Guard and imposed a curfew, which proved insufficient to restore order given the sheer devastation wrought by the hurricane.

In addition to destroying about 90 percent of the island's buildings—leaving many of its fifty-five thousand residents bereft and/or homeless—the hurricane severely damaged communications systems, making it difficult for Washington-based officials to confirm conditions on the island. Accordingly, ham radio operators communicated much of the information Washington officials relied upon to assess the situation on the ground, which included panicked reports of "machete-armed mobs."

While ham radio operators shared reports of armed gangs, fleeing tourists told rescue teams coming ashore from the mainland of "chaos, long and heavy automatic weapons fire, robbers with machetes and prisoners—including murderers—on the loose." One news report verified white tourists being heckled by black crowds, as one woman told the *New York Times*: "They followed us down the road shouting, 'Whitey, go home!'"

———

WITH VIOLENT ROCKING UNDERFOOT, WHIPPING GUSTS, INUNDATING TIDES, OR forest-felling flames, disasters dismantle the illusion of safety. Disasters reveal that physical constructions and the peace they represent are truly as unstable as social ones. As disasters uproot all tangible indication of law and order, they also alleviate the pressure of the boot that is violence and its threat—the looming enforcement that, together with law, restrains human action. In the seeming absence of law and order, fear rushes in to fill the void, and with it age-old narratives that, in the case of black disaster victims, do not necessarily represent the mythic pre-law man, but rather the potential insurrectionist poised to seize an opportunity to become victor in the imagined zero-sum game, and finally triumph in bloody revenge.

SUCH ACCOUNTS WERE LIKELY ENHANCED BY ISLAND RACIAL TENSIONS that long preceded the hurricane's landfall, as about 85 percent of St. Croix's inhabitants at the time were black and tended to occupy jobs in a tourist industry that serviced mostly white seasonal visitors. Also, radio operators reported that hundreds of inmates broke out of a hurricane-damaged prison, escalating both the fears and projections of violence of civilians stranded by the storm. Though a number of the island's residents had in fact armed themselves in the aftermath of the hurricane, in the end there were few reports of injuries or fatalities arising from interpersonal violence—which included, as reported in the *Washington Post*, an American dentist struck on the head by a two-by-four while trying to photograph the looting, and a store owner fatally shooting an alleged looter.

AMID THE EERIE SILENCE LEFT IN THE WAKE OF A DISASTER, RUMOR ALSO rushes in to fill the apparent absence of law and order. Propelled by fear, rumor exaggerates present danger through grand narratives that justify dread. Rumors also proliferate like the forest fires that may be prone to instigate them, felling common sense and reason as they overwhelm the imagination. Rumor is the medium for underlying beliefs about the "true" nature of selfish and warlike human beings—beliefs that swell and break through the surface formalities that purport to respect the freedom and equality of all persons, and sweep them away.

WHILE THE EXTENT OF PERSONAL VIOLENCE ON ST. CROIX MIGHT HAVE
been exaggerated at the time, it is undisputed that widespread looting did occur after the hurricane, with not only civilians but also
local police, National Guard troops, and even prominent officials and
local leaders having participated. (Among the persons later charged
for theft and/or larceny were a former St. Croix senator and the vice
president of a bank, each of whom was made an example of by prosecutors who could not possibly charge all of the thousands actually
involved.) One witness told the *Associated Press* that he had seen "a
National Guard truck filled to capacity with all kinds of stuff in it."
A law enforcement official told the *Washington Post* that "a guy with
a National Guard uniform told me to go into a store and 'take what
you need.' Why? Because the National Guard was looting, too." Some
shop owners even reportedly invited looters into their stores, noting
that their losses would be covered by insurance.

Some of the pervasive looting was need-oriented, engaged in by
residents who were running out of food and other necessary provisions. The mass pillaging, however, was not only for essential items,
but also things like toaster ovens, televisions, refrigerators, and laun-
dry dryers, transforming a foraging expedition into a carnivalesque
spree. According to the *Washington Post*, "The plunder started on
the day after the Sunday night storm, as panicked islanders sought
to stock up on food. It quickly degenerated into a free-for-all grab of
all sorts of consumer goods that some witnesses likened to a 'feeding
frenzy.'" The Coast Guard dispatched a vessel to help evacuate tourists, and a representative of the U.S. Armed Forces' maritime branch
reported that two of the first forty set to embark were so eager to flee
that they swam out to meet it.

The atmosphere in the wake of a disaster, similar to that of a riot, is often more carnivalesque than violent, representing a rare opportunity for disaster victims to flout so-called natural order and gain access to spoils that would be socioeconomically out of reach. Yet, as is also the case during a riot, crimes against property, and not against people, largely represent the disruption of "peace" and "order." That the call to restore law and order amid a disaster is more about deep-seated fear than fact does little to prioritize safeguarding actual people over property.

—————

PRESIDENT BUSH ULTIMATELY DEPLOYED ABOUT 1,100 MILITARY POLICE from bases in Texas, Missouri, North Carolina, and Louisiana to restore order on the island, as well as more than one hundred federal marshals and FBI agents "to protect federal personnel and property." Federal troops—some armed with machine guns and M16s—were installed in the downtown area of the island's commercial district, and order restored. While some reports credit such order to military presence, others have claimed the looting was quelled because there was nothing left to steal.

Though the presidential proclamation was silent on whether it had been made at the request of territorial governor Alexander Farrelly, a spokesperson for President Bush claimed that it had. Farrelly, however, insisted that he had not made any such request. Farrelly further thought the proclamation and tenor of the military response was heavy-handed, disproportionate to the actual level of unrest he claimed he witnessed on the ground. Farrelly told the Associated Press that there was "some looting" but that there was "no near state of anarchy" in the Virgin Islands, adding that he should know because he was in the streets every day. Federal law enforcement officers substantiated the governor's statements, agreeing that media reports had exaggerated the disorder on the island with "reports of rioting and of roving, machete-wielding gangs bent on murder."

As for perceptions of legitimacy on the ground, *Newsday* reported that "[s]ome residents expressed bitterness that the cargo planes carrying military police did not transport food and building materials instead," noting that in the hurricane's immediate aftermath numerous people on the island were inquiring where they could find drinking water. Some territorial officials also criticized the federal military deployment, which they argued diverted necessary resources from relief missions to security operations. Nonvoting House of Representatives member Ron de Lugo criticized the media reportage of the disruption on the island, "denounc[ing] the television networks, *Time Magazine*, *The New York Times*, *The Wall Street Journal*, *The Miami Herald*, *The Chicago Tribune* and other news organizations, accusing them of concentrating on the looting and exaggerating the extent of civil disorder."

ALTHOUGH IT PREVAILS IN THE IMAGINATIONS OF MANY MEMBERS OF THE public and government officials alike, the Hobbesian state of nature is only one narrative for framing human behavior in the immediate aftermath of a major disaster. Another one has been corroborated by numerous studies—that the people affected strengthen their social ties by helping one another and engaging in altruistic behaviors. As studies have shown, instead of panicking and fleeing a disaster site, many people in such situations tend to help rescue other victims. Evacuees file out of threatened structures in a calm and orderly fashion and do not stampede over one another to save themselves. Meanwhile, those completely unaffected by a disaster tend to willingly volunteer to assist the trapped and injured. Also, much of the initial disaster relief is provided by the people themselves, who do not tend to passively await assistance from relief organizations or the government. In other words, there tends to be order absent the semblance of "order."

―――――

IT WOULD BE THE DAY AFTER HE DISPATCHED TROOPS TO ST. CROIX THAT President Bush would declare the U.S. Virgin Islands a "disaster area" under the Robert T. Stafford Disaster Relief and Emergency Assistance Act, which is generally applied to coordinate the federal response to either natural disasters such as hurricanes, floods, and brush fires, or man-made disasters. Federal relief under the Stafford Act would include both short- and long-term monetary aid, as well as immediate assistance to local officials in their efforts to save lives and alleviate suffering. The Federal Emergency Management Agency (FEMA) coordinates federal disaster response in accordance with the Stafford Act, whereby items such as food, plastic sheeting, and electric generators, among other essentials, were eventually distributed on the island. Notably, although federal troops can be deployed pursuant to the Stafford Act in the wake of a disaster, they would not—as they would under the Insurrection Act—have powers akin to local law enforcement, such as search and seizure or making arrests.

In the United States, a "major disaster" has a legal definition, set forth in the Robert T. Stafford Disaster Relief and Emergency Assistance Act, which collapses acts of God and man-made disasters into one: "any natural catastrophe (including any hurricane, tornado, storm, high water, wind-driven water, tidal wave, tsunami, earthquake, volcanic eruption, landslide, mudslide, snowstorm, or drought), or, regardless of cause, any fire, flood, or explosion, in any part of the United States, which in the determination of the President causes damage of sufficient severity and magnitude to warrant major disaster assistance [. . .]."

In due respect for the U.S. federalist system, such events technically are to be administered at the most local level possible, with additional assistance requested from federal officials after such resources
have been exhausted. So, if there were a large explosion in a city, the
city's mayor would be responsible for disaster response and, if overwhelmed, would then request assistance from the governor, who, if
overwhelmed, would then request supplemental help at the federal
level from the president. Only the governor's formal request for federal help under the Stafford Act triggers such assistance, including
supplementing search-and-rescue efforts and emergency loans. The
stated intention behind such federal assistance is "alleviating the damage, loss, hardship, or suffering caused" by "major disaster."

DISASTERS ARE FRAMED IN NARRATIVES THAT MANUFACTURE THE
responses to them. Just as the word of law calls forth and justifies
violence and its threat, the word of law, in the case of a disaster, can
also mitigate the extent of violence disaster victims are subject to,
reframing what could easily be a mission to shoot and kill into one
to search and rescue. The extent of violence deemed by the State to
be warranted amid a disaster is less an indication of actual danger on
the ground than of whether persons on the ground are considered to
be victims or perpetrators.

ON AUGUST 24, 1992, PRESIDENT GEORGE H. W. BUSH PROCLAIMED A "MAJOR
disaster" pursuant to the Stafford Act—the same day Hurricane
Andrew made landfall in South Florida with winds at an estimated
175 miles per hour. The Category Five hurricane especially devastated
South Dade County, a suburban part of the Miami metropolitan area
where the population at the time was about 70 percent white (mostly
of Cuban descent).

Florida governor Lawton Chiles had declared a state of emergency and activated the Florida National Guard to assist local law enforcement, which included riot police dispatched to help secure areas reportedly besieged by looting. Among the Guard's activities was to help riot police to erect barricades around downtown Miami's commercial district, which happened to border two of the city's poorest and mostly black neighborhoods, and help enforce a curfew announced by Dade County officials. At the height of the looting, Governor Chiles dispatched National Guard troops to secure the Cutler Ridge Mall, which ultimately served as the Guard's base.

Though official statistics on the extent of the looting remain uncertain, news stories of that time highlighted an atmosphere pervaded by fear and perceived lawlessness—with reports of signs painted on homes and other buildings reading "Loot and I'll Shoot" or "Looters will lose body parts"; at least one man presumed to be a looter was shot dead by a South Florida resident. Local law enforcement, on the other hand, apparently took a far less aggressive approach to deterring looters. One news article reported witnessing officers stopping the car of an alleged looter, removing stolen merchandise from the vehicle, then sending the driver away. The primary mission of the state Guard was to deter rather than detain looters. As commander of the Florida National Guard, Major General Ronald Harrison, informed the *Chicago Tribune*: "Our mission is to help people, provide security and help in search and rescue, not make arrests." Accordingly, Harrison also told reporters that while the state National Guard under his command carried live ammunition, their weapons were not loaded when they stood guard.

———

DISASTERS THREATEN TO STRIP ALL EMPERORS BARE, MOCK THE VANITY of any assumed authority to govern. When disaster strikes, only vulnerability reigns. To regain control and reestablish a sense of order in the wake of a disaster might entail restoring the appearance of order. Just as a robber who holds up a bank with a fake gun nonetheless calls forth violence and its threat, so do law enforcers with unloaded artillery intimidate the would-be lawless. However, the question is raised—which disaster victims are subjected to actual violence, and which only to its threat.

THREE DAYS FOLLOWING THE HURRICANE'S LANDFALL, AT LEAST ONE South Florida resident voiced dissatisfaction at the National Guard troops guarding shopping centers while storm victims were still in need of vital aid. "Where the hell is the cavalry on this one?" asked a woman named Kate Hale to rolling television cameras. "We need food, we need water, we need people. If we do not move food and water into the south end in a very short period of time, we are going to have more casualties." Hale further noted that Miami-Dade County had an emergency response team that responds within ten to twenty-four hours to earthquakes in Mexico and hurricanes in the Caribbean. "Why can't we get some help when it happens in our own country?"

Soon thereafter, Governor Chiles asked the federal government to send additional active-duty troops to Florida under the Stafford Act—without, notably, also making a request under the Insurrection Act, which would have conferred law enforcement powers on such troops. And like the Florida National Guard, they were deployed to help create the appearance of force rather than to use force. As reported in the *Miami Herald*, members of the 82nd Airborne Division—who were armed with M16 rifles that were not loaded—were confronted by an armed gang in South Dade County. Though the confrontation was diffused, a captain of the division recalling the incident noted that "[o]ne of these times, somebody's going to call our bluff and somebody will get shot."

THERE IS A THEORY OF DISASTER THAT CONSIDERS THE EXTENT OF THE devastation left in its wake to be symptomatic of preexisting conditions on the ground. In this line of thought, an earthquake, tornado, or flood does not simply cause devastation, but also reveals the devastation underlying it in the form of, say, faulty infrastructure, inept politicians, or ineffective policies—all of which would be otherwise masked by a semblance of order. The response to the COVID-19 pandemic in the United States, for example, revealed not only an individual's susceptibility to becoming infected by a virus, but also stark socioeconomic inequality and a broken healthcare system. The ongoing man-made disaster that is racism is among those preexisting conditions revealed in crisis, which stirs up recurring themes as it levels the sense of "progress."

CRUDE, EMPTY, FRAGILE SHELL

In *The Wretched of the Earth*, Frantz Fanon states that all national projects are ultimately frail. "Instead of being the coordinated crystallization of the people's innermost aspirations, instead of being the most tangible, immediate product of popular mobilization, national consciousness is nothing but a crude, empty, fragile shell," Fanon writes. "The cracks in it explain how easy it is for young independent countries to switch back from nation to ethnic group and from state to tribe—a regression which is so terribly detrimental and prejudicial to the development of the nation and national unity."

The "crude, empty, fragile shell" also represents the "order" that is fractured in the midst of a disaster. And yet when "order" is understood to mean property that is undisturbed—perhaps freshly painted, and even assiduously manicured—the crude, empty, fragile shell may be nothing more than a shiny object.

PRESIDENT GEORGE W. BUSH WANTED TO INVOKE THE INSURRECTION ACT
as part of the federal response to Hurricane Katrina, which was at
Category Three intensity when it made landfall in Louisiana on the
morning of August 29, 2005. The hurricane damaged levees erected
to protect New Orleans—already situated below sea level—from
flooding, a breach which soon left about 80 percent of the city under
fifteen feet of water. The hurricane also debilitated transportation in
New Orleans and damaged the city's communications infrastructure,
which left scant reliable channels for local and state officials to share
information about the situation on the ground. Amid this disaster, an
estimated fifty thousand residents who had not evacuated before the
storm hit were still trapped in the city, marooned without access to
food, drinking water, and other critical provisions.

"Why no massive airdrop of food and water?" CNN news anchor
Soledad O'Brien asked on a broadcast aired five days after the hurricane hit. "In Banda Aceh, in Indonesia, they got food dropped two
days after the tsunami struck." O'Brien here was channeling mass
frustration with delayed relief efforts. With official communication
systems down, much of the reporting about the aftermath of the hurricane that devastated New Orleans was being transmitted via news
and social media, with dramatic images of stranded residents navigating flood waters on makeshift floats or waving for help on rooftops.
Some were even worse: corpses floating in floodwater. By contrast,
depictions of a robust corps of first responders engaging in a large-
scale search-and-rescue mission were glaringly absent.

Two days before the storm hit, Governor Kathleen Blanco had
requested that President Bush declare a "major disaster" under the
Stafford Act, which would trigger the federal government to provide
funding and other assistance to Louisiana state and local officials

working on relief efforts in coordination with FEMA. Blanco had also already activated the state National Guard to assist in the aftermath of the hurricane—four thousand soldiers by the time the hurricane made landfall and the remaining seventeen hundred the next day. However, these were not enough and no more were available: some thirty-two hundred of Louisiana's Guardsmen had been deployed to Iraq. On the day of landfall, the state troops on hand became overwhelmed when storm waters flooded their headquarters, cutting off their communications and disabling their vehicles. Guard officials reported that they were preoccupied with evacuating their command center and rescuing troops who could not swim in the rising water. With transportation in and out of New Orleans compromised, additional National Guard troops volunteered by governors of nearby states, including Mississippi and Alabama, were not able to arrive in significant numbers until the fourth day after the storm hit.

THE FRAILTIES DISASTERS EXPOSE ARE NOT ONLY SYSTEMIC, BUT ALSO personal. Disasters pose a psychic challenge for the individuals faced with them. They force the question of where one's sense of safety is invested. When I fasten my inner sense of security to the physical structures that, like a brisk arm knocking chess pieces off a board, disasters throw into disarray, the more prone I am to projecting my fears onto the devastation on the ground. The extent of preexisting fears not only magnifies the extent of a given disaster, it can also trigger a sense of helplessness and overwhelming desire for some external authority to rush to the rescue. Just as a calamitous act of God can bring even the most staunch atheist to his knees in prayer, disasters also incite an outcry among even the most disaffected citizens for governmental forces to save them, like a superhero in an action movie.

SEARCH-AND-RESCUE, HOWEVER, WAS NOT THE TELEGRAPHED PRIORITY
of such troops, as Governor Blanco stated at a September 2 press
conference announcing the arrival of three hundred members of the
Arkansas National Guard in New Orleans: "These troops are fresh
back from Iraq, well trained, experienced, battle-tested and under my
orders to restore order in the streets. They have M-16s and they are
locked and loaded. These troops know how to shoot and kill and they
are more than willing to do so if necessary and I expect they will."
Indeed, black residents stranded in New Orleans in the immediate
aftermath of the hurricane were mostly portrayed by the media as having formed violent armed gangs, supposedly including rooftop snipers
and perpetrators of pedophilic rape. Fox News anchor John Gibson
stated at the time that there were "[a]ll kinds of reports of looting, fires
and violence." He went on: "Thugs shooting at rescue crews. Thousands of police and National Guard troops are on the scene trying to
get the situation under control. Thousands more on the way. So heads
up, looters." In turn, Fox reporter David Lee Miller added: "As you
so rightly point out, there are so many murders taking place. There
are rapes, other violent crimes taking place in New Orleans." Gibson,
however, thereafter stated, "[W]e have yet to confirm a lot of that."

The Superdome—the sports-stadium-turned-haven during
the hurricane because of its relatively high ground and enormous
capacity—was a particular site of exaggerated speculation, transfig-
ured through rumor into a domain of murder and rape. New Orleans
mayor Ray Nagin himself claimed it was the effective headquarters of
"hundreds of gang members." Up to ten people did die in the Superdome in the aftermath of the hurricane, according to news reports;
however, such casualties were a result of neglect rather than violence—
crimes of omission rather than of commission. If this is so, where did
all of the misplaced conjecture come from? With communications

systems largely shut down, rumor and exaggeration filled the vacuum left by a lack of reliable information exchange, thereby recharacterizing a mission of search-and-rescue as one of shoot-to-kill.

Certain media reports that were not prone to repeating exaggeration nonetheless displayed racial disparities in the reports of hurricane victims. Two different images of hurricane victims in major newspapers—one featuring two white people wading though flood waters as some provisions they were dragging floated behind them, and the other showing a black person doing exactly the same thing—notoriously bore different captions: under the white flood victims, "Two residents wade through chest-deep water after finding bread and soda from a local grocery store [. . .]," while under the black flood victim, "A young man walks through chest deep flood water after looting a grocery store in New Orleans." In any event, while looting was pervasive after the storm, reports of ensuing violence were largely inflated by the media. Five years later, in 2010, the *New York Times* reflected on such media reports, acknowledging their distorted portrayal of events. "The narrative of those early, chaotic days—built largely on rumors and half-baked anecdotes—quickly hardened into a kind of ugly consensus," reported the *Times*, that "poor blacks and looters were murdering innocents and terrorizing whoever crossed their path in the dark, unprotected city."

In retrospect, the rumors that proliferated in New Orleans also overshadowed reports of attacks on black hurricane victims by law enforcement and white civilians—violence which was, in the end, the most pervasive in the storm's aftermath. On September 4, six days after the hurricane hit, police officers fatally shot two African American men and wounded four others on the Danziger Bridge. None of the shooting victims were armed, though police officers claimed they had been responding to reports of gunfire on the bridge.

Subsequent news reports revealed vigilante violence in Algiers Point, a largely white enclave within the predominantly black district of Algiers that is accessible via ferry and two bridges. Whereas levees girding New Orleans from flooding were breached due to the hurricane, Algiers Point levees remained secure against Mississippi River waters, creating a dry haven for "refugees" evacuating New Orleans. The National Guard, moreover, had designated the Algiers Point ferry landing as an official evacuation site for those seeking refuge from flooding, and patrolled it heavily. Yet bodies of black men—with bullet wounds—were found lying in the streets among wreckage strewn by the hurricane.

As *ProPublica* reported in 2008, a group of white Algiers Point residents collaborated to protect their neighborhood from an influx of "refugees," blocking off roads leading into the area, stockpiling weapons, and patrolling in pickup trucks. "The newly formed militia," reported *ProPublica*, "a loose band of about 15 to 30 residents, most of them men, all of them white, was looking for thieves, outlaws or, as one member put it, anyone who simply 'didn't belong.' " At the time, some newspaper reports in 2005 had referred to the armed group as "the ultimate neighborhood watch," yet subsequent reporting recast the makeshift militiamen as perpetrators of, not protectors against, violence. *ProPublica* later reported that at least eleven African American men were shot in Algiers Point after the storm, with all the shooters allegedly white.

———

THE ORDERLY FAÇADE MASKING DISASTER: THIS WAS THE "ORDER" I WAS supposed to appreciate being raised in. The silence usually sounded like cawing crows or coos of mourning doves, the periodic rumble of mail or garbage trucks, or the buzz of lawnmowers. That was during the day. At night I would hear crickets. When some of my parents' friends would visit, having traveled all the way from the city where they still lived, I would often overhear them say that the place was so "peaceful." I never had any appreciaton for any of these pleasant

façades. It was as if I were always jaded by my quaint, tree-lined environs, which repulsed me and from which I could not wait to escape.

In the midst of the apparent order in Long Island, it's no coincidence that among the sole incidents of racism I remember being publicly sanctioned was the time when three high schoolers—two white
Americans and one student from Colombia—took it upon themselves
to burn a nine-by-six-foot cross on the lawn of one of their black
classmates. According to news reports at the time, the three teens'
decision came about while they were smoking marijuana together one
day when one suggested, without seeming fanfare, that "they burn a
cross on a black man's lawn." Hand-wringing and federal civil rights
lawsuits ensued, with my high school principal telling news reporters
that he was "shocked and surprised" and a Suffolk County legislator
stating that "[t]here is no place for this type of prejudice." I wouldn't
go so far as to say their dismay was mere performance, only that they
seemed to view the burning cross as some alien matter that fell out of
the sky, tarnishing the idyllic suburb, rather than a totem that merely
symbolized that which was prevalent yet denied, murmured behind
closed doors, and thick in the otherwise abiding silence.

AT THE TIME OF THE DISASTER, IT WAS THE EXAGGERATED REPORTS OF
violence by and among black residents of New Orleans that had
impressed themselves upon President Bush. On August 30, the day
after the hurricane struck in Louisiana, Governor Blanco informed
reporters that she had requested additional federal troops from the
president to restore law and order in New Orleans, as well as, the
following day, the mobilization of forty thousand additional National
Guard troops from other states to help supplement the state's thinned
ranks. Blanco's request was within the parameters of the Stafford
Act and its disaster-relief provisions, already in effect. Concerned
over media reports of looting and violence in New Orleans, President

Bush did not want to deploy additional troops to Louisiana without investing them with law enforcement powers—i.e., the authority to, among other things, search suspects, seize evidence, and make arrests. In other words, the president wanted to deploy such troops under the Insurrection Act, which would not only have conferred law enforcement powers on the troops, but also would have technically made the president, rather than the governor, commander in chief of their mission.

Governor Blanco, for her part, objected to invoking the Insurrection Act. It was not that the governor was keen to avoid the specter of standing soldiers and the violence they threatened. Rather, she was resisting the Bush administration's move to strip her role as ultimate commander in chief of the National Guard. In the end, the governor prevailed; additional troops were deployed five days after the hurricane hit—well into the crisis in New Orleans.

Like predecessors including presidents John F. Kennedy and Lyndon B. Johnson, President Bush was hesitant to employ federal military intervention without the blessing of the Louisiana governor, once again elevating public perception as a key element in federalist politics. As Bush wrote in his 2010 memoir *Decision Points*: "If I invoked the Insurrection Act against her wishes, the world would see a male Republican president usurping the authority of a female Democratic governor by declaring an insurrection in a largely African American city. That would arouse controversy anywhere." He continued: "To do so in the Deep South, where there had been centuries of states' rights tensions, could unleash holy hell."

Following the Hurricane Katrina debacle, in October 2006 Congress enacted the John Warner National Defense Authorization Act for Fiscal Year 2007, which would have constituted routine appropriations legislation but for an amendment to the Insurrection Act that was buried within it. The legislation amended the Insurrection Act to allow the president to unilaterally federalize the National Guard and/

or deploy federal troops in any U.S. state or territory when "domestic violence" erupts "as a result of a natural disaster, epidemic, or other serious public health emergency, terrorist attack or incident, or other condition [. . .]." However, after facing strong opposition from all fifty U.S. governors for, among other things, radically usurping the authority of state governors and subverting the posse comitatus restrictions that limit federal military involvement in state affairs, the amendment was repealed in January 2008.

As much as Hurricane Katrina wrought disaster, it uncovered disaster—among other calamities, the age-old dilemma of black Americans in the United States living in a country within a country. Indeed, with most of New Orleans underwater, news reporters referred to the city as a "third-world country" and to its mostly black residents stranded in attics and other makeshift shelters as "refugees." As reported by the Associated Press, critics "argued that 'refugee' implies that the displaced storm victims, many of whom have been black, are second-class citizens, or not even Americans." Overlaid by the wreckage of physical disaster, the underlying disaster (manifested in rumor and "excessive use of force" and extralegal killings) cast black evacuees of the hurricane as both relief-seeking and rioters, and as innocent victims and dangerous insurgents.

CHAPTER 8

The Beginning and the End

History is the grand story of purported progress, a collective tale of peoples who definitively move forward, ever marching toward some desired horizon. History in this sense is measured in linear time—a straight line barreling ahead to connect a sequence of events that advance society from past to present to future. History, though, is also doomed to repeat. Like each day marked by the successive rise and set of the sun, history is cyclical, and our clocks and calendars mere constructs, futile attempts to imprint man's "order" onto nature's infinite rhythms.

So, what is called the "past" is relived again, the same missteps made into familiar pitfalls.

History, though, happened a really long time ago. And yet history also happened only just yesterday. History, then, is a temporal illusion, an optical trick of some telescopic effect, which zooms in or out on past events. And, in the end (or in the beginning), everyone knows that the contents of history depend on the perspective of the one writing it, the "victors," as they say. History, however, also depends on the one reading it, in other words, to the ones subjected to it. Like light, history takes shape based on the disposition of its observer. In all these senses, history is a kind of ideology—that totalizing and illusory perception that can appear as smooth as a paved street or as sturdy as a building.

And yet there is another version of history, one verified by science. In this sense—the scientific view of the past—history is not just a prisoner of perception. History, rather, is made up of disparate moments suspended in space-time—a matrix constituted by three-dimensional space and that "indefinite progress of existence and events in the past, present, and future" defined as time. History, in this scientific sense, is not a selected series of events that crawls past like the endless scroll at the bottom of a television screen. History is also not a series of events that seems to rotate on a sundial, marking the hours by the cyclical rotation of shadow and light. History according to science is made up of events only seemingly located in the "past," "present," and "future," but which in fact are each locked within space-time at specific coordinates, like a house fixed in space at a particular address—the moments that constitute history, according to science, exist simultaneously. In other words, all of history is happening right now.

To translate science into metaphor, every given event within history is like writing on a palimpsest—every other writing that was made "before" is that which has already been effaced, but of which traces nonetheless remain.

———

ON MAY 1, 1992, PRESIDENT GEORGE H. W. BUSH ISSUED A PROCLAMATION under the Insurrection Act regarding "conditions of domestic violence and disorder" in Los Angeles, California. He was responding to the riots sparked in the city after four white Los Angeles police officers—Theodore Briseno, Stacey Koon, Laurence Powell, and Timothy Wind—were acquitted of charges for their involvement of the brutal beating in March 1991 of Rodney King, a black motorist the officers had pulled over and arrested after a high-speed chase.

Unusual for the time, a bystander recorded King's beating with a handheld video camera. The footage of the police officers kicking and pummeling King with batons as he lay crumpled on the ground was widely televised in an unprecedented visual display of evidence of police brutality. After a jury acquitted all four officers charged with assault and use of excessive force, riots broke out and escalated into six days of unrest throughout Los Angeles. In one spectacular incident of retributive violence, a white truck driver named Reginald Denny was pulled out of his vehicle by a group of black men and brutally beaten.

The day President Bush issued the proclamation, he delivered a national televised address denouncing the riots. "What we saw last night and the night before in Los Angeles is not about civil rights. It's not about the great cause of equality that all Americans must uphold. It's not a message of protest," said Bush. "It's been the brutality of a mob, pure and simple. And let me assure you, I will use whatever force is necessary to restore order." Having been advised that the main instigator of the riots was opportunistic gang activity, President Bush did not express much sympathy with the outrage of rioters.

Multiple narratives proliferated in the news media, representing a wide spectrum of sympathies. As Ronald Jacobs writes of news coverage at the time in *Race, Media, and the Crisis of Civil Society: From Watts to Rodney King*: "[S]imple (i.e., non-contextualized) descriptions of the uprisings in the *Los Angeles Times* and *Chicago Tribune* described the rioters as largely composed of criminals and opportunists, while the *New York Times* described the scene as reminiscent of a 'street party or a carnival,' and ABC News described the 'rage' as 'mindless, infectious and random.'" However, as Jacobs points out, initial news reports about the riots tended to place more blame on the Los Angeles Police Department than on the rioters themselves, whose public demonstration of outrage was largely reported in the context of frustration with police brutality.

Such coverage contrasted with the narratives that predominated in initial news reports of the Watts Rebellion, sparked August 11, 1965, when a white police officer arrested a black motorist for suspected drunk driving; the arrest drew a crowd of some two to three hundred observers who set off a spate of rioting that lasted for five days and resulted in thirty-four deaths, more than one thousand injuries, and about $40 million in property damage. As Jacobs in *Race, Media, and the Crisis of Civil Society* wrote of Watts: "Within the mainstream press, the similarities mainly concerned the descriptions of the rioters and their actions, which were described as being 'irrational,' 'hysterical,' and 'indiscriminate.'" The *Los Angeles Times* and the *Chicago Tribune* for their part reiterated a position that the Watts riots themselves represented a breakdown of "law and order."

Given the relative sympathies of mainstream news reports of the 1992 uprising in Los Angeles, Bush's own law-and-order rhetoric was criticized at the time for revealing less concern about the context in which the riots emerged than the lawlessness of the rioters. As Jacobs cites, the *New York Times* was among them:

> The comments [by Bush] spread over eight hours, left the impression that the White House was scrambling to keep atop public reaction to the verdict in the brutality case. As the day progressed, the President moved further from his initial expression of "frustration" about the King verdict and began condemning the rioters. In his last appearance of the day . . . the President did not mention the verdict at all. . . . On Wednesday evening, as smoke first began to curl above Los Angeles, Mr. Bush had told reporters only that "what's needed now is calm and respect for the law."

Bush, as Jacobs also notes, was described at the time as being more concerned about appearing in control of riot response than on identifying and addressing its root causes.

Despite Bush's forceful televised rhetoric casting rioters as a violent mob, behind the scenes the president had been unsure about how to go about invoking the Insurrection Act, despite the prior episode in response to Hurricane Hugo. As recalled by David F. Demarest Jr., Bush's assistant and White House communications director, the president asked an aide how to go about federalizing the National Guard. When the aide responded that he didn't know and advised Bush to call Secretary of State Colin Powell, Demarest overheard the president's end of the telephone conversation. After ending the phone call, Bush confirmed: "Colin says, 'All you've got to do is say it.'"

The thirty-five hundred federal troops deployed under Bush's order did not arrive in Los Angeles until the fourth day of the riots, by which time they had largely subsided. In the end, sixty-three people were killed and property damage in the city was estimated to approximate one billion dollars.

MODEL DEFENDANTS

One evening in college I was a passenger in a car full of friends driving in a beat-up car on the South Side of Chicago. I can't remember much about the occasion's inciting incident other than that it was both innocuous and jovial, a routine case of barely legal adults venturing off campus toward some festivity on the North Side. When the lights of a police car flashed from behind and signaled for our vehicle to pull over, the driver groaned and acquiesced as we slowed to a crawl and hugged the sidewalk. We hadn't been speeding or anything, at least not as far as I could tell, but there was admittedly one passenger too many in the five-seater—that would be me, as I was picked up last. Could that at most mean a ticket? Some kind of fine? We would soon find out. The driver rolled down the window, poised to deliver some prerehearsed excuse for the police officer outside his door, then quickly stiffened.

"Put your hands on the steering wheel!" the police officer yelled, gun pointed at my friend. After a tense exchange involving the careful production of a driver's license and registration, the driver was brusquely ordered out of the car. Then, one by one, the rest of us passengers were also ordered out of the vehicle, patted down, and instructed to raise our hands. Once outside the car, I saw at least five other police officers standing in wait, guns pointed at us.

———

HANDS UP! DON'T SHOOT! WAS ONE OF THE RALLYING CRIES OF PROTESTers who gathered in the summer of 2014 after police officer Darren Wilson killed Michael Brown in Ferguson, Missouri, shooting the eighteen-year-old at least six times. At the time of the shooting, on August 9, Wilson was in pursuit of Brown on suspicion of theft from a local convenience store. While some witnesses have claimed that immediately prior to the shooting Brown had started to rush Wilson, other witnesses insist that, after Wilson shot him once in the back, Brown stopped running, turned around, and held his hands up.

Brown's guilt or innocence in respect to Wilson's allegations is far less interesting to me than the contesting media narratives that inevitably arose to frame the killing. As Brown's case gained more news attention, it was the dead teenager's character that was scrutinized: the *New York Times*—noting his drug and alcohol use, shoplifting, and writing of rap lyrics that were at times "vulgar"—reported that Brown was "no angel." By contrast, a *Times* article about Brown's killer, Wilson, described him as a "well-mannered, relatively soft-spoken, even bland person who seemed, if anything, to seek out a low profile." In response to significant public criticism about describing Brown as "no angel"—including by one social media user who found the same descriptor once used in the newspaper to describe Al Capone—the *Times* issued a formal apology.

Before Brown, Trayvon Martin was subjected to similar media

narratives. After self-appointed neighborhood watchman George Zimmerman accosted, shot, and killed seventeen-year-old Martin as he was walking back to his father's house in Sanford, Florida, narratives swiftly arose to frame Martin as a suspect in his own killing. In early news reports, Martin was portrayed as a suspicious "guy" who frightened Zimmerman, who acted in self-defense, and the Sanford police department attributed to Zimmerman screams heard on a 911 call made from a bystanders huddled in their suburban home. Sanford police even submitted Martin's corpse to drug and alcohol testing, rather than Zimmerman, the shooter, as per standard practice. Weeks later, Martin's parents helped reframe the national media attention brought to the incident, emphasizing that Martin was a "kid," a "child" whose only crime was to have bought Skittles and Arizona Iced Tea. And it was Martin who was screaming in pain and fear as he tried to fend off Zimmerman, the gun-toting adult. Martin's 140-pound weight was also emphasized in this new narrative, as compared to the hulking 250-pound Zimmerman, who was recast as a wannabe cop who managed to get his hands on a gun despite prior charges for domestic violence and assaulting a police officer while resisting arrest. Martin's grades also did narrative work, as he was recast as a cheerful A and B student.

The roles of Martin and Zimmerman in the media narratives oscillated between the role of victim and perpetrator depending on the signifiers highlighted in the story line. Though the media narrative later started to tip in Martin's favor, I watched as pundits like Geraldo Rivera attempted to mobilize an ominous signifier in order to weigh public opinion on the other side, highlighting Martin's hoodie as sufficient to inspire suspicion and Zimmerman's citizen's arrest.

The notion of a model plaintiff is familiar, recalling how Claudette Colvin refused to relinquish her seat on a bus in Montgomery, Alabama, nine months before Rosa Parks did, but was not similarly championed by the NAACP because, among other reasons, she had been a pregnant teen. The understanding among civil rights activists at the time was, of course, that it would not be sufficient to argue on behalf of a black plaintiff's case; the black plaintiff herself would be put on trial, and would need to possess an unblemished track record in order to have a chance at having her claims considered on their merits and, perhaps, at achieving justice. Whether a civil or criminal matter, and whether plaintiffs or alleged victims of a crime, black Americans are forever model defendants. And the presumption of innocence is not one of those principles that can be enforced at the other end of a gun.

———

IT WAS A SURREAL POSITION TO BE IN, NOT ONLY STANDING THERE BEFORE five or so gun-wielding cops, but knowing that if one of us made one false move we could all end up dead. I was still a college student and not yet a lawyer, so thoughts of my "rights" or what might have constituted sufficient "reasonable suspicion" to warrant pulling us over did not come to mind. Rather, I felt that odd sensation that I sometimes would feel when standing at the edge of some very tall precipice. But, right then, hands raised before the police officers and their guns, instead of stopping myself from jumping I had to suppress the overwhelming sensation to make some erratic move or even dart toward them and yell "Boo!"

I had been the only black person in the car full of white passengers, a marker that one of the officers, another black woman, commemorated by calling me "Miss Thang." That said, I did not feel more or less safe, my bemusement notwithstanding. The police officers eventually drew back their weapons after each of us, one by one, produced our university IDs. The police officer who had inspected them with a creased brow eventually informed us that the beat-up blue station wagon we were driving in "fit the description" of one that had been reportedly involved in a burglary. Soon thereafter, we were "free to go."

AFTER MICHAEL BROWN'S SHOOTING, PROTESTS SPREAD THROUGHOUT Ferguson, along with rioting, which prompted Missouri governor Jay Nixon to issue a curfew and call forth the state National Guard—the first time a state governor had called out the National Guard since the LA riots over twenty years earlier. Some officials, including Lt. Gen. Russel Honoré, who had served as the Joint Task Force Katrina commander, called on President Obama to invoke the Insurrection Act in response to the unrest in Ferguson. However, the Obama administration did not do so; the president sought to distance himself from sanctioning the domestic use of military force. Heavily armed members of the Oath Keepers, for their part, turned up in Ferguson and organized patrols to defend local businesses against rioters.

The Ferguson unrest brought national attention to the use of military gear by local law enforcement, which, optically at least, diminished the effective difference between the spectacle of standing soldiers and civilian police officers. As reported at the time, Obama instead called for a review of the use of military equipment by local police forces and warned that blurring the lines between military and local law enforcement would be "contrary to our traditions." He also sent Attorney General Eric Holder to Ferguson to monitor the events on the ground to confirm whether National Guard troops were "helping or hindering the situation." The city had become a site of contention among militarized police, peaceful protesters, and provocateurs who damaged property and taunted police officers who in turn used smoke bombs, tear gas, flash grenades, and rubber bullets to disperse the crowd.

In this light, the question of federal military intervention seemed negligible. What difference is there, someone might ask, between militarized police and federal troops. One answer is training: Army soldiers are generally mandated to undergo more rigorous drills and formal training than local and state police officers. In that light, perhaps federal troops, together with any National Guardsmen under federal command, would be more likely to adhere to rules of engagement established for their deployment and less likely than police officers to engage in the arbitrary use of force.

These technicalities are not unimportant, but they overlook one overarching factor—the overall framing of the mission. When property, in such a mission, is the purported victim, then anyone on the ground who is not also clad in an official uniform is automatically suspect—if all peaceful protesters are presumptive rioters, the matter of training is a secondary issue to whether such persons are framed as perpetrators by default.

BACK IN THE CAR, AND CRUISING UP LAKE SHORE DRIVE TOWARD THE North Side, everyone was silent. I suppose what we had just gone through was objectively scary, but I wasn't rattled or afraid. The most appropriate word I can find to describe this incident is "surreal." I knew what was happening was really happening, but at the same time it felt like some kind of a dream. My bizarre urge to taunt the police officers with a sudden movement was not exactly suicidal, but more an attempt to wrest narrative control over the event by forcing it to a logical conclusion.

Although that was my first personal encounter with the police, I had zero sense of them as officers appointed to serve and protect me. By that time, whenever I returned from college to visit home in Long Island and was subject to the sliding stares of some neighbors standing by the screen doors to watch me as I walked past their houses, I readily expected to be one day apprehended and questioned by the police in my own neighborhood. To be held up and perhaps even shot by police officers seemed like a natural progression from the quotidian experiences of surveillance and suspicion that I was already accustomed to.

Yet, though the situation was dreamlike, it wasn't happening in an actual dream, in which I had a chance of perhaps assuming supernatural powers and wresting control from my captors. Dead victims of police violence have no agency, and risk being mere props in a narrative established for them. I would not, as in an actual dream, have the opportunity to set the record straight.

ALMOST SEVEN MONTHS AFTER BROWN'S KILLING, THE DEPARTMENT OF Justice provided context to the deadly incident in a 2015 report summarizing its findings regarding its investigation of the Ferguson Police Department. The report found, among other things, that about 90 percent of documented force used by the department was used against African Americans—who also accounted for 85 percent of vehicle stops, 90 percent of citations, and 93 percent of arrests despite comprising 67 percent of Ferguson's population. The Department of Justice also documented evidence of racism within the police department, citing email correspondence among police supervisors and court staff that stereotyped African Americans as criminals, with one message "that joked about an abortion by an African-American woman being a means of crime control."

WORDS LIKE "RACISM," "DISCRIMINATION," OR "OPPRESSION" HAVE THEIR utility, but they don't quite describe what I consider to be the fundamental grievance of having to navigate the United States as a black person—and that is the constraint imposed on my narrative agency. In the form of systemic injustice and the deputies who reinforce it, this constraint, as Toni Morrison has pointed out, "keeps you explaining, over and over again, your reason for being."

As Morrison continues: "Somebody says you have no language and you spend twenty years proving that you do. Somebody says your head isn't shaped properly so you have scientists working on the fact that it is. Somebody says you have no art, so you dredge that up. Somebody says you have no kingdoms, so you dredge that up. None of this is necessary. There will always be one more thing."

Living as a model defendant, against whom any and all allegations are presumed to be true, presumptively guilty before I even begin to tell my own story, I am relegated to mining history in order to construct a counternarrative in which to situate and preemptively defend myself.

———

ON APRIL 25, 2015, RIOTS ERUPTED IN BALTIMORE, MARYLAND, AFTER A twenty-five-year-old black man named Freddie Gray died of a spinal cord injury after his arresting officer battered him in a police van. Word of certain social media postings had spread, with talk of mass reprisals against Gray's killing with a "purge—a term derived from a 2013 dystopian film named *The Purge,* dramatizing one fictional day in the year when all laws are suspended and mayhem rules. In the days leading up to this social media threat of riots, protests had already been underway, tinged with violence enacted by what the city's mayor called "a small group of agitators." The worst, however, was expected to come on April 27, the day of Gray's funeral and the posted date of the "purge."

The online chatter of school-aged posters disseminated a digital flyer detailing the "purge," which was to begin at 3 p.m. at the Mondawmin Mall before continuing into downtown Baltimore. In response, the Baltimore Police Department shut down public transportation in the area and blockaded roads surrounding both the mall and the high school located directly across the street. Further, police in riot gear prevented students let out from school for the day from boarding any available buses and cordoned them on the school grounds.

"The majority of my students thought what was going to happen was stupid or were frightened at the idea," a teacher from the high school told reporters. "Very few seemed to want to participate in 'the purge.'" The police, for their part, had already mobilized around the department-issued consensus that the students were composed of "various gangs" who had "entered into a partnership to 'take out' law enforcement." Accordingly, the police adopted a preemptive strategy and staged a showdown with students at the high school before any "purge" could be prompted. As one witness reported of the students, "They weren't doing anything. No rock throwing, nothing. . . . The cops started marching toward groups of kids who were just milling about." By 3:30 p.m., hemmed-in students started to throw bottles and bricks, injuring an officer. More violence and, subsequently, looting ensued. Arguably, and in hindsight, the worst of the Baltimore riots were incited by the very squadron of police officers who emerged to suppress unrest before it ever began, failing to distinguish between reality and rumor, thus turning rumor into reality.

———

I SOMETIMES FEEL TRAPPED IN THE KIND OF NARRATIVE DESCRIBED BY Roland Barthes, in *Mythologies*. This narrative—or as Barthes calls it, myth—distorts rather than lucidly reflects reality, even though it may appear authentic to many who behold it. "Myth does not deny things," writes Barthes, "on the contrary, its function is to talk about them simply, it purifies them, it makes them innocent again, it gives them a natural and eternal justification, it gives them a clarity which is not that of an explanation, but of a statement of fact."

So, if the association of black people with criminality is reconstituted, in such a myth, as an eternal fact, then to fear black people becomes logical, simple even. Black people, within this myth, are scary because they are scary, like spiders or the dark. Yet because, as Barthes has also pointed out, tautology is a "double murder"—a deadly affront to both rationality and language—the fear incited by this myth essentially has no real meaning, no grounding, apart from its attachment to blackness.

Although certain myths maintain their enduring meaning, they do adapt to the times in which they are circulated. Where, say, during the antebellum period, it was narratively sufficient to simply fear Negroes, after the Civil War where formal "equality" was incorporated into the myth, such fear was instead attached to different words which signified black people without referring to them directly—to words like "crime," or, later, "inner cities" and the "low-income housing" located in them. In this way, metonymy aids and abets myth.

———

WHEN DISCUSSING THE BALTIMORE RIOTS THAT APRIL, OBAMA FOR HIS part decried the "criminals and thugs who tore up the place," stating they were distracting from the substantive issue of police brutality. The president later doubled down on his comments, expressing through a spokesperson that he didn't regret using the term.

"Whether it's arson or, you know, the looting of a liquor store [. . .] those were thuggish acts," Obama spokesperson Josh Earnest told reporters at the time, denying the word carried any racial connotations.

DEADLY PERFORMANCES

At 12:53 a.m. on May 29, 2020, President Trump tweeted: "These THUGS are dishonoring the memory of George Floyd, and I won't let that happen. Just spoke to Governor Tim Walz and told him that the Military is with him all the way. Any difficulty and we will assume control but, when the looting starts, the shooting starts. Thank you!" Trump signaled his inclination to invoke the Insurrection Act in this incendiary message, which was made two days before his press conference announcing his willingness to do so and his cryptic stand before St. John's Episcopal Church's door.

The threat was consistent with the promises of Trump's campaign, during which he positioned himself as the "law and order" candidate after the 2016 fatal shooting of five police officers in Dallas. In line with his promise, the then-president made a similar tweet in January 2017: "If Chicago doesn't fix the horrible 'carnage' going on, I will send in the Feds!" Citing gun violence and an escalating murder rate, Trump repeated his threat to send federal "help" to Chicago a number of times over the next several months.

The "law and order" slogan, of course, was not new, but was popular code in the late sixties, deployed by both George Wallace and Richard Nixon, who leveraged white resentment among the "silent majority" about the civil disobedience of Martin Luther King Jr. and other "outside agitators" who challenged civil rights violations in the South. As exit polls underestimated Trump voters because many kept their inclinations secret from pollsters, a new silent majority of sorts was presumably susceptible to similar jargon, albeit more than forty-five years later.

History, in a sense, was happening all over again. In the documentary *13th*, Ava DuVernay dramatizes the resonance of Trump's "law and order" candidacy in a haunting montage of black protesters being shoved by angry white mobs, juxtaposing black-and-white footage of historical civil rights protests with present-day scenes from Trump's campaign rallies. "I love the old days," Trump states in a voice-over, an aside made at one of his rallies. "You know what they used to do with guys like that in a place like this . . . they'd be carried out in a stretcher." Cheers from Trump's audience are then heard rising in the background.

═══════

I NEVER WATCHED THE VIRAL VIDEO SHOWING DEREK CHAUVIN KNEEL ON George Floyd's neck for upward of nine minutes. Even so, I couldn't avoid seeing still images from the recording, or Chauvin's dead-eyed poker face staring directly into the camera, hands in pockets as he crushed his knee into the back of Floyd's neck. With his steady gaze and his casual posture, Chauvin seemed to be challenging the viewer, taunting all of us digital eyewitnesses; he seemed to be saying with his eyes, "What are you going to do about it?"

The answer to this question—"What are you going to do about it?"—was, in my mind, a paradox. The answer to this question was both "nothing" and "something." *Nothing* because the clip of Chauvin's nine-minute torture and asphyxiation of Floyd was not being shared in real time, only after the fact. It's always too late to do anything to actually help the person being accosted or murdered in these videos. *Something*, though, because to watch something like that and do nothing is to be as much of a monster as Chauvin embodied in the video. *Something*, because *there but for the grace of God . . .*

That said, I didn't join the protests so much as witness them, taking my cue whenever given to, say, kneel upon command, appropriating Chauvin's deadly act and refashioning it as one of solidarity. The ubiquitous smartphones held up all around, sometimes aimed in my direction, kept me out of the moment and even more conscious of my presence and movements. I found that I could not any longer simply *be* at a protest, melt into the crowd, unselfconsciously chant on cue, forget myself for a larger issue. At these protests, it was as if I could only appear.

There were, however, respites from this diffidence. One day, walking away from an assembly on trans rights in New York's Washington Square Park toward the commotion all of us overheard at the park's edge, I sympathized with the young woman who sat crying on the ground, lifting her head now and then to squint and allow someone standing nearby to pour a bottle of water into her eyes. I asked two guys what had happened and was told the cops had pepper-sprayed some folks who had been marching. I was quickly moved out of that moment and back into observer mode when a white woman quickly weaved her way in our direction and screamed, "White bodies to the front!"

Another time, walking one day up Cadman Plaza toward the

Brooklyn Bridge, I couldn't lose myself in the chanting ("No justice, no peace! Fuck the racist police!"). Instead, I catalogued the slogans, whether makeshift and drawn on cardboard or more elaborately designed. *Racism Is a Pandemic. Silence Is Betrayal. White Silence = Violence.* Then, as I danced at a drum circle at Grand Army Plaza, my eyes scanned the crowd, watching a young woman move from person to person, offering herbal remedies, or intermittently checking on the man who had climbed the large bronze statue of two nude figures, perched between the male and female heads and waving a multicolored flag. I was too busy scanning my environment for details, too aware that I was living history.

———

NEWS REPORTS OF TRUMP'S TWEETS COMPARED HIS RHETORIC ABOUT shooting looters with that of former Alabama governor George Wallace, the infamous staunch segregationist who defied school desegregation at the height of the civil rights movement. When asked during his 1967 presidential campaign how he would address urban violence, Wallace responded: "Bam, shoot 'em dead on the spot! Shoot to kill if anyone throws a rock at a policeman or throws a Molotov cocktail."

———

THE LAW IS THE PROVINCE OF REFORM, NOT REVOLUTION. EVEN IF REPRE-senting a wannabe revolutionary, a lawyer would have to do so within the present legal construct, tinkering here and there in an already-built house, where a revolutionary would have preferred to simply burn the house down. Therein lies the disjuncture of what, for me, became the most singular moment of the uprisings, five days after Derek Chauvin killed George Floyd.

On Friday, May 30, 2020, thirty-one-year-old public interest lawyer Urooj Rahman filmed an interview before the Barclays Center in Brooklyn, New York, amid massive protests in the city against police brutality.

"This shit won't ever stop unless we fucking take it all down," Rahman said to the interviewer almost a quarter after midnight, according to the cell phone that glowed in her hand. "We're all in so much pain from how fucked up this country is toward Black lives. This has got to stop, and the only way they hear us is through violence, through the means that they use. 'You got to use the master's tools.' That's what my friend always says."

Later, around 1 a.m., Rahman was captured by a photographer leaning out of a car driven by Colinford Mattis, another lawyer, throwing a Molotov cocktail made of a gasoline-filled beer bottle, its neck stuffed with lit toilet paper, through a broken window of an abandoned cop car.

———

FOR THEIR PART, GOVERNORS OF NORTHERN U.S. STATES, LIKE JAY NIXON in Minneapolis and Andrew Cuomo in New York, objected to Trump's threatened invocation of the Insurrection Act. In the meantime, certain officials representing southern states, including Arkansas senator Tom Cotton and Texas governor Greg Abbott, voiced their support for Trump to use the Act. In the wake of Trump's address, Governor Abbott announced that "protest agitators" who engaged in looting and violence within the state of Texas would be subject to federal prosecution. In a joint statement made with four Texas U.S. attorneys, Abbott warned that "Texans must be able to exercise their First Amendment rights without fear of having agitators, including those coming from out-of-state, hijack their peaceful protest."

———

UROOJ RAHMAN AND COLINFORD MATTIS: BOTH CHILDREN OF IMMIGRANTS to the United States, Rahman of Pakistani parents, and Mattis of Jamaican. Both lawyers, Rahman representing indigent clients in eviction proceedings, and Mattis working at a white-shoe law firm at the time of the incident. Both idealistic and committed to public interest and other nonprofit legal work. Both native New Yorkers, from Brooklyn. There is obviously more to Rahman and Mattis than the tantalizing juxtaposition of a sworn lawyer throwing a Molotov cocktail. In their personal histories, I saw the attempt to work one's way up in the legal construct, perhaps attain aspects of the Immigrant Dream, perhaps watch their peers conflate their personal achievements with social progress. I also recognized the inevitable frustrations of having one's ideals confined to a legal straitjacket, as even the hope of facilitating widespread systemic reform is reduced to celebrating intermittent and fleeting victories.

Rahman and Mattis were eventually arrested and face federal charges including arson, conspiracy, and the use of explosives, with penalties of forty-five years to life imprisonment. Although their alleged crimes would have typically been adjudicated at the local level, federal prosecutors elected to take on the matter and elevate the young lawyers as poster children exemplifying the violent nature of what were, even then, largely being referred to as "peaceful" protests. As defendants, Rahman and Mattis would be shoehorned into narratives that supported their case, flattened into model defendants who would have to advertise their academic pedigree, peddle their modest upbringing, reframe their unbridled and principled anger into a lapse of judgment that would be understandable for anyone who was carried away in the moment, or with the mob. In other words, Rahman and Mattis would be, once again, lost in yet another narrative that was not of their making, all in an effort to counteract the argument that they were violent insurgents.

———

RHETORIC ABOUT "PROTEST AGITATORS" IMMEDIATELY RECALLED HOW southern lawmakers from the antebellum period to the civil rights movement censured "outside agitators" for crossing state lines to "cause trouble" in service of abolition or desegregation, thereby detracting attention from the injustices of slavery and Jim Crow. The statement also served as a legal justification for Trump to invoke the act unilaterally, a power that is conditioned on any "insurrection, domestic violence, unlawful combination, or conspiracy" either causing the deprivation of constitutional rights or obstructing the enforcement of federal law. Such southern officials, in this case, abdicated a fidelity to states' rights in favor of federal intervention.

———

ADHERENCE TO FEDERALISM AND MINIMAL FEDERAL INTERFERENCE IN state affairs is supposed to be one of the central concerns of conservative politicians. Taking an ahistorical view of states' rights—overlooking how this policy position flourished in order to defend the state-regulated institutions of slavery and segregation against federal intervention—conservative purveyors of federalism often take quantum leaps back to the *Federalist Papers*, appropriating the enumerated concerns of antifederalists as their own.

But perhaps this is only the case when federalist principles are a cover for their political preferences. Given the spate of activity among Texan Republican lawmakers that clamored to identify federal laws any riotous "agitators" might have been violating to justify the deployment of federal troops under the Insurrection Act, the veneer of respectability given to abstract arguments for federalism has completely worn off. Federalism, in this light, is not some lofty principle, but a mere tool.

———

ALTHOUGH, AS REPORTED IN THE *NEW YORK TIMES*, TRUMP AIDES WENT AS far as drafting proclamations to deploy active-duty troops, Trump in the end did not invoke the Insurrection Act in response to the uprisings that erupted after George Floyd's killing, as higher-ups in the military echelon opposed the move, including defense secretary Mark Esper, who publicly stated that he did not support deploying active-duty forces to quell civil unrest for now. "The option to use active-duty forces in a law enforcement role should only be used as a matter of last resort and only in the most urgent and dire of situations," Esper stated in a news briefing. "We are not in one of those situations now."

Not long thereafter, a bill was introduced in the House to amend the Insurrection Act to reinsert congressional oversight over the Act's invocation and to require that—prior to any dispatch of federal troops—the president, the Secretary of Defense, and the Attorney General make a certification to Congress that the events warranted the deployment, along with the intended scope and duration. The bill also stated that any authorized deployments would be terminated within fourteen days unless extended by joint resolution of Congress and permitted certain individuals to seek court-ordered relief from them.

Although President Trump did not invoke the Act—and instead, according to the *New York Times*, urged governors present on a conference call to "dominate" the protesters through the National Guard—his administration did devise a means of federal intervention in the protests against police brutality in Portland, Oregon. In an executive order signed on June 26, 2020, Trump authorized the deployment of federal military police to protect monuments and statues that constitute "federal property." The preamble to the order cited "a sustained assault on . . . government property" and stated that "[m]any of the rioters, arsonists, and left-wing extremists who have carried out and supported these acts have explicitly identified themselves with ideologies—such as Marxism—that call for the destruction of the United States system of government." Issued amid the toppling of statues commemorating Confederate heroes, the order specifically cited the pulling down of one statue of Ulysses S. Grant in San Francisco, stating that "to [vandals], it made no difference that President Grant led the Union Army to victory over the Confederacy in the Civil War, enforced Reconstruction, fought the Ku Klux Klan, and advocated for the Fifteenth Amendment, which guaranteed freed slaves the right to vote."

Under this authority, federal military police, including agents from the Department of Homeland Security and customs and border patrol, were deployed to defend federal property from vandalism and destruction—an authority which translated into federal agents clashing with protesters on the ground.

———

IF FEDERALISM IS NOT SOME IMMUTABLE HIGHER PRINCIPLE BUT RATHER a tool wielded depending on the political proclivities of the one wielding it, then it makes sense that Trump's sympathies during the summer uprisings of 2020 were more in line with George Wallace than with Lyndon B. Johnson. Similarities between Trump and George Wallace seem to extend beyond the president's incendiary tweet. Though on the surface of events Wallace's stand in the Alabama schoolhouse door was defeated by federal military intervention, in the governor's own estimation at the time, his theatrical showdown with the federal government ultimately played out in his favor. Prior to that particular spectacle, when state officials had cautioned Wallace that his defiance could invite the mob violence that had flared up at Ole Miss, not to mention federal troop deployment, Wallace reportedly replied that "[t]he first day they bring federal troops into this state, I'm gonna run for president."

Wallace was well aware that his blustering against federal intervention would consolidate the political support of Alabama's white segregationists. Theatrically defiant, the southern Democrat was determined to make a show of defiance against "federal interference" in order to rile up support from his white racist base. "Wallace had found the key to electoral glory," writes Robert J. Norrell in *The House I Live In: Race in the American Century*. "Tell white southerners what they wanted to hear, say it belligerently, and then bask in their adoration."

There is further indication that Wallace's defiance was a form of political theater. Before ever becoming governor, Wallace learned the hard way during his failed 1958 gubernatorial race that positioning himself to white voters as a moderate who was conciliatory on racial equality was a losing battle. Having lost that initial race in part by denouncing his opponent's ties to the Ku Klux Klan, Wallace thereafter ramped up his divisive racial rhetoric to propel himself to victory in his 1962 campaign. Indeed, the oft-quoted byword of his inaugural speech is "Segregation now! Segregation tomorrow! Segregation forever!"

Upon actually becoming governor, however, Wallace was apparently more devoted to grandstanding than to the day-to-day running of state affairs; as a consequence, Wallace's administration was characterized by patronage, as his appointees regularly doled out state funds to their friends and political allies. Instead of concerning himself with such matters, as Jeffrey Frederick described in *Stand Up for Alabama: Governor George Wallace*, Wallace instead devoted himself to a "nonstop, twenty-four-hour-a-day, three-hundred-sixty-five-day-a-year, four-year campaign."

WHAT BEGAN AS BLACK LIVES MATTER PROTESTS AGAINST POLICE BRUTALity transitioned, in Portland, into protests against fascism, as federal military police were not merely a specter of authoritarianism but also forced protesters away from certain federal sites that were a hotbed for demonstrators, such as federal courthouses, and reportedly even snatched protesters into unmarked vans. Such Portland protesters were also gathered in news reports under the moniker "Antifa"—referring to a decentralized antifascist and -racist movement that uses both nonviolent and violent tactics as part of its social justice objectives— and thereby transformed, by connotation, from peaceful protesters into provocateurs. Like the age-old "outside agitators," Antifa became a bogeyman, a code word for unprincipled anarchy and disruption of "law and order." Although the intensity of the protests eventually waned, despite the efforts of diehard activists who continued to put their bodies on the line to challenge state and local authority, the executive order issued by Trump was in effect for six months from signing.

IN THE END, EVERYTHING IS PERFORMATIVE—THAT IS, UNTIL SOMEONE ends up killed. Watching the police gathered at the perimeter of the marches or behind strategically placed barricades, it was clear to me that the mass photo opportunity that was the summer 2020 uprising could quickly transition into a stage of mass violence. I was also immediately reminded of my disdain for that repeated phrase: "peaceful protesters." During the uprising, the "peaceful protester" became the new "unarmed black person," as if danger was automatically imputed to any "protester" or "black person" unless qualified by an unthreatening adjective. The term "peaceful protester" normalized the true menace, the actual source of danger, the various levels of law enforcement poised to exercise their invested authority to inflict violence on those whose actions they deemed illicit.

GIVEN THE WIDESPREAD REPORTS OF EXCESSIVE USE OF FORCE BY RIOT police during the uprising, the irony is that Trump could very well have proposed invoking the Insurrection Act to protect the First Amendment rights of peaceful protesters to assemble, echoing the deployment in support of the civil rights protesters who marched from Selma to Montgomery. However, like federalism, the Insurrection Act is also a mere tool, the invocation of which to suppress "domestic violence" or enforce civil rights ultimately depends upon whether, in the case of the 2020 uprisings, protesters in support of black lives are framed as perpetrators or victims. It was as if George Wallace himself instead of Lyndon B. Johnson was in the White House. And the irony is that when addressing black Americans who called for statues of Confederates to come down, Trump stated, "If you don't understand your history, you will go back to it again."

Exodus

After a mostly white mob stormed the U.S. Capitol on January 6, 2021, and threatened to disrupt the Electoral College certification of the presidential election, beating a Capitol Police officer in its midst, some Republican spokesmen were loath to call its participants "insurrectionists." Donald Trump himself characterized the Capitol rioters as posing "zero threat, right from the start," and went on to state that "[s]ome of them went in, and they are hugging and kissing the police and the guards," and that they were waved in and out of the Capitol by said police. Wisconsin Senator Ron Johnson also remarked after the January 6 riot that "[t]his didn't seem like an armed insurrection to me. When you hear the word 'armed,' don't you think of firearms?"

Later, at a February 23 hearing on the Capitol attacks, Johnson further supported his stance by citing a piece in *The Federalist* by J. Michael Waller. In D.C. at the time of the attacks, Waller observed many attendees of the "Stop the Steal" rally he encountered on Constitution Avenue that day, and writes that "some were indignant and contemptuous of Congress, but not one appeared angry or incited to riot." The *Federalist* article also puts the blame for later violence on agents provocateurs who were members of Antifa, insisting that the lion's share of those present at the Capitol that day were "peaceful" protesters. That this characterization proved to contrast sharply with confirmed facts of the siege is far less interesting to me than the narratives put forth to minimize the threat posed by Capitol rioters and rehabilitate them as "citizens."

So, what's in a name? An "insurrectionist," by definition, is someone who has engaged in an act or instance of revolting against a civil authority or an established government. However, many of those participating in the riots on that fateful January 6 considered themselves to be "patriots," by definition vigorously supporting their country and prepared to defend it against enemies and detractors. Among such rioters, as indicated by the subsequent indictments, were members of the Oath Keepers; some of them reportedly directed fellow Capitol infiltrators toward the Senate wing in order to stop the certification of the presidential election.

Although those who stormed the Capitol building that day may have been cast by the news media and beyond as insurrectionists, they consider themselves to be patriots. They also interpreted President Trump to be their strongman, or hype man. A number of rioters later claimed that they were rallying at the Capitol that day at Trump's instruction. After giving thanks to "hundreds of thousands of American patriots who are committed to the honesty of our elections and the integrity of our glorious republic," Trump urged his supporters to "stop the steal." In addressing the crowd, he said, "[Y]ou're the people that built this nation," and "[y]ou're not the people that tore down our nation." At some point during Trump's speech, in which he denounced the election results as fraudulent, the crowd started chanting: "Fight for Trump!"

Upon facing federal charges for their involvement in the riot, some participants claimed in their defense that they were just following Trump's instructions. One woman arrested for participating in the riot told a journalist that she traveled to the "Stop the Steal" rally because the president said, "Be there." "So I went," she continued, "and I answered the call of my president. When speaking to reporters, Al Watkins, a defense attorney for one of the rioters, referenced "the months of lies and misrepresentations and horrific innuendo and hyperbolic speech by our president designed to inflame, enrage, motivate." Such defenses reiterate the charges against Trump after the House of Representatives adopted an article of impeachment against him for incitement of insurrection, including his infamous remark at a presidential debate aimed at the Proud Boys, a right-wing extremist organization: "Stand Back and Stand By." The defenses are also corroborated by the mobilization of "Trump's Army," as referred to in the president's campaign materials, to engage in poll-watching missions across the country to report any voting irregularities.

After the Senate voted to acquit Trump at the impeachment trial, the NAACP filed a civil law suit on behalf of Mississippi congressman Bennie Thompson under the Civil War era Ku Klux Klan Act of 1871, accusing Trump, former New York governor Rudy Giuliani, and the far-right extremist group the Oath Keepers of conspiring to incite a riot on January 6 with the intent to prevent Congress from certifying the presidential election. The same legislation that Ulysses S. Grant used during Reconstruction in response to Ku Klux Klan violence against freedmen in the South was resurrected to claim that Trump and his coconspirators mobilized his supporters to effectively suppress the black vote, which according to polls turned out to be critical in swaying the election in favor of Trump's opponent. Of course, due to the pandemic, the suspense-ridden electoral process involved a high proportion of mail-in ballots due to stay-at-home advice; when tabulated in crucial swing states like Michigan and Georgia, such ballots came largely from cities like Detroit and Atlanta, where the population is predominantly African American.

In the case of the Capitol "insurrection," then, violence and its threat was a product of the "word," but just not a lawful one. The substance of the allegations against Trump, at his impeachment trial and beyond, was that his word incited and channeled extralegal violence against the very government he headed, in favor of his retaining power. Also, when the president declined to name those who stormed the Capitol "insurrectionists," he effectively aided and abetted the violence once it started on January 6.

It's true that the Insurrection Act does not need to be invoked by the president in order to authorize federal military intervention in the District of Columbia, which lacks statehood. However, as commander in chief of the D.C. National Guard, the president and his administration could have directed that this be done once riots were sparked at the Capitol. Although local commanders of the National Guard are invested with the limited authority to take immediate military action in certain emergency situations where there is not sufficient time to obtain the requisite approvals, in the case of the "Stop the Steal" rally the Pentagon had restricted the authority of the D.C. National Guard commander before the riot, requiring higher-level sign-off in order to take such immediate action.

The commander, according to the *Washington Post*, did not get any approval for over an hour after receiving desperate calls from the Capitol Police, which meant that active-duty guards were diverted from their prescribed mission that day of directing traffic to help secure the Capitol for about three hours after pleas for help. In a call between the Capitol Police the day of the riots, the Pentagon, and local city officials, the Capitol Police chief made an urgent request for two hundred National Guard troops, and in response an Army official replied that "the 'optics' of soldiers inside the Capitol building was not something they wanted." In other words, such conversations reflect the historical reticence of federal officials to use military intervention in local affairs; however, at the same time, in failing to take timely action, they effectively sanctioned extralegal violence by omission.

One obvious parallel involves the 2017 rally held in Charlottes-ville, Virginia, to oppose the proposed removal of a statue of Con-federate General Robert E. Lee, which drew counterprotesters who gathered to oppose the many white nationalists and neo-Nazis parad-ing on that day. Refusing to denounce the white nationalist contingent at the rally, Trump remarked that there were "very fine people on both sides." Of course, it was at this rally that a white nationalist drove his car into a group of counterprotesters, killing a young activist named Heather Heyer. The violent nature of the rally attendees, however, was not limited to this deadly attack.

I watched a video of the rally that later surfaced, showing a man sporting a gray bandana across his brow and, over a blue "wife-beater," a bulletproof vest. He had just stepped down some external stairs amid fellow neo-Nazis and white nationalists, but he was not carrying one of the tiki torches that would come to symbolize the inflamed anger of so many mostly white men who gripped them as they too descended upon Charlottesville on August 21, 2017. Rather, it was a black man—off-screen with other counterprotesters—who carried an improvised torch, its flames that lit the right side of the frame. I watched the bullet-proofed man move toward these flames and yell something unintelligible yet reminiscent of a racial slur, then draw a handgun and fire. Satisfied, the bullet-proofed man turned to rejoin his brethren on the parade route, lined, reportedly, with state troopers. Not one officer moved to apprehend the shooter.

That the Charlottesville shooter's bullet struck the ground and did not harm anyone is a happy accident that offers no justification for the failure of law enforcement to respond to his criminal act. Both the shooting and Heyer's murder highlighted not only the violence of the white nationalist protests in Charlottesville, but also the rather lax approach to maintaining law and order. "There was no police presence," one counterprotester told the *New York Times*. "We were watching people punch each other; people were bleeding all the while police were inside of barricades at the park, watching. It was essentially just brawling on the street and community members trying to protect each other."

Similarly, Michigan police did not use force against the group of armed mostly white men who stormed the state's capitol in Lansing during demonstrations opposing pandemic lockdowns. The crowd gathered at an "American Patriot Rally" on April 30, 2020, including men dressed in camouflage and carrying AR-15 rifles, rushed into the Capitol building and attempted to disrupt a meeting being held by lawmakers discussing stay-at-home orders. "I love freedom," one member of the crowd said at the time. "In America, we should be free." Another demonstrator was quoted as calling the lawmakers inside the capital "Redcoats." As for media narratives framing the event, numerous news reports at the time referred to those gathered at the Michigan capitol as "protesters," technically highlighting the fact that they assembled to voice an objection to the lockdowns but, unlike use of the word "riot" or, of course, "insurrection," failing to describe the violent nature of the crowd. Trump, for his part, remarked that they were "very good people."

Narratives about such events are always contesting as well as contested, and the utterances made by lawmakers and presidents are regularly disputed and denied by the listening public. However, when those who have the power to wield violence (and its threat) to enforce the law engage in such characterizations, their words amount to more than just talk. They are, in themselves, a kind of legal interpretation, and in the case of federal military intervention, the absence of a proclamation under the Insurrection Act—despite a given incident fitting the textbook definition of "domestic violence" or "unlawful obstruction" or "insurrection" that may give rise to its invocation—does constitute an official action, even if by omission.

The parallels between the scant use of force by law enforcement in incidents involving armed and mostly white demonstrators and the excessive use of force against unarmed black people and protesters who assemble to proclaim that their lives matter are obvious. And this disparate outcome can be traced back not only to the country's original sin, but also the prevailing definition of the original citizen. Where even the concept of a "black citizen" was an oxymoron at the founding of the country, the concept of the "white citizen" was already naturalized, preceding the Constitution insofar as being white was already a prerequisite for being considered a citizen under existing state law.

Taking into consideration that being white and male were also initial prerequisites to be called forth as a posse or be conscripted into the militia, these qualities were not only originally imbued in the very idea of a "citizen" but also the personhood of one who was authorized to enforce the law. The "white citizen," then, was not only the original citizen, but also inherently a "lawman." Perhaps this is why armed white men, whether white nationalists or right-wing militiamen, presume to call themselves "patriots"—recalling the revolutionary founding fathers—despite committing acts of terror in the name of the flag.

The reluctance among certain politicians to call them "insurrectionists" or even "terrorists" may not only be a matter of reflexive bias or a performative dog whistle, but also a product of the enduring concept of the white citizen as an enforcer of law, and therefore less susceptible to being interpreted as on the wrong side of it. This concept, of course, is as enduring as that of a black person in the United States being effectively interpreted as inherently suspicious and dangerous—ever the potential insurrectionist, a status that is the by-product of the original sin, rendering black people in America as permanent outlaws.

"EMERGENCIES HAVE ALWAYS BEEN NECESSARY TO PROGRESS," WROTE VICtor Hugo. "It was darkness which produced the lamp. It was fog that produced the compass. It was hunger that drove us to exploration." Perhaps if one were to replace the word "emergencies" with "insurrections," then the very same statement would seem just as true. Using the Insurrection Act and federal military intervention as a guide through history, it becomes clear that certain key events lauded for advancing the civil rights of black Americans are, in their own way, concessions in an ongoing war.

That the Thirteenth, Fourteenth, and Fifteenth amendments, as well as the country's very first civil rights legislation affirming equal protection under the law, were all enacted after a bloody civil war are well-known illustrations of this argument. Federal military intervention was also critical to enforcing such fledgling rights during Reconstruction, when black suffrage and elections of black politicians flourished. It's also clear that the Civil Rights Act of 1964 and the Voting Rights Act of 1965 were each passed after incidents that were deemed to merit federal military intervention under the Act, the first after George Wallace's stand in the schoolhouse door, and the second after Bloody Sunday marred the sanctioned march of civil rights protesters from Selma to Montgomery.

However, this ongoing war is marked by concessions that also constitute regression. The Posse Comitatus Act of 1878 was one such concession, marking the end of Reconstruction and the use of federal troops to enforce the civil rights of black Americans in the South, leaving in its wake a lacuna of enforcement in which white paramilitary groups like the Ku Klux Klan could once again rise and reassert racial dominance through terror. In this light, the absence of federal military enforcement similarly characterizes the unofficial "insurrection" at the U.S. Capitol on January 6, where rioters seeking to disrupt the certification of the election were also effectively seeking to suppress the black vote that was critical in turning the election away from Trump's favor. When Trump's national security advisor Michael Flynn advocated for the president to invoke the Insurrection Act in order to demand a "revote" of the election under military supervision, such a proclamation of "insurrection" threatened to interpret the exercise of the black vote as a form of domestic violence that warranted suppression.

"Progress," through this lens, has been a series of advancements and retrenchments in a warlike contest. Even symbolic victories in this ongoing war, the most significant in recent history being the election of Barack Obama, were then followed by white supremacist regression, such as the presidency of Donald Trump, the insurrectionist in chief who with the support of his followers effectively rebelled against the election of the first black president.

The nature of this "progress" is also reflected in the interpretive pendulum of the Insurrection Act, insofar as it swings back and forth between its use to suppress so-called race riots and to enforce civil rights. The use of the Act is, ultimately, a reflection of the precarious status of black citizens. The "black citizen" in the United States is akin to the unstable image highlighted in Ludwig Wittgenstein's *Philosophical Investigations*, which in the flicker of an eye can be seen as either a duck or a rabbit. Similarly, and despite the formal advances toward "equality" and "freedom," black citizens have not emerged from the interpretive paradox of being deemed at once person and property, both ward and enemy of the state. Black citizens, then, are blurred and distorted in this double vision, where we are paradoxically both victims and perpetrators, both relief-seeking and rioters, both integrated and insurgent.

———

PERHAPS HISTORY ISN'T ALWAYS PROPAGANDA, AS W. E. B. DU BOIS ONCE wrote, but the presentation of history is always an argument. As in a court of law, where lawyers give the same set of facts a different slant depending on the party they represent, history is, at bottom, a persuasive narrative. As evident from *The 1776 Report*, issued through a commission authorized by President Trump, governmental authorities do not only mandate meaning through violence and its threat, but promulgate their own narratives—an attempt to not merely make and enforce law, but shape the context in which the law is generally understood and obeyed. Whether one accepts as gospel *The 1776 Report*, which emphasizes the principles of equality and liberty celebrated in the founding documents of the United States, or *The 1619 Project*, conceived by journalist Nikole Hannah-Jones for *The New York Times*, which centers the practice of slavery and its aftereffects, reflects one's stake in the ongoing battle to name the world and establish the prevailing narrative framework through which we make meaning within it.

Just as the legal construct does not fully occupy the field of meaning, there is never one History, but multiple histories, as many histories as there are people, as many narrative commitments as there are narrative possibilities. And even as we traverse these many narratives and the parallel worlds they create, there is always a new narrative, a new world, waiting to emerge, perhaps on the verge of materializing from the otherworldly terrain of dreams.

———

BEFORE THE ABOLITIONIST AND ACTIVIST HARRIET TUBMAN ESCAPED from slavery, navigating back and forth through secret routes and safe houses called the Underground Railroad to ferry about seventy enslaved people to freedom, she would have dreams. As recounted to Sarah Hopkins Bradford in *Harriet Tubman, Moses of Her People*, "[S]he used to dream of flying over fields and towns, and rivers and mountains, looking down upon them 'like a bird' [. . .]." As it turned out, these were more than dreams—they were premonitions, as when Tubman escaped northward, she saw along her way the many places she had first sighted during her dream state.

In Tubman's day, freedom was largely a matter of geography, of taking flight to a free state or Canada or beyond. As the legal construct has evolved, formally dissolving slavery, then segregation, and erecting frameworks for affirming formal rights, the narrative arc toward freedom also has shifted, from one whose plot takes place on an outer terrain to an inner one. And assuming one's narrative agency, or true freedom, may no longer be a matter of tweaking the legal construct, or being volleyed back and forth between progress and retrenchment, or even nobly laboring to assimilate into the American Dream. It may be as simple as validating one's own individual dreams, and, from there, seeking signs for every next step, each one taken as if under a torchlight in the pitch dark.

ACKNOWLEDGMENTS

This book is the product of research I first conducted during a fellowship at Columbia Law School; I am very grateful to Mark Barenberg for being instrumental in coordinating it. I am grateful to Sherally Munshi and Daniel Steinmetz-Jenkins for the critical discussions about the subject during that fellowship that helped guide my thinking at the time, as well as to Patricia Williams for inviting me on a number of occasions during my fellowship to present the subject in her seminars. I am also indebted to Navid Khazanei and Kitty Austin for publishing the resulting law-review article I wrote on the subject, "Paradoxes of Sovereignty and Citizenship: Humanitarian Intervention at Home," in the *CUNY Law Review*. If it hadn't been for the urging of Zafir Buraei and Amisha Patel I would not have written a piece about the Ferguson uprisings, "Humanitarian Intervention at Home," which was accepted for publication in the *Los Angeles Review of Books* by Tom Lutz, and caught the attention of my kind, patient, and thorough editor, Alane Mason, who has been an early and steadfast champion of this work. Many thanks are also due to my erstwhile agent Katie Zannechia, who helped polish my proposal for submission, and to Khazanei, again, and New School librarian Paul Abruzzo for indispensable research assistance. I'm grateful for funding I received in the early stages of this research from the Wiliam Nelson Cromwell Foundation, and, later, from the Robert B. Silvers Foundation. For providing a room of my own throughout this process, I'd like to thank Joan Gurley and Shaniqua Gordon. For helping me to clear mental blocks, organize myself, and focus, I thank Bri Monroe and Jackie Simek. For moral support, I thank Andy Faranda and Alina Mason, who listened to me discuss all things "insurrection" through-out this process; my beloved father, James Allan, who would have been proud to see this work finally materialize; and, lastly, I thank my mother and biggest fan, Tuzyline Allan, who read my manuscript in its various stages and offered essential feedback that this book is all the better for incorporating.

FURTHER READING

Agamben, Giorgio. 2005. *State of Exception*. Translated by Kevin Attell. University of Chicago Press.

Aptheker, Herbert. 1983. *American Negro Slave Revolts*. 6th ed. International Publishers.

———. 2006. *Nat Turner's Slave Rebellion: Including the 1831 "Confessions."* Dover Publications.

Barthes, Roland. 1957. Reprint 2012. *Mythologies*. Translated by Richard Howard and Annette Lavers. Hill and Wang.

Baudrillard, Jean. 1994. *Simulacra and Simulation*. Translated by Sheila Faria Glaser. University of Michigan Press.

Bennett, Lerone, Jr. 2003. *Before the Mayflower: A History of Black America 1619–1964*. 7th ed. Johnson Pub.

Blight, David W. 1989. *Frederick Douglass' Civil War: Keeping Faith in Jubilee*. Louisiana State University Press.

Boritt, Gabor S., ed. 1996. *Why the Civil War Came*. Oxford University Press.

Bradford, Sarah H. 1886. Reprint 2012. *Harriet Tubman: The Moses of Her People*. University of North Carolina Press.

Brown, Robert L. 2010. *Defining Moments: Historic Decisions by Arkansas Governors from McMath through Huckabee*. University of Arkansas Press.

Bush, George W. 2010. *Decision Points*. Crown.

Carmichael, Stokely, and Mumia Abu-Jamal. 2007. *Stokely Speaks: From Black Power to Pan-Africanism*. Lawrence Hill Books.

Cleaver, Eldridge. 1971. Reprint 1991. *Soul on Ice*. Delta.

Cover, Robert M. 1995. *Narrative, Violence, and the Law: The Essays of Robert Cover,* edited by Martha Minow et al. University of Michigan Press.

Csicsek, Alex. 2011. "Spiro T. Agnew and the Burning of Baltimore." *Baltimore '68: Riots and Rebirth in an American City.* Edited by Jessica I. Elfenbein, Thomas L. Hollowak, and Elizabeth M. Nix. Temple University Press.

Davis, Angela Y. 2019. *Women, Race & Class.* Penguin Books.

Davis, David Brion. 1975. *The Problem of Slavery in the Age of Revolution 1770–1823.* Cornell University Press.

Du Bois, W. E. B., and Henry Louis Gates Jr. 2014. *Black Reconstruction in America.* Oxford University Press.

Dunbar-Ortiz, Roxanne. 2018. *Loaded: A Disarming History of the Second Amendment.* City Lights Books.

Egerton, Douglas R. 1993. *Gabriel's Rebellion: The Virginia Slave Conspiracies of 1800 and 1802.* University of North Carolina Press.

Fanon, Frantz. 2004. *The Wretched of the Earth.* Translated by Richard Philcox. Grove Press.

Fehrenbacher, Don E., and Ward M. McAfee. 2002. *Slaveholding Republic: An Account of the United States Government's Relations to Slavery.* Oxford University Press.

Foner, Eric. 2002. *Reconstruction: America's Unfinished Revolution, 1863–1877.* Perennial Classics.

Ford, Lacy K. 2011. *Deliver Us from Evil: The Slavery Question in the Old South.* Oxford University Press.

Frederick, Jeff. 2007. *Stand Up for Alabama : Governor George Wallace.* University of Alabama Press.

Freehling, William W. 1990. *The Road to Disunion: Secessionists at Bay, 1776–1854,* Volume 1. Oxford University Press.

Freire, Paulo. 2018. *Pedagogy of the Oppressed.* Bloomsbury Academic.

Ginsberg, Benjamin. 2010. *Moses of South Carolina: A Jewish Scalawag during Radical Reconstruction.* Johns Hopkins University Press.

Gregg, Richard B. 2018. *The Power of Non-Violence.* Cambridge University Press.

Grenier, John. *The First Way of War: American War Making on the Frontier, 1607–1814.* Cambridge University Press.

Hadden, Sally E. 2003. *Slave Patrols: Law and Violence in Virginia and the Carolinas.* Harvard University Press.

Hamilton, Alexander, James Madison, and John Jay. 2003. *The Federalist Papers.* Introduction by Garry Wills. Random House.

Eyes on the Prize [videorecording]. 2006. *America's Civil Rights Movement.* Directed by Henry Hampton, Julian Bond, and Steve Fayer. Produced by Blackside. WGBH TV and Home Video PBS.

Hegel, Georg Wilhelm Friedrich. 2017. *Phenomenology of Spirit.* Cambridge University Press.

Hobbes, Thomas. 2017. *Leviathan.* Penguin Classics.

Horne, Gerald. 2015. *Confronting the Black Jacobins: The U.S., the Haitian Revolution, and the Origins of the Dominican Republic.* Monthly Review Press.

Ignatiev, Noel. 2012. *How the Irish Became White.* Taylor and Francis.

Jacobs, Ronald N. 2000. *Race, Media and the Crisis of Civil Society: From the Watts Riots to Rodney King.* Cambridge University Press.

James, C. L. R. 1963. Reprint 1989. *The Black Jacobins: Toussaint L'Ouverture and the San Domingo Revolution.* Vintage Books.

Johnson, Nicholas. 2014. *Negroes and the Gun: The Black Tradition of Arms.* Prometheus Books.

Jordan, Winthrop D. 2012. *White Over Black: American Attitudes Toward the Negro 1550–1812.* University of North Carolina.

Joseph, Peniel E. 2014. *Stokely: A Life.* Basic Civitas.

Katagiri, Yasuhiro. 2001. *The Mississippi State Sovereignty Commission Civil Rights and States' Rights.* University Press of Mississippi.

Keith, LeeAnna. 2008. *The Colfax Massacre: The Untold Story of Black Power, White Terror, and the Death of Reconstruction.* Oxford University Press.

Kelly, George Armstrong. 1966. "Notes on Hegel's 'Lordship and Bondage.'" *Review of Metaphysics* 19 (4): 780–802.

King, Martin Luther, Jr. 2010. *Why We Can't Wait.* Beacon Press.

King, Martin Luther, Jr. 1991. *A Testament of Hope: The Essential Writings and Speeches of Martin Luther King, Jr.* Edited by James M. Washington. HarperCollins.

Klarman, Michael J. 2016. *The Framers' Coup: The Making of the United States Constitution.* Oxford University Press.

Knowles, Helen J. 2007. "The Constitution and Slavery: A Special Relationship." *Slavery & Abolition* 28 (3): 309–28.

Le Bon, Gustave. 1895. Reprint 2010. *The Crowd: A Study of the Popular Mind.* Dover.

Leviathan, Or the Matter, Form, and Power of a Commonwealth, Ecclesiastical and Civil (Matter, Form, and Power of a Commonwealth, Ecclesiastical and Civil). 2015. Directed by Hobbes Thomas. Blackstone Audio.

Locke, John. 1988. *Two Treatises of Government*. Cambridge University Press.

Lupo, Lindsey. 2011. *Flak-Catchers: One Hundred Years of Riot Commission Politics in America*. Lexington Books.

McAdam, Doug, and Karina Kloos. 2014. *Deeply Divided: Racial Politics and Social Movements in Post-War America*. Oxford University Press.

Morgan, Edmund S. 2003. *American Slavery, American Freedom: The Ordeal of Colonial Virginia*. W. W. Norton.

Morris, Aldon D. 1986. *The Origins of the Civil Rights Movement: Black Communities Organizing for Change*. Free Press.

Newton, Huey P. 1998. *War Against the Panthers: A Study of Repression in America*. Harlem River Press.

Norrell, Robert J. 2005. *The House I Live In: Race in the American Century*. Oxford University Press.

Olmsted, Frederick Law. 1860. Reprint 2015. *A Journey in the Back Country*. Andesite Press.

Parsons, Elaine Frantz. 2015. *Ku-Klux: The Birth of the Klan during Reconstruction*. University of North Carolina Press.

Pearl, Matthew. 2016. "K Troop." *Slate*.

Risen, Clay. 2009. *A Nation on Fire: America in the Wake of the King Assassination*. John Wiley & Sons.

Schwantes, Carlos A. 1982. "Protest in a Promised Land: Unemployment, Disinheritance, and the Origin of Labor Militancy in the Pacific Northwest, 1885–1886." *Western Historical Quarterly* 13 (4): 373–90.

Smith, Carl. 2008. *Urban Disorder and the Shape of Belief: The Great Chicago Fire, the Haymarket Bomb, and the Model Town of Pullman*. University of Chicago Press.

United States National Advisory Commission on Civil Disorders. 1988. *The Kerner Report: The 1968 Report of the National Advisory Commission on Civil Disorders*. Pantheon Books.

Waldstreicher, David. 2009. *Slavery's Constitution: From Revolution to Ratification*. Hill and Wang.

Wallace, David. 1980. "Orval Faubus: The Central Figure at Little Rock Central High School." *Arkansas Historical Quarterly* 39 (4): 314–29.

Webb, Samuel L., Margaret E. Armbrester, Albert P. Brewer, and David E. Alsobrook. 2014. *Alabama Governors: A Political History of the State*. University of Alabama Press.

Wittgenstein, Ludwig. 2004. *Philosophical Investigations*. Cambridge University Press.

INDEX